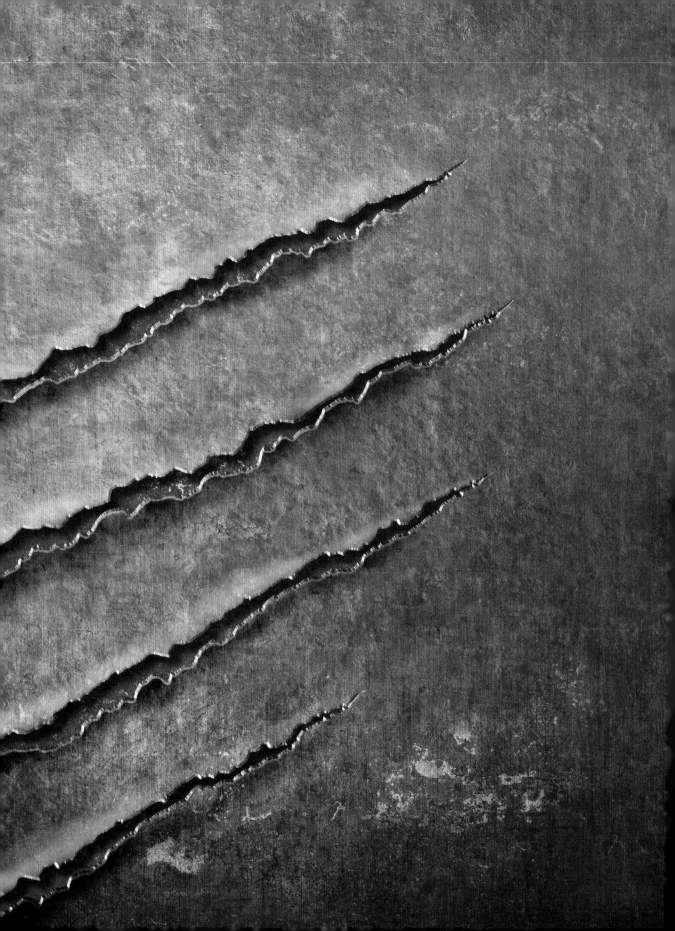

UPDATED
EDITION

MARTIN POPOFF

with

Blaze Bayley · Rich Davenport · Bobby "Blitz" Ellsworth

Marty Friedman · Matt Heafy · Tim Henderson · Chris Jericho · Jimmy Kay

Sean Kelly · Mike Portnoy · Franc Potvin · Kirsten Rosenberg

Brian Slagel · Nita Strauss · Ahmet Zappa

Contents

*Introduction and
Discographic Notes* *6*

1 Iron Maiden 8

2 Killers 24

3 The Number of the Beast 40

4 Piece of Mind 56

5 Powerslave 70

6 Somewhere in Time 84

7 Seventh Son of a Seventh Son 98

8 No Prayer for the Dying 114

9 Fear of the Dark 128

10 The X Factor 142

11 Virtual XI 156

12 Brave New World 170

13 Dance of Death 184

14 A Matter of Life and Death 200

15 The Final Frontier 214

16 The Book of Souls 230

17 Senjutsu 246

About the Author *262*
About the Contributors *263*
Author Bibliography *266*
Index *268*
Photo Credits *271*

Introduction

Can't say I was Eddie-on-the-spot with *The Soundhouse Tapes*, and for that I blame the fact I was from a small town in British Columbia, one ocean and one very large continent away from Iron Maiden's hunting grounds—the prey being any other New Wave of British Heavy Metal (NWOBHM) band that would dare stumble into their path on their way to renaissance rock dominance.

But there I was at Quintessence Records in Vancouver, paying $14.99 for my import copy of *Iron Maiden* on May 28, 1980, snatching up on that same trip (what I was doing on an eight-hour car drive away from home during the grade-eleven school year is beyond me) a copy of Saxon's *Wheels of Steel* for $16.

Getting home to Trail, I'm sure I was struck by how Saxon still had at least one leg warmer–clad toe in the '70s, while this other band that I knew was already soaking up all the oxygen in the scene was all about the new decade, Steve's long struggle through the second half of the '70s notwithstanding (how were we even to know such things back then?).

Thus began a dizzying bout of Iron Maiden mania. *Killers* was purchased through my work at the local record store, Kelly's (no price recorded for posterity), on May 30, 1981, followed by the *Maiden Japan* EP, $3.99 on December 12, 1981. *The Number of the Beast* was snagged at A&A Records in Vancouver on a trip my dad made to visit me during first-year university, where I had been lonely and stressed, having (long story) put three-fifths of my eggs in one basket for an experimental arts program called Arts One, wherein the prof decided to give almost everybody some variation of C minuses. In any event, me an' Pops went to, I believe it was, three Vancouver Canucks playoff games.

Back to Maiden, *The Number of the Beast* was purchased brand new for $4.97 on April 7, 1982. Flash forward to May 26, 1983; *Piece of Mind* ran me $7.99 at Sam the Record Man in Victoria. *Powerslave*?

$6.99, September 20, 1984, at A+B Sound in Victoria. Then *Live After Death* for $9.99 on November 27, 1985, at Cheapies Records in Hamilton, Ontario, now that I found myself submerged in the MBA program at McMaster. Thanks for indulging me the use of my green Duo-Tang record purchase record that I'd lost for fifteen years and only recently found.

I'll hit you with one other date. The first time I ever saw Iron Maiden live was with Saxon and Fastway supporting in Spokane, Washington, July 24, 1983. Again I'll blame the lapse on coming from the boonies, nowhere near the rock 'n' roll tour circuit. But what a show; to this day I rank *Piece of Mind*, *Power & the Glory*, and *Fastway* as titanic equals and, strangely enough, in my opinion the best records of the three bands' respective catalogs.

Grind forward a few weeks and then some and here we are, in a position to celebrate together this legendary band that is still vital, making the same kind of music they brought us in the heady days of the NWOBHM, from which they quickly leapt ahead, thanks to determination, talent, personality, a pile of creativity, Rod Smallwood, and Derek Riggs and Eddie.

For those unfamiliar with the structure of the *Album by Album* series, this book is a follow-up to similar tomes I've written on Rush, AC/DC, and Pink Floyd—the concept being the assembly of a panel of deep fans and experts from all walks of life, and a subsequent jaw session over each of the band's studio albums. What resulted for these folks, in many cases (because they told me so), for myself for sure, and hopefully for you the reader, is a rekindling of the love affair you might have had for this band at one point, since dimmed in the sensory overload that is modern digital life.

Like I say, that's certainly been the case for your intrepid moderator, because, I gotta tell ya, during the long journey through the Maiden catalog with these folks, many of them friends and all at least acquaintances through the years (save for the two women I had not known before, Nita Strauss and Kirsten Rosenberg, as well as Ahmet Zappa—all delightful), I've come out the other end affirming something I'd suspected for many years: even though for an old man like me there's no way that anything else the band makes will ever usurp the deep sentimental love I have for the first five Iron Maiden records, absolutely nipping at their heels and hugely enjoyable near start to finish are the last four albums.

Alas, *Brave New World* I like about as much as I did during the excitement we all had as we interviewed the guys and wrote about the reunion in our mag *Brave Words & Bloody Knuckles* eighteen years ago. But land sakes, *Dance of Death* and *A Matter of Life and Death* . . . I used to sneer at the similarities in those titles, but now the word "death" in an Iron Maiden record title is synonymous with top-shelf quality—with these two albums, it's almost code for the elixir of youth.

And dammit, I love it when that happens. I love it when a heritage act I grew up with can keep me engaged with their new music. In this light, I put Maiden in the same camp as Motörhead, Deep Purple, Cheap Trick, Kiss, and, as the next generation goes, Metallica, Megadeth, and Overkill. (Saxon and Accept ain't doing too bloody badly, either.)

Anyway, thanks for allowing me these introductory musings. I hope you enjoy reading the thoughts of my esteemed and knowledgeable panel as much as I did gathering them. It was an absolute joy getting told and resold seemingly one minute to the next on the many deep virtues found all over the vast Maiden catalog, especially, as I say, across the astonishing run of superlong and involved records since Bruce bounced back. With that happy thought lingering, I now ease myself into the comparatively passive moderator's seat and present to you *Iron Maiden: Album by Album*.

Discographic Notes

A few notes on the presentation of the album credits:

Credits and citations of all types, where available, are reproduced to be in the spirit of the earliest UK issue of the album.

Albums up to and including *No Prayer for the Dying* get the vinyl-related Side 1/Side 2 designation. After that, to reflect full immersion into the CD age, that designation is dropped.

Song timings are cited as per the earliest issue of the album from any territory. If not available on UK issue as was the standard, I went next to the US or Canadian issue from the same year.

Where there are discrepancies on writing credits or song spellings and punctuations, back sleeve took precedent over record label.

Writing credits that distinguish between music and lyrics are not common with Maiden; hence the comma is used so as not to cause errors, especially when more than two names are listed.

Performance and production credits are as cited on the earliest issue.

No further demarcation has been cited for single-song or occasional performance or vocal on a track, nor for producers of certain sessions where we could have started breaking things up.

Songs are not in double quotes in the track listings to promote neatness.

Other liberties were taken, decisions made as the situation required.

1 Iron Maiden

with Bobby "Blitz" Ellsworth, Marty Friedman, and Brian Slagel

SIDE 1
1. Prowler 3:56
(Harris)
2. Remember Tomorrow 5:20
(Harris, Di'Anno)
3. Running Free 3:22
(Harris, Di'Anno)
4. Phantom of the Opera 7:02
(Harris)

SIDE 2
1. Transylvania 4:09
(Harris)
2. Strange World 5:43
(Harris)
3. Charlotte the Harlot 4:14
(Murray)
4. Iron Maiden 3:43
(Harris)

Personnel: Paul Di'Anno—lead vocals; Dave
   Murray—guitar; Dennis Stratton—guitar, vocals;
   Steve Harris—bass, vocals; Clive Burr—drums
Produced by Will Malone
Recorded at Kingsway Studios, London
Released April 14, 1980

Note: The US and Canadian release added "Sanctuary" (Iron Maiden), 3:19.

Despite the instant smash impact of Iron Maiden's self-titled debut, no one could say this band hadn't paid their dues. With roots all the way back to 1975, Steve Harris and a rotating cast were creating a new wave of British heavy metal long before anybody thought to stick capital letters on that term.

The slow rise through the pubs—with many of these songs in the set—resulted in the band's first bits of pre-LP product, namely the legendary long-form seven-inch indie release *The Soundhouse Tapes*, and marquee positioning on what is essentially NWOBHM's kickoff release, the first of the two *Metal for Muthas* compilations, which Iron Maiden opened with "Sanctuary" and, in fact, velvet-roped themselves as the only band with two tracks on the comp, adding the majestic "Wrathchild" to Side 2.

Metal for Muthas arrived February 15, 1980, with the self-titled debut album set to frighten the shops two months later, a rapid rise pretty much assured with the laser-focused Rod Smallwood as manager. It didn't hurt that Iron Maiden had the five-way personnel magnetism to make these anthems translate live.

However, the production values of *Iron Maiden* left something to be desired. Although not distractingly bad like a few tragic examples from the NWOBHM (Raven, Fist, and Tygers of Pan Tang come to mind), it was a bit thin, urgent, and punky, which nonetheless suited the high energy and even frantic music as well as the aggressive growl and nonchalant cool emanating from the man at the mic, Paul Di'Anno. The album was recorded in thirteen days and

Opposite:
Eddie down for the
count. Left to right:
Clive Burr, Adrian Smith,
Paul Di'Anno, Steve
Harris (seated), and
Dave Murray.

produced by an apparently disinterested and not exactly pedigreed Will Malone, which (again, silver lining) led Steve Harris to get involved in production, an invaluable asset down the line in terms of his substantial input with Martin Birch, and later self-production and co-production roles.

But no amount of subpar knob-jobbing could stop these stage-tested songs. Again, personality and high relief distinguish the record. Opener "Prowler" was surprisingly punky, as were youthful anthem "Running Free" and "Charlotte the Harlot." "Remember Tomorrow" and "Strange World" showed that when one of these new-generation metal bands made quiet music, it was going to be morose and creepy in deference to the masters, Black Sabbath and bridge band Judas Priest. "Transylvania" tacitly suggests greatness, for only the audacious and talented would stick an instrumental on their first album. As a sort of pedal-to-the-metal deference to Harris's progressive rock roots, there was the band's first literary/cinematic epic in "Phantom of the Opera," with title track, although brief, managing prog flourishes as well.

Comparisons with the great Black Sabbath are underscored in the title track. Here was what was to become the first-generation-defining metal band of a new decade issuing in spring 1980 an album named after themselves, with a song named after the album, named after the band—just like Black Sabbath, which issued its groundbreaking debut in spring 1970. Both albums addressed horror themes straight between the eyes—literally, with scary occult figures staring right at you from the record jackets.

But let's not get carried away. Black Sabbath invented heavy metal, while Iron Maiden was pretty much a brash version of Judas Priest circa *Sad Wings of Destiny* through *Stained Class* and, frankly, nowhere near as good or trailblazing (this is a point I will never cede: despite how awesome *Iron Maiden* is, innovation is not one of its ticked boxes, outside of, arguably, the cover art). Black Sabbath, by 1980, was a completely new band with Ronnie James Dio at the helm, while Judas Priest was busy dumbing themselves down with *British Steel*, voluntarily

Iron Maiden's self-funded debut release, *The Soundhouse Tapes*, released November 9, 1979.

abdicating their throne, with Steve Harris and an equally battle-ready Paul Di'Anno all too willing to seize the jewel-encrusted mace.

And there was no question Iron Maiden was doing exactly that, with its blistering support-slot disrobings of Priest and Kiss, with its boasts on that very subject, with *The Soundhouse Tapes*, with the Metal for Muthas tour, with a nice flow of picture-sleeve singles that built a narrative for the band's mascot, Eddie, and most notably with the dark mystique crafted by the composition and sequencing of the tracks on *Iron Maiden*. And, which, let's not forget, drove a small but vocal army of headbangers insane in North America as an import for a magical four months before the record received official stateside release. That US version would add "Sanctuary," a bit of an outlier that made me prefer my copy of the original as sacrosanct, the way Eddie intended it, a record second only to *Angel Witch* (by Angel Witch, featuring "Angel Witch") in the canon of the finest NWOBHM records of all time.

MARTIN POPOFF: To start, I'm interested in how Iron Maiden first entered your lives. How did you find out about them?
MARTY FRIEDMAN: When the NWOBHM started, my good friend John Lackey—still friends today—could not get enough of anything remotely British metal. There were a few import record stores in the Maryland/Washington, DC, area and they had all sorts of NWOBHM albums and singles. We—especially John—would buy anything that looked metal, and that first Iron Maiden album could only be metal with that jacket.

Looking back, most of those bands sucked. Regardless, they had this sound and look we just loved. Songwriting and musicianship were not the top criteria in our minds at the time. We just ate all of it up. We spent a lot of money buying seven-inch records for one shitty bonus track, and we still loved it, because the sound was so new and so much more exciting than hard rock was back then.

Iron Maiden was different for several reasons. The cover artwork didn't look cheesy like the other bands', but it still told you the record was gonna be metal. You were proud to have that cover lying around your room, as opposed to, say, Styx.

An early print ad showing Iron Maiden at the top of the bill at the Marquee in London.

POPOFF: How about you, Brian, on the other coast?

BRIAN SLAGEL: I was a big-time tape trader, and a friend in Sweden sent me an AC/DC live tape from somewhere, live in 1980, and said, "Hey, there's this band you might like, just put out a single called *The Soundhouse Tapes*, named Iron Maiden." And he put that, the three songs, on the end of the tape. And that began my lifelong obsession with Iron Maiden. I heard that and went, "This is the most amazing thing I've ever heard." So I started getting information about who they were, what was going on over in England, and became obsessed with the NWOBHM and Iron Maiden.

POPOFF: What was special about Iron Maiden versus the '70s bands you knew? Or other NWOBHM bands for that matter?

SLAGEL: Growing up, being a huge metal fan, I loved all that '70s stuff. I heard Deep Purple's *Machine Head*, which completely changed my life, when I was eleven, and got into all that stuff. I loved AC/DC and Priest—everybody from that period. But with Maiden, there was just something there I hadn't heard before. Because I was a big punk rock fan as well, maybe it was the mixture of metal and punk. It just seemed different, cutting edge, fresh, interesting. It immediately clicked with me.

BOBBY "BLITZ" ELLSWORTH: I was exposed to Iron Maiden and the majority of the New Wave of British Heavy Metal when Overkill started. When D. D. Verni, Rat Skates, I, and a guy named Robert Pisarek formed Overkill, these guys really exposed me to more of that. It was sometime around 1981 and my first thoughts were, this seemed to stand out on its own, above its precursors. I remember being at rehearsal and these guys were so excited about it, before I knew it the songs from *Iron Maiden*, and eventually *Killers*, were in our cover set. It was quite an influence on us and quite a slap on the side of the head for me.

Three other metal LPs of the era that give *Iron Maiden* a run for its money: Black Sabbath's *Heaven and Hell*, Judas Priest's *British Steel*, and the eponymous debut album by Angel Witch.

Opposite:
Getting ready to hit the road, 1980. *Left to right:* Clive Burr, Paul Di'Anno, Dennis Stratton, Dave Murray, and Steve Harris.

FRIEDMAN: I was already in this career as a guitarist before I heard Maiden; my path was already set. But when I heard Maiden, I knew I had to up my heavy metal game. Because what I was playing up 'til then was more like punky aggressive hard rock that was kind of like metal. At that time, when you thought of metal, you thought of motorcycles and Steppenwolf and hippie stuff, really. And so Maiden was like, wow, this kind of sounds like punk, but it's pretty heavy and the guitar is pretty cool. It made the music I was making heavier. But that's not just Maiden—that's probably all the NWOBHM.

POPOFF: And maybe we had no way of knowing, but Maiden had paid their dues.

SLAGEL: Just like all the bands from that scene. That scene started out of nothing. It was really a reaction to the punk rock movement and disco and all this other nonsense at the time. And it came out of nowhere, this whole NWOBHM scene. Iron Maiden was the first thing I heard, and then I started hearing everybody else after that. But, yeah, when Maiden came up, they played pubs and clubs for years and nothing really happened. It *looked* like it was a fast ride, but they played for years and not a whole lot happened. They got the first album out on a major label and it went from there.

The *Metal for Muthas* album, released February 1980, featuring Iron Maiden's "Sanctuary" and "Wrathchild."

POPOFF: There are all sorts of future classics on the record, but the first big song was "Running Free," the first single coming out a couple months ahead of the album. Why do you think that was worthy enough to be the first single?

FRIEDMAN: This was probably the most mainstream song on the album, with the cool sing-along chorus. It sounded like punk rock from the mid-'70s with harmony lead guitars. It was fresh at the time.

ELLSWORTH: When you're talking about metal in general and evoking that emotion, you're talking about individualism and the celebration of it, and "Running Free" quite obviously ticks all those emotional boxes. This was a great introduction to a great new band. "I'm running free, yeah!"

The band's first single for EMI, "Running Free," released February 1980.

One thing I always remember about that era of Iron Maiden was that the lyrics were quite often from a first-person perspective. "Running Free," you could call the song "*I'm Running Free*," just like it says in the lyrics. But, later, it kind of changed into more of a "we" thing. Sure, there was individualism, but I think Di'Anno sang more in terms of "I." Dickinson sang in terms of "I," but also "we," which extended it.

SLAGEL: "Running Free" had the bigger "hooks," where you could sing along and it would stick in your brain. So I get why that would be the single, although I think they put out, like, a thousand singles from that record and I have all of them [*laughs*]. But it's also an easy subject. A lot of the other stuff is more medieval, and this is more youthful, angsty. Again, it was that punk attitude but couched in a metal vibe.

Iron Maiden fans get into the spirit at the Metal for Muthas tour, Lyceum, London, February 10, 1980.

POPOFF: Speaking of punk, the narrative was always that Maiden was different because of Paul Di'Anno—that there was something punky about him, with his short hair and leather jacket.

SLAGEL: Certainly. He definitely dressed more like a punk rocker, especially in the early days. As a guy who loved '70s metal but also punk rock, I loved the merging of those two scenes, with Paul's look and even the way he sounded. He sang more like a punk rocker. He didn't sound like Halford or Ian Gillan or any of those guys.

FRIEDMAN: He looked cool, had a manly voice, and just oozed punk and metal combined, which was how I fashioned myself back then. He had an emotional way of singing without being a sissy, which is of top importance when you are fifteen. There are very few metal voices I like. I'm not into the high tones—kept me off the Rush bandwagon because of that high voice, although I absolutely admire them to the end of the earth. But I can't hang with high tones. This also coming from a guy who, in the early '80s, had high-tone singers and shit like that, so don't kill me.

But Paul Di'Anno had a manly voice, and heavy metal is manly music. Plus I just thought he had a lot of emotion. It wasn't about technique and it wasn't operatic. That high-voice stuff just sounds so cheesy to me, even when it's done well. On the first two albums, the vocals were just so manly, and it didn't seem contrived. It didn't seem like they cared about even making it! It seemed like they were just doing it. It was so cool.

ELLSWORTH: I was learning to sing at the time, so Paul was not necessarily someone who was groundbreaking. But I always liked his punky presentation, and I always thought that presentation was more important than, say, musically correct performance. This was metal—we were trying to evoke emotion. And that's what I got out of Paul Di'Anno—that it wasn't about being musically correct. Because what was happening around him seemed musically correct, he became kind of the counterpart to that Steve Harris/Clive Burr, where those two seemed like they were charging forward. It was almost like Di'Anno brought the storm, the dark cloud over the top of that musical perfection.

Harris leans into Di'Anno at the Lyceum, February 10, 1980.

Stratton strikes a pose; the Lyceum, London, February 10, 1980.

POPOFF: What did you think of "Sanctuary" being added to the US edition of the album?
ELLSWORTH: I didn't know there were two versions at that time. But, yeah, to this day, that song has impact for Overkill—we just released our eighteenth record and covered "Sanctuary" as a bonus track. We're still carrying those beginnings with us so many decades later. "Sanctuary" is just this simple, emotional song, and that emotion was evoked through the riff and through the vocals. I agree with you it's really the odd one among the group. But it's probably the one with the most energy, or at least punk or rock 'n' roll energy. That's probably why someone like Paul shines on a song like that.

SLAGEL: It was a great song, number one, and, growing up in the '70s and being a huge AC/DC fan, I was not unaccustomed to albums coming out in the US that had different songs on them. Great song—the more the merrier for me.

POPOFF: At the opposite end of the spectrum from "Running Free" and "Sanctuary" is the longest song on the album, "Phantom of the Opera."
SLAGEL: Definitely my favorite song by far on that record. I love long, epic songs. The subject matter was amazing amid this progressive, Rush-meets-Jethro Tull, all-over-the-place sort of stuff. That song completely blew me away. Everything I ever wanted in a metal band was on that record. It was fast, it was heavy, it had medieval lyrics, and it had that medieval look—with the album cover. Everything was just kind of perfect.

FRIEDMAN: What an arrangement, and so progressive. The drumless intro is classic, and it really sets things up in a great way. To me, this was the heavy metal equivalent to "Free Bird," with lots of repeating guitar clichés, which are absolutely fantastic when used in an inspired context—"Hotel California," "Layla," and "Free Bird" come to mind, right? As far as I was concerned, "Phantom of the Opera" was the first time this many guitar clichés were repeated so many times. Repetition is key when making memorable music, and this was the most impressive metal guitar song out there at the time.

POPOFF: And of course there's an instrumental, "Transylvania."

FRIEDMAN: At the time there were practically no triplet-based heavy rock instrumentals. This was probably one of the earliest cases of that whole "widdly widdly" syndrome as the English press often called it. That's the sound of triplets being played rapidly on lead guitar. At the time this was super impressive, especially to a young teen. But it hasn't really aged that well, if only because it inspired so many poor replicas over the years.

SLAGEL: Definitely, "Transylvania" was cool. An instrumental wasn't something we normally heard back then. There were, maybe, a couple I remember. And I didn't miss that there were no vocals. And then there's "Iron Maiden," which I've heard a billion times now. But when it first came out, it was more like, "Wow, this song is really great." "Prowler," the first song, doesn't get a lot of love these days, but that opening riff is so unique. It kind of transitions into this heavy punk-meets-metal thing. If I was going to invent and create the perfect heavy metal band, this is what it would sound like. But I'll stick with "Phantom." It's always fun hearing that song live. They play it every time, but I don't get bored of it, so the riff must be pretty good.

Iron Maiden's second EMI single was "Sanctuary," released May 1980.

POPOFF: Are the roots of thrash buried somewhere in a song like "Phantom of the Opera"?

ELLSWORTH: I think so, in regard to the ferocity it's played at. Thrash metal is about evoking an emotion, but there's still got to be that element of musical perfection. Ultimately, when you press play or put the needle down, the emotion was what mattered. And that was the success of a song like that. It's not really about deciphering it or pulling it apart.

POPOFF: As counterpoint to the ferocity of that song, there are these two dark dirges in "Strange World" and "Remember Tomorrow." Although, granted, "Remember Tomorrow" rocks out as well.

ELLSWORTH: These are really the birth of those Metallica-type ballads, with the depressive approach but still a type of celebration at the end. Musically, "Remember

A ticket from the band's show at the Rainbow Theatre in London, June 20, 1980.

Tomorrow" had a lot more nuts than, for instance, the melodic Sabbath or Purple. This was something that still had balls. A song like "Remember Tomorrow" became a template for what followed with many thrash bands.

"Remember Tomorrow" and "Strange World" set the bar higher, or at least in a different place. They gave the record contrast. Everything didn't have to be on ten like "Running Free" or "Charlotte the Harlot." You could go up and you could go down; there were hills and valleys. It made for an interesting way of presenting a new heavy band.

FRIEDMAN: It was classy to have contrast between a quiet verse and a heavy chorus. Little did they know this would become one of the biggest and longest continuing clichés in heavy metal music. It was fun to play along with as a teen guitarist because, during the mellow part, you could actually hear your own guitar. Although when I found out that Harris was a big prog fan, it was kind of a letdown, because I always hated that *Star Trek* stuff. Up until then I just saw Maiden as this brand-new entity playing slamming energetic metal with guitar harmonies and cool song titles.

SLAGEL: I was totally into it. Growing up in the '70s and being into Elton John and a bunch of other stuff that was a bit more mellow, I loved that dynamic of having these fast, heavy songs with a real punky vibe and then this melodic mellow stuff that breaks things up. All those influences on them, particularly Steve, were also big influences on me. So the fact they were doing that was perfect for me. They were taking all the best parts of all the bands I loved and putting them into this band.

POPOFF: And speaking of Steve, in this band, the bass player is the leader. How does that affect things?

SLAGEL: Really, out of every band I grew up with in the '70s, it was always the guitar player who wrote everything. Geezer wrote most of the lyrics for Sabbath, obviously, and there's Geddy Lee in Rush, but Harris, that was his band and he was writing those songs—and from the bass perspective. You can hear the bass a lot louder than in other stuff. When I was a dumb kid, I didn't even know what a bass guitar was. I didn't even hear it [*laughs*]. When you start hearing it, it's like, "Oh, I get it now." It's a different perspective to have a guy like that writing and being the focal point of the band as far as the writing goes. He also plays guitar, but he's a phenomenal bass player.

FRIEDMAN: I was always more impressed by Steve's songwriting and arranging than his bass playing. I found it too busy at times and rarely liked the bassists who copied him too closely. That said, he plays some wonderful stuff, and overall it adds to the charm of the band.

ELLSWORTH: Maiden was a bass player's dream. Bass became a lead instrument, not put in the background as support, but right out front. The Motörhead philosophy of everything louder than everything else—these guys did that—which was an eye-opening experience for those in the metal community—this idea of the bass front and center. For a bass player, oh my God, this is pure heaven.

POPOFF: How would you assess Will Malone's production job on the album?
SLAGEL: Honestly, what they were doing with the music was so groundbreaking I didn't notice. I was drinking in all the NWOBHM stuff at that point and hearing all this stuff that was so raw and not perfectly recorded. These bands were doing this with zero money. Production-wise, *Iron Maiden* was a little bit better than the norm. It wasn't perfect, but it sounded good. In 1980, when it came out, it was perfectly

Backstage at the Reading Festival (with Eddie), August 1980.

In October 1980, to bridge the gap between its first and second albums, Iron Maiden released a cover of "Women in Uniform" by the Skyhooks.

fine for me. Even if I listen to it now it sounds fine. But, clearly, they went on to use the greatest producer of all time in Martin Birch.

POPOFF: Can I get an "amen" that arguably there's one NWOBHM record that's better than *Iron Maiden*, namely another self-titled debut, *Angel Witch*?

FRIEDMAN: Yes, I liked *Angel Witch* even better than *Iron Maiden* at the time, but I honestly can't remember why. Possibly because it was scarier and the lead guitar was more impressive to me. Maiden's guitar arrangements were way more impressive, but their lead solos were a bit pedestrian.

SLAGEL: I think you could argue there were a few bands from the New Wave of British Heavy Metal—Diamond Head, obviously being another—bigger than Iron Maiden for a minute. And obviously they were a massive influence on Metallica too; they could've turned the corner.

But a lot of Maiden's success was because they had a phenomenal manager. You have to have good people around you. Metallica would not be as big as Metallica is if they didn't have a ton of amazing people around them—management, agents, all that—and Maiden had the same thing. Soon as Rod Smallwood got with them, he knew how to work the system, how to make them big, how to get the best of everything they were doing on the business side. And Steve Harris, being a smart guy as well, that's really what propelled them faster than a lot of those, along with being a phenomenal band.

The *Live!! + one* EP, released in Japan in November 1980, featured four songs recorded at the Marquee in London in July.

POPOFF: Finally, I know we've touched on it, but what do you make of Eddie and that album cover? Eddie turned out to be an icon, and here's our first look at him in all his green, pasty glory.

ELLSWORTH: Well, it's the first time I ever thought of getting a tattoo, I'll tell you that much [*laughs*]. This was visually different. And, quickly, all young bands, to some degree, wanted to be Maiden, or at least have that impact, and we all knew part of that impact came from Eddie. I don't think we wanted, necessarily, to copy them, but soon thereafter our band, Overkill, had a mascot too. So, from the audible to the visual, Maiden was a template for guys our age.

Lofty ambitions. *Top row, from left:* Di'Anno, Murray, Harris. *Seated:* Burr and Smith.

POPOFF: So Overkill had good ol' Chaly. Marty, you guys in Megadeth had Vic Rattlehead.

FRIEDMAN: Absolutely. Eddie turned out to be a great thing for Maiden, and it turned out to be an identifying point for every metal band. It's like, you gotta have one. But for me, at the time, I really didn't care about that, other than the fact that the Maiden covers looked so fucking cool. Which shows you how much I know [*laughs*]. I had no idea that Eddie—and all the mascots, really—put some money in the pockets of the people doing it. It was brilliant, but, at the time, all I cared about was the music.

SLAGEL: Back then it was pretty shocking to have this crazy-looking zombie on the cover of an album with that logo, and the kind of evil, dark, British background. And it absolutely stood out. When I first saw the cover, I thought, "Oh my God, this is insane." Especially being on a major label as they were at the time. And you're right: You knew it was a heavy metal album. You didn't have to guess. In the '70s, I would buy albums based on the covers. When I discovered Rush, it was because I looked at *2112* and went, "Oh, maybe this is heavy metal." And it kind of was. But there was no mistaking that when you got *Iron Maiden* home—it was going to be heavy.

2 Killers

with Marty Friedman, Jimmy Kay, and Mike Portnoy

SIDE 1
1. The Ides of March 1:48
(Harris)
2. Wrathchild 2:54
(Harris)
3. Murders in the Rue Morgue 4:14
(Harris)
4. Another Life 3:22
(Harris)
5. Genghis Khan 3:02
(Harris)
6. Innocent Exile 3:50
(Harris)

SIDE 2
1. Killers 4:58
(Harris, Di'Anno)
2. Prodigal Son 6:05
(Harris)
3. Purgatory 3:18
(Harris)
4. Drifter 4:47
(Harris)

Personnel: Paul Di'Anno—vocals; Dave Murray—
    guitar; Adrian Smith—guitar; Steve Harris—
    bass; Clive Burr—drums
Produced by Martin Birch
Recorded at Battery Studios, London
Released February 2, 1981

Note: The US and Canadian release added "Twilight Zone" (Murray, Harris), 2:33.

First off, *Killers* is Iron Maiden's *Van Halen II*—the work of a band confidently coming into its own while pulling together a second record full of songs honed over the hard-clubbing years. And if the band considered these songs the B pile, no one noticed, thanks in large part to the arrivals of producer Martin Birch (at the height of his powers) and Adrian Smith on guitar, replacing Dennis Stratton.

Only "Prodigal Son" and "Murders in the Rue Morgue" are new songs, the former neither here nor there, save for its sincere acoustic guitar. But the latter is one of the band's most dynamic and sparkly compositions ever—stuffed with melody and personality, very much of an Adrian Smith vibe although Steve is credited alone, as is the case with every last track except "Killers."

Indeed, Steve's dominance in the writing distinguishes *Killers*, as does the fact that this is the only Maiden album with two instrumentals. Of more interest is the contrast with the debut, particularly the tough, closer-to-correct production values and the more effective melding of heavy metal with the band's proggy ideas. In other words, the outcome is brighter, more accessible, and less flat-out creepy than the debut—*Iron Maiden* is wine and downers while *Killers* is pints at the pub.

Comparison continued, unlike *Van Halen II*, *Killers* was a creative triumph; similar to *Van Halen II*, the album didn't particularly advance Maiden's career, nor did it hatch many hits or enduring classics. Still, none can deny the heavy metal seduction of "Wrathchild," the track that put Steve on the map with that clarion call of a bass line and put his band on the map with its inclusion on the historic first *Metal for Muthas* album. The aforementioned "Murders in the Rue Morgue" sits in many a Maiden fan's top ten, and "Innocent Exile" should have been

bigger. "Another Life" is another deep-cut classic; these especially making *Killers* a respected Maiden record—both for its songcraft and its singular and twin leads.

On a different tack, "Purgatory" and "Killers" both suggest proto-thrash (although down the street, Raven was doing this to greater effect), while *Killers* retains ties to the band's pubby punkiness via the breakdown section of "Another Life" and the totality of the closing track, "Drifter."

Add it up, and, outside of a short intro, there are nine tracks on *Killers*, and only the mellow one is more than five minutes long. The durations indeed contribute to the record's sense of immediacy, but, again, one might conjecture, more of that comes from Martin Birch's lively and midrange-dominant sound, something he brought to both Blue Öyster Cult with *Cultösaurus Erectus* and *Fire of Unknown Origin*,

A band portrait taken around the time of the release of *Killers*, featuring new member Adrian Smith (*second right*).

and to Black Sabbath with *Heaven and Hell* and *Mob Rules*, even if quite oddly and enigmatically, all four of those records champion midrange in different ways.

But please excuse the inside baseball; for really, what arguably matters most is again the notion that *Killers* is Part II of Maiden working through its tried-and-tested material en route to a clean slate—cleaner than anticipated, given the switcheroo about to take place at the lead singer position.

MARTIN POPOFF: Let's start with this: How were you introduced to *Killers*?
MARTY FRIEDMAN: The day it was available in the US, my bro and I drove to downtown Washington, DC, to be sure we could get a copy. It was not like there would be dozens in stock. Maybe three or four copies, if we were lucky. And then we saw that cover—which looked so amazing, especially with the glossy cardboard stock that some UK albums had. No US albums were printed on that kind of stock, and it just looked so superior.

The cover was way cooler than the first album, so, of course, we had no doubt that the album contents would be even better than the debut. I was right in guessing that—to me everything about *Killers* was superior to the debut. Sonically it sounded higher budget, the songs were arranged better, performed better; the guitar tones were juicier and heavier. If I liked the debut, I loved *Killers*. The debut sounded kind of low budget and underground, but *Killers* sounded mainstream, which led us American kids to believe that the UK was so cool that heavy music, like Maiden, was mainstream [*laughs*]. In the US at that time, Fleetwood Mac was the norm and no one knew who Maiden was.

And as a young guitarist, it was rare to find new stuff cool enough to want to learn what was going on with it. *Killers* was stimulating. I learned all the songs and even the B-Sides from the ultra-rare import singles. The guitar work was really fun to learn. It was not so challenging that it made me want to give up, but still cool enough to try to master it. I played along with this album as much as I did the debut.

POPOFF: The big difference is the replacement of guitarist Dennis Stratton with Adrian Smith.
MIKE PORTNOY: I'd say Adrian joining the band made somewhat of a difference, but it was very subtle at this stage. I think Adrian's involvement in the band years down the road would be more and more apparent. But, for this album, I think it really established a strong dual guitar team with Adrian and Dave. And I think the songs on *Killers* started to show their more progressive leanings and less of the punk rock side. The first album had a nice

combination of both. You had the punk rock side of "Sanctuary" and "Prowler," but then you had "Phantom of the Opera" as well. I guess they established that punk, prog, and metal formula, maybe one-third each [*laughs*].

FRIEDMAN: I thought Adrian was a tastier, more thought-out kind of player compared to Dave Murray, but, at the same time, Murray had more of a distinctive sound. You could pick out Murray from other guitarists because he's just doing trills all the time, you know [*laughs*]. He does trills, like, in every solo. But whatever it takes to stand out.

If I can pick out who it is just from hearing a solo, the goal is realized. But if I were to have one of the two guys do a guest solo on my record, I would go for Adrian, because he's tastier and seems more concerned with his note choice.

Producer Martin Birch, who began a long and fruitful association with Iron Maiden on *Killers*, is shown here at Record Plant, New York City, 1976.

Murray rocks out (with Di'Anno in the background) at Pointe East in Lynwood, Illinois, June 26, 1981.

POPOFF: I've talked to Paul Di'Anno many times, and he's got a distinct dislike for *Killers*. **Jimmy, you've interviewed him a few times as well. Where's his head these days on** *Killers*?

JIMMY KAY: According to Paul, he's a little disappointed in the songs going from the first album to the second album. But I think it's the other way around. Martin Birch has brought them to another level here. Black Sabbath and Deep Purple invented heavy metal, whereas I really do believe, with *Killers*, Maiden redefined heavy metal, and everything takes off from there. You've got Paul Di'Anno with his fabulous, street, angry, raspy voice, and the music is just a wall of metallic sound, in the sense that it's a bottom-heavy album.

Also, there's a conceptual theme in *Killers* that isn't present in the first album. But there is also similarity in that they're all old songs from back to 1977. Of course, with Martin, the production values are much stronger than the songs of similar vintage on the debut.

Paul Di'Anno disagrees. He thinks there's not a lot of energy on these songs. I think the songs are just as strong, even if you gotta think they put their favorites on the first album. And if you look at "Killers," the song itself, it's a brilliant piece of work because it doesn't follow the typical structure of any song. It's sort of like verse, bridge, verse, bridge, solo, bridge, verse. And the album's not called *Killer*—the album is called *Killers*. Because there's either suicide or serial killing or murder everywhere. I don't know if it's consciously or subconsciously a theme with Steve, who wrote ninety-five percent of the album.

Even the album cover, right? The first album cover, you see Eddie and he's just sort of that punk rocker in the streets. Here you've got Eddie with the axe. And you see Charlotte the Harlot up in the hotel room, and you see the Ruskin Arms in the distance. But you know, he's murdered another victim. That would be the most iconic album cover for them. When anybody thinks of Iron Maiden, or at least Eddie, they think of either *The Number of the Beast* or *Killers*. It's a piece of art. And when you listen to the song "Killers," it directly evokes the imagery of that album cover.

PORTNOY: Martin Birch, to my ears, was the George Martin of Iron Maiden. He was absolutely crucial to their sound. *The Number of the Beast* was like the end of the punk rock and the entrance of Bruce, and a little more progressive songs. And then *Piece of Mind* was the next logical step. But even though they are all quite different, Martin

Di'Anno on stage at Pointe East, a few weeks into Iron Maiden's first US tour.

Birch's mixes and productions back in the early '80s were the best in the business. He was the go-to guy for clean, early heavy metal productions. Before this, he did Black Sabbath, Blue Öyster Cult, and Whitesnake, which all sounded crystal clear.

POPOFF: With *Killers*, how was Maiden stacking up against their NWOBHM brethren?
FRIEDMAN: It was just more listenable. The other stuff had the same spirit, but the guitar playing, to be frank, was pretty bad [*laughs*]. Most of the NWOBHM, the playing and the songwriting, overall, it didn't make you want to listen to it so many times. You'd buy it because it was new and fresh. I had all those seven-inches and you'd just buy them because the NWOBHM was so fresh. You'd get A II Z, for example, and you'd say, "Wow, this is heavy," and you'd listen to it twice and then listen to *Killers* fifteen times. The other bands didn't have the quality or the well-produced

The band takes a breather backstage at Pointe East.

sound or the cool guitar riffs—and the cool album covers and the cool song titles. It all kind of sounded the same, and for some reason, Maiden just did it better.

POPOFF: What are some of the highlight tracks for you on the record?
KAY: I love "Murders in the Rue Morgue." It's typical Steve Harris, where there's always a twist. It's based on Edgar Allan Poe's short story. We assume he's a tourist, because he doesn't speak French. He stumbles upon two bodies that are women, and he's got blood on himself but he didn't kill them. And then the people, they sort of spot him and accuse him, so he runs to Italy. But the last line is the key: "My doctor said I've done this before." He actually was the murderer. He just wasn't aware of it.
Friedman: "Murders in the Rue Morgue" is my favorite too. I always liked fast music, and this was the fastest on the album. And Di'Anno had the coolest voice. It was punk, it was metal, it was rock, and it never seemed forced or contrived.

POPOFF: Even "The Ides of March" is about killing.
KAY: That's right, the fifteenth day of March is the assassination of Julius Caesar. And it's crazy but even the other instrumental, "Genghis Khan," if you listen to it carefully, it's about murder, right? It's Iron Maiden's "YYZ" [*laughs*]—it's broken down into three movements. From what I hear, Steve Harris wanted to create a sort of battle song. The first part is the march into battle while the second movement is the faster part. As they are in battle, it speeds up. And then the third part is the victory. If you really listen carefully, it breaks down into those themes.
PORTNOY: Having an instrumental like "Genghis Khan" was those guys showing their chops and dexterity. We all know Steve was a big '70s prog fan.

POPOFF: "The Ides of March" gives way to the record's biggest track by far, "Wrathchild."
FRIEDMAN: I wonder if *Killers* was maybe the first of many metal albums that started with an instrumental anthem. I was teaching guitar back then, and I must have made a fortune teaching this song, not only to guitarists but to bass players too. Great vocals, and what a classic heavy metal riff.
KAY: One thing people have missed on "Wrathchild"—look at the opening line, where he's born into greed and dominance

"Purgatory," released June 1981, was the last Iron Maiden single to feature Paul Di'Anno.

Steve Harris and his Fender Precision bass on tour in the United States, July 1981.

and his mother is a queen and he's never seen his father. And the word "wrathchild" is actually a made-up word, "wrath" being angry and "child." And he's looking for his father. But what people miss is, the original 1977 version was called "Rothschild," as in the Rothschilds, one of the richest families in the world. So originally it was about the Rothschilds, according to what I'm told. The lyric has this boy looking for his father he never knew. I can see that happening in these rich billionaire families. They probably changed the wording around because they were worried that maybe something would happen to them. But there's a picture the old drummer, Thunderstick, has—he was later in Samson, with Bruce—of an old demo tape with "Rothschild" written on it.

POPOFF: I've always viewed "Killers" as the heaviest song on the album. There's a classic Iron Maiden gallop to it, but then it switches to parts that seem to presage thrash.
PORTNOY: I can see that. I love "Killers." I remember getting the *Maiden Japan* EP around this time, and it had the live version of "Killers" plus "Innocent Exile" and "Wrathchild." The title track is one of the essential Di'Anno-era songs. And

"Murders in the Rue Morgue" and "Wrathchild," I guess those are the three off this album that still occasionally get pulled out and played.

With Dream Theater, we got to play "Killers," with Paul Di'Anno singing, at a show in Salzburg in 1995. That was incredible for me because, when I was with Dream Theater back in those days, we got to play with both Bruce and Paul at different points.

KAY: The song "Killers" was written from different perspectives. Paul told me that, at the beginning, it's in third person, and as the song progresses, it goes to the first person—the killer himself. And at the end of the song, another little twist, "God help me, what have I done?" He loves to kill but he's regretting it.

By the way, another cool song is "Prodigal Son." It talks about Lamia, a demon. When I was a young kid, the album didn't come with the lyrics, so I didn't know who Lamia was. I didn't even know what Paul Di'Anno was saying. The narrator is begging Lamia, this female demon who eats children, this Greek mythical figure, for his soul back from the devil. Pretty morbid but, oddly, this is Maiden gamely using acoustic guitars, which they would barely ever pick up again—almost never.

POPOFF: Analyze the Maiden gallop.

PORTNOY: Well, that's all coming from Steve Harris more than the drummer. It's all coming from the bass. Many of the riffs and rhythms that Steve writes on the bass have that galloping shuffle. Nicko was able to lock in with that perfectly. Clive did as well, but I think most of that chug is coming from the bass.

One great debate among metal fans is Iron Maiden versus Judas Priest. That was like the Beatles versus the Rolling Stones in the '60s or Sabbath versus Zeppelin in the '70s. Iron Maiden versus Judas Priest was the debate in the '80s. And I think the biggest difference between the two was the bass. In Iron Maiden, you had an absolute virtuoso on bass. You had two amazing singers, Bruce Dickinson and Rob Halford. You had two great double-guitar packages. And you had great drummers. But really, it was the bass players that kind of separated the two. Steve

Harris was a complete virtuoso and, to this day, one of the great bass pioneers.

Comparing the guitarists, Adrian and Dave play a bit more progressive and melodic. K. K. Downing and Glenn Tipton are more like traditional, old-school English guitar players, whereas I think Dave and Adrian were pushing it more and trying to go to newer places. The great thing about Maiden is they played a lot of melodies in place of the vocals. At times when the vocals aren't singing, they play guitar melodies and harmonies, whereas in Priest it was more just riffs. This came in handy much later when Maiden put Janick Gers in as a third guitar player and started touring as a three-guitar band. Suddenly, you could have two guys playing twin leads with one guy playing rhythm underneath. As crazy as it may seem to have three guitar players in a metal band, it makes a lot of sense musically.

FRIEDMAN: I saw Maiden open for Priest on the Point of Entry tour. I thought *Point of Entry* sucked balls and was the death knell for my beloved Priest. Nothing was further from the truth. Maiden was great, with lots of youthful energy, but they played everything way too fast, which sounds amateur in arenas. Priest came on and showed everyone, without question, who the metal gods were that night. Even the sellout songs from *Point of Entry*, like "Desert Plains" and "Hot Rockin'," sounded mammoth compared to Maiden's sort of bumblebee buzzing guitars. Priest opened with "Solar Angels," and, moving through their set, they kind of wiped away the memory of Maiden's set—which was sad for me, because I was there to see my new favorite band show the old dogs the wave of the future. But Priest schooled them pretty badly that night.

POPOFF: Funny. Marty, would you say Maiden perfected the heavy metal gallop?
FRIEDMAN: The gallop was my least important, least favorite thing about the band [*laughs*]. The gallop was like . . . how cool is a gallop?

Truth be told, and this is a very important point, Maiden fans are usually around fourteen or fifteen when they're just picking up an instrument, when they first discover a band like that. And then they hear something that sounds impossible,

Opposite:
Di'Anno on stage at the Palladium in New York City, July 1981.

but then when they try to play it on their instrument, they realize that maybe it's hard, but it's not impossible.

If you're a fifteen-year-old, you go listen to a band like, say, Yes, and you can pretty much say it's impossible. But when you hear Iron Maiden, it's like, "Well, if I practice this, there's, like, a mechanical way to do this." And that's so important, because if you're fourteen or fifteen, you don't have a girlfriend, you're not very popular, you've got plenty of time to work on mechanics. And then you think these rock stars are even cooler because they're just nailing this stuff you're having such a hard time with.

I think Iron Maiden was an absolutely perfect level of playing to inspire kids to play an instrument. When I was in Megadeth, I always thought our shit was too hard, our music too difficult. It's not going to inspire kids the way Metallica would. Metallica will play the same riff many times over and over, where Megadeth would play five riffs where there should be one riff. I always thought we needed to simplify it.

And Iron Maiden was probably the perfect balance for inspiring kids, and what's more important than that? Especially in rock and heavy metal. You want to have music that, when kids hear it, they think, "I wanna play, I wanna play." And I think in Megadeth, the overall assault was almost like we were trying to impress people. Rather than impressing people, it's more important to inspire people. This is coming from a guy who just released an album with the most insane guitar work of all time. You'll notice a lot of things I say, I contradict myself.

POPOFF: Of note, "Twilight Zone" was added to the North American version of *Killers*, just like "Sanctuary" was added to *Iron Maiden*.
KAY: Paul Di'Anno told me that with "Twilight Zone," they really jammed up that song, and it probably represents one of his best vocal deliveries. If you listen to the chorus, he's going from his chest voice to his head voice, back to his chest voice, in a really high sort of register. It's really difficult to do. And he said he really, really practiced in the jam session before they recorded that. He also told me he learned a lot of techniques from Martin Birch, which he uses to this day.

Above:
The "Twilight Zone" single was released exactly one month after *Killers* on March 2, 1981.

Below:
A print ad for the band's November 1981 show at the Rainbow Theatre in London—a homecoming of sorts after many months touring Europe and the United States.

Opposite:
Murray and Smith at the Palladium, where Iron Maiden made its New York debut with a run of three shows in July 1981.

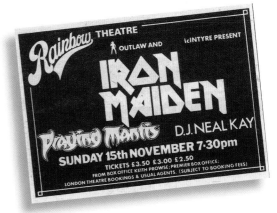

POPOFF: Ultimately, the big deal with *Killers* is, you've got the two guitarists who would establish that twin-lead trademark that pretty much defines Maiden's sound.

FRIEDMAN: For sure. At the time maybe you'd get the Allman Brothers or some kind of mellow rock with an occasional double-lead solo. Brian May deserves some credit, too, with all that harmonizing he overdubbed with himself. But Maiden was all harmonies, all the time, and in a metal context! Brilliant!

So, yeah, Maiden's harmony twin guitars were groundbreaking and a definite precursor to all the metal subgenres to come. Harmonizing a solo guitar line in thirds is the biggest staple of death metal and all kinds of intense metal. It is the easiest, most theoretically basic way to harmonize two guitars, allowing young metallers to "sound metal" just by playing the same line the other guitarist is playing, but up a step-and-a-half. Crack the Sky, a Maryland prog band, was already doing this, and even a bit more adventurous harmonizing, at the time, so I immediately recognized this basic harmony interval. And Maiden used this exact interval on every guitar line to the point where it really defined their sound.

I don't know, I kind of fell off the bandwagon as soon as Maiden started doing everything that is probably what made them famous. I think what it must be is, what they've done is pretty much the absolute identity of heavy metal—as a cliché. But not in a bad way. Like when you think of heavy metal, you think of harmonizing guitars, high-tone vocals; you think of *Star Trek* lyrics. And Maiden did it first, and they did it at a very major level. And they did it really, really well when nobody was

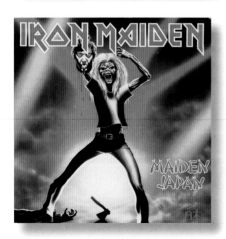

doing it well at all, and they continue to do it well. It's like the Ramones. They didn't stray from the formula, and, so, if you like that formula, you're going to go back again and again. I totally get it.

But it's so funny, back in 1981, I felt Maiden was very underground and way too cool to be popular. I felt exactly the same about Metallica, which shows what I know. I thought Metallica would never get signed. I thought Iron Maiden was the greatest thing ever, but only my two friends and I would ever, ever hear about them. It just continued to boggle my mind as they got bigger and bigger, of course, to my delight, because heavy metal was getting popular. But when I was listening to the first two records, I was like, "This is just so out there, no one's ever going to get into this."

POPOFF: Why do you think Paul Di'Anno was fired from the band? And what does Paul think after all these years?

KAY: Paul's side of the story was he was upset about how the *Killers* album, specifically the production, came out. He thought it was too glossy. Plus, the songs didn't have the spirit of the first album, which he loves. The reason he didn't show up to gigs when he was on tour was because he was so upset at the direction of the band. He was losing interest.

Of course, Steve's side of things is different. Steve is sort of like, "This guy is not taking the band seriously—he doesn't want to tour, he's partying too much." And then Bruce Dickinson said Paul was out-and-out fired because they wanted somebody better. So take your pick.

But there's something about Paul. He's got a character that everybody loves. You don't know if he's telling you the truth, but he's got this persona. He's funny, man. He's funny as hell. He's a guy you want to hang out with and just listen to him talk. He might not be the most responsible guy in the world [*laughs*], but, man, he's a great person to hang out with. And let's never forget, there was something about his voice. I don't think you could deliver all these songs about killers and murder and have a clean tenor singer. It had to be Paul's voice—his voice matched these lyrical themes. Paul Di'Anno just had to do Iron Maiden's first two albums. I just couldn't imagine it any other way.

The Number of the Beast

with Bobby "Blitz" Ellsworth, Franc Potvin, and Brian Slagel

SIDE 1
1. Invaders 3:20
(Harris)
2. Children of the Damned .4:34
(Harris)
3. The Prisoner 5:34
(Smith, Harris)
4. 22 Acacia Avenue 6:34
(Harris, Smith)

SIDE 2
1. The Number of the Beast .4:25
(Harris)
2. Run to the Hills. 3:50
(Harris)
3. Gangland. 3:46
(Smith, Burr)
4. Hallowed Be Thy Name. .7:08
(Harris)

Personnel: Bruce Dickinson—vocals; Dave Murray—
    guitars; Adrian Smith—guitars, backing vocals;
    Steve Harris—bass, backing vocals; Clive Burr—
    drums
Produced by Martin Birch
Recorded at Battery Studios, London
Released March 22, 1982

It was a heavy metal happenstance perhaps destined to be. Fireplug Bruce Dickinson had proven himself, hands down, the greatest singer and most enigmatic front man of the New Wave of British Heavy Metal. Not through the wobbly early Samson albums, but certainly by the time of that band's raging classic, *Shock Tactics*, a record that, in this writer's view, stands as Dickinson's greatest vocal showcase. And he was smart as a whip to boot.

Iron Maiden was having vaguely articulated problems with its own lead singer, Paul Di'Anno. He was a bit scary, partied a bit too hard, didn't seem to buy fully into this heavy metal thing. And, on the path toward creative differences, Steve Harris wanted to explore a direction that would demand more thespian and technical skills from the man at the mic.

Cue the summit at the Reading Festival between Dickinson and Maiden manager Rod Smallwood, where heavy metal headlines were made. Bruce jumped ship, right into the waters of a warm-up tour of Italy, a gig at the Rainbow in London to introduce him to the home crowd, and writing sessions for which he couldn't be credited due to contractual obligations with Samson.

The Number of the Beast was rush-recorded on antiquated equipment at Battery Studios in the space of five weeks. Stories abound of the studio lights flickering on and off and equipment inexplicably going on the fritz. And then there was Martin Birch's van accident with a group of nuns, with the repair bill coming in at £666!

The unideal, and possibly haunted, sessions resulted in a roughly edged album roiling with energy. Many fans as well as the band consider "Invaders" and "Gangland" subpar, with Harris ruing that "Gangland" was included on the album instead of the

superior "Total Eclipse." And though it's unspoken (golden goose and all that), "Run to the Hills," the band's breakthrough hit, with its frantic but fragile gallop, ain't much better than the aforementioned.

But the rest of the album represents an exciting, youthful type of stadium rock. "Children of the Damned" and the title track are epic and dramatic, with "Hallowed Be Thy Name" possessing those qualities and more, a deathly heavy metal tale playing out in the mind of an excited metal kid cheering on the first band of his own generation. Rounding out the record, "The Prisoner" and "22 Acacia Avenue" are barnstorming classics, proving that once the material from the club days had run out,

Backstage at the Rosemount Horizon near Chicago for the Beast on the Road tour, September 1982.

the quality writing would continue, with Harris and Adrian Smith (now writing for Maiden for the first time) tailoring the songs to the talents of its new front man.

Grumbling about a couple duff tracks (and perhaps a lack of dynamics in the production) aside, *The Number of the Beast* thrilled the market with devilish glee. Amid a thriving heavy metal environment fired by Priest, Ozzy, Ronnie James Dio–led Sabbath, and the ascendant Scorpions, "Run to the Hills" rocketed up the charts in both Canada and the United States, aided by a self-deprecating and comedic video. As the band flipped from club to theater to headline status, debate raged about this evil group of youngsters from the UK—its mascot now powerful enough to puppeteer the devil.

The Number of the Beast went platinum in the United States and the UK, while Canada sent the record soaring to triple platinum, with assorted gold discs around the world filling out the story. Frankly, those certifications seem low for what is one

Dickinson performing with his previous band, Samson, at the 1980 Reading Festival.

CHAPTER 3

of the most famed and celebrated heavy metal albums of all time, propelled partly by the iconic album cover art, still a T-shirt favorite among all the Eddies that have been created more than forty years later.

MARTIN POPOFF: Brian, I have to start with you, because you are on record consistently calling *The Number of the Beast* the greatest album of all time by anybody! First off, what happens when Maiden gets themselves a new singer?
BRIAN SLAGEL: Right, obviously, I was very, very familiar with Bruce, because he was in a band called Samson, another big band from the NWOBHM that had put out a couple of decent records and had some pretty good success in England.

To backtrack a little bit, I saw Iron Maiden in 1981 in Houston, Texas—the first time I'd ever seen them. They weren't playing the West Coast on that tour, so I had to fly to Houston. They were opening for Priest and that's as far west as they got. And then they added some dates of the very end of that tour, playing at Long Beach Arena, opening for UFO.

I'd made some inroads with the record company because I had the fanzine at the time. I was interviewing Steve, and, weirdly, it's the only time I ever met Steve Harris in thirty-whatever years. Sort of funny. I've been in the same room with him countless times, but I just never . . . I couldn't . . . and I'm friends with Rod Smallwood and all the other guys.

Anyway, they came to open for UFO, and my friend John and I interviewed Paul Di'Anno at that gig. And he said, "I'm leaving Iron Maiden after this show." We're like, "What?! Are you crazy?" He said, "Yeah, I want to do something more melodic." We were devastated. Like, wow, this is pretty crazy. So it certainly wasn't a surprise when it happened. I think he asked me not to tell anybody, so we never mentioned it. But it's funny, because a few years later he moved to LA and he was dating a girl who was good friends with the girl I was dating at the time, so I hung out with him quite often.

When Bruce joined, it was like, oh, okay, Bruce from Samson—pretty good choice. But people don't remember that was very, very controversial when *The Number of the Beast* came out. I was still working at the record store, and I would say half the people hated it and hated Bruce and loved Di'Anno and refused to even listen to that record or give it the time of day. I would say at least half the people that were into Maiden said no, because we sold tons and tons of *Killers* records. So it was extremely

Samson's *Shock Tactics*
LP, released May 1981.

controversial when they got him. But I loved that record from the moment I put it on. Still to this day, as you say, it's my all-time favorite record. And I love Bruce—I think he was the perfect guy to have for that band. Obviously [*laughs*].

POPOFF: And Franc, this all happened pretty fast, right?
FRANC POTVIN: Definitely. *Shock Tactics* comes out in May of '81; Reading is in August; Paul is gone in September, playing his last show in Denmark on September 10; and then Bruce played his first show in, what, October 1981, in Italy? So Bruce finished the Killers World Tour. They were considered warm-up shows. And then the single "Run to the Hills" came out in February 1982.

So think about it: They play their first show together and it's the wrap-up to the *Killers* tour. Maiden had just played their first North American headline gigs in June, in Montreal and Toronto. It's amazing how things were changing so quickly back in the day. Now five years ago feels like a year ago.

So, yeah, I guess the record must've been rushed. Now that I'm thinking of the timeline that way, and given that most of the songs weren't actually written. Because there are barely any songs on *Killers* that weren't from the '70s. And they were kind of like B songs, in a way, from their catalog, which ended up being the A songs to a lot of people. But for *The Number of the Beast*, they were basically all brand-new songs. It was the first time Adrian Smith wrote for the band too. So he brings something new. Bruce, apparently, wrote more than is shown and had something to do with "Run to the Hills."

SLAGEL: I think in a lot of cases, when you make records really quickly, it works out well. *Machine Head*, by Deep Purple, was made extremely quickly. We [Slayer] made *Show No Mercy* in ten days. Black Sabbath made those records quickly. You can overthink things and take too long. So being rushed, sometimes, is better. The music is what it is, and you don't have time to rethink or overthink stuff.

And clearly you don't want to make a record that's, "Oh, this is a perfect record; this is the greatest record we ever made." Because then you're stuffed. What do you have to prove after that? So I like the fact that Iron Maiden didn't think it was perfect. But, to *me*, there are zero elements of that record that are not perfect—it's the greatest album ever made in the history of music ever after [*laughs*].

POPOFF: Blitz, as a heavy metal singer, what did you think of Maiden's new vocalist?

BOBBY "BLITZ" ELLSWORTH: First off, it's not easy to replace a singer because the identifiable quality that most bands have is their singer; that becomes the band's individuality. Because guitar tones, et cetera, can overlap between bands. And these guys also had a strong bass/drums relationship, and then they add Bruce Dickinson to it. As a fan, you're nervous about the idea, but it seemed to be an absolute step up. We're not looking back. This is what it is from now on. This guy may not work in every band, but, for this stuff, this guy works and has the perfect presentation, demeanor, and talent for it.

As for technical skills, I noticed as a singer that Dickinson could sing with power—but also sing with melody within that power. If this guy was going to do a departure at the end of the line, "Oh, oh" [*singing higher*], it was perfect. The biggest problem is shifting gears. How do you go from third gear to fourth gear smoothly? Most guys have to stop. Well, this guy could do it in transition. And it was instantly noticeable on the record. For instance, the scream in "Run to the Hills"—where he kind of builds it from a low note all the way up to the end—it sounds like he has more. Usually when guys do that, you're all the way out and that's all you have. You either reach it or you don't. But he always sounded like he had more, and that was always really attractive in his presentation.

SLAGEL: I think what Bruce added was more melody versus the sort of punk attitude that Di'Anno represented. Bruce's singing was more of the classic Rob Halford/Ian Gillan style, over a superheavy metal background. He still had some grit, obviously, but the screams and the high-end melodic stuff were really what made it amazing. Now it was superheavy, fast music with this very melodic lead singer. Again, to me, Iron Maiden was now the perfect heavy metal band, and *The Number of the Beast* was the perfect heavy metal album.

Iron Maiden has released fan-favorite "Run to the Hills" as a single three times over the years: first in its original incarnation in February 1982, and then in live versions in 1985 and 2002.

POTVIN: Bruce Dickinson would not have said to Rod Smallwood, "I want to be in that band" had *Killers* and *Iron Maiden* not been made. If Bruce didn't like the band, he wouldn't have said, "One day, I'm going to sing for that band." And let's face it, I do love Samson, don't get me wrong, but I don't think the songwriting was there. I think the two were meant to be together in the history of metal, just like Lars and James meeting was meant to be. Consequently, I think *The Number of the Beast* is essential to the history of metal.

POPOFF: Okay, into the record. One could say "Hallowed Be Thy Name" is the showcase song for the deep fan, but "Run to the Hills" was the showcase, of sorts, that introduced the band to a wider audience.

SLAGEL: Clearly that was the breaking point for the band, the song that got them to the next level. Because it had a strong chorus, it had the video that MTV played like every five seconds [*laughs*]. But it makes sense that would be the song—and actually it's probably the only song on the record that would have had a chance of any radio play. So it became their big single off that record.

ELLSWORTH: When I think of Bruce Dickinson, I think of a guy who knows his history. He knows where he's coming from, knows his country and the world, and he brings that to the studio and to the stage. And there's something very glorious about that when it comes to presentation. I said it earlier, that when you sing in terms of "I"— I am depressed, I am evil, I am out of my mind—that's one thing; but "Run to the Hills" is totally different. It's this story of European immigration and American armies taking the United States from the original inhabitants. Anybody who knows that is not thinking just in terms of self, but beyond self. He essentially brings in grandeur, and that subliminally sneaks into your head; you say this is bigger than just me—this is us. And I think that kind of grandeur gives the songs weight.

"The Number of the Beast," released April 1982, was the second single to be drawn from the album of the same name.

POTVIN: It's not one of my favorites, but I think it's good. The solo is great; it's got that old Dave Murray style, like the solo in "Killers," with that wah-wah tone to it. It's interesting to have a British band singing about the extermination of American Indians, right? And half the song is the white man's perspective and half the song is the natives' perspective. That's the song that broke them in North America, so from that standpoint, without "Run to the Hills," would there be an Iron Maiden in North America? Because Maiden never exploded in

Europe with *The Number of the Beast* the way they did here. Especially in Canada and especially where I'm from, in Quebec.

Clive Burr—who would soon depart the band— on stage during Iron Maiden's return to the Palladium, New York City, June 29, 1982.

POPOFF: What about Clive Burr's performance as opposed to what we would hear from his replacement, Nicko McBrain?
POTVIN: Clive's a little more on the beat or ahead of the beat and less behind the beat than Nicko tends to be. I was just listening to a Lars Ulrich interview, and Lars pretty much does snare rolls all the time. And if you think of how Clive was on "Hallowed Be Thy Name," Lars said Clive's drum rolls are pretty much literally his style.

Clive could be credited, in a way, with introducing punk rock–style beats to classic metal. Those beats probably existed before, with Doug Samson before him, because most of the songs on *Killers* were new. But a lot of people view *Killers* as punk-meets-metal and proto-thrash. So Clive's a transition between classic metal and thrash. I think he's really important in the speeding up of music, and he

definitely influenced a lot of people. Listen to live versions, and some, I thought, Nicko did better, where he came in and did it a little differently with the ride cymbal a little looser and playing behind the beat.

SLAGEL: Phenomenal. I was a massive fan of Clive's from day one. I love, absolutely, love, love, love his drumming. Nicko is an amazing drummer but he's never replaced Clive in my opinion. There is something about Clive's style. He played really fast stuff and it was intricate but he kept a really interesting beat to it. The style reminds me a little bit of Slayer's Dave Lombardo when Dave started to play; he played just a tiny bit off and that made it work. And Clive had some of that same vibe, where, if you put a click track on it, it might not be absolutely perfect—but it was perfect for these songs.

ELLSWORTH: Clive is part of that energy they have when they lock up—him and Steve. And by playing on the front end of the beat, you're always going to have that happen. It almost appears as if the train is about to come off the tracks. But the idea is to have the engineer keep that train on the tracks. There's an excitement to that, a feigned energy. That's my thought on playing ahead of the beat. I saw them live for the first time on *The Number of the Beast*, with the guys from Overkill, somewhere in Westchester, New York, a 2,500-seater, and they were the headliner. I honestly don't remember who the first band was. These were the days when we would be out in the parking lot rolling our own and drinking beers because we couldn't afford them inside. I remember coming in for Maiden and pushing our way to the front. It was unseated, as I recall.

So we got pretty close to the front, which was an unbelievable experience, with Bruce Dickinson's swinging hair and the foot on the monitor and the wrestling boots, the whole thing. The amount of energy generated . . . you thought the album had energy, but—when you saw it live, when things were happening—there was energy all over the place. It wasn't different just audibly, it was different visually too.

And after that, we were poking and pulling things from Iron Maiden and saying, "How great is this?" I remember when I saw them, saying, "I'm taking that and taking that, too, and I'm taking that." [*laughs*] I remember the singer in Gama Bomb, a guy named Philly Byrne, he was commenting after a show on how I performed. And I said it as simply as I could: "I didn't invent any of this. I just stole all the good stuff." And a lot of that comes from Bruce Dickinson.

A print ad for the 1982 Reading Festival, with Iron Maiden and the Michael Schenker Group given joint top billing.

Opposite:
Dickinson looks out across the audience during Iron Maiden's headline set at the Reading Festival, August 28, 1982.

POPOFF: We'd be remiss if we didn't talk about "Hallowed Be Thy Name," which one might call the first song of Maiden's modern era, where all the ingredients are there, and at a highly creative level.

POTVIN: It shows the epic side, the quiet side, it has that signature guitar harmony, it has deep-thinking lyrics about mortality—beautiful melody through all its passages. Bruce is showcasing his skills and vocal range, and it's just great. I believe it's Steve Harris's favorite song too. And that's the first song I heard from that album. My cousin Caroline, who was maybe a couple years older than me, she was like, thirteen, fourteen—she was already over Maiden—and she gave me her vinyl and she said,

"You have to listen to this," and the first song she put on was "Hallowed." She said, "This is the best song from Maiden—listen to it." And I can still visualize that moment. I still own that vinyl she gave me. And it's not just sentimental. To this day, I think that it's their best song.

ELLSWORTH: Well, the first thing I think about is the twin lead—which the precursor is Brian Robertson and Scott Gorham, right? I'm not going to say Adrian Smith and Dave Murray ripped a page from their book, but for sure they loved those Thin Lizzy harmonies and then took them way beyond, made them central to the song—it becomes a song within a song. That was one of their greatest qualities, using the guitars that way after building everything around the bass and drums.

And "Hallowed Be Thy Name," that's Bruce's ultimate depiction of sadness in a vocal presentation. One of the cool things about being a vocalist is evoking those emotions and having them come across to the listener. If you sing it like you believe it—and you believe it yourself—you're probably going to be attractive to other

people with that presentation. "Hallowed Be Thy Name" and "Run to the Hills" and the title track—you really have three separate characters on these, and to be able to distinguish between those characters is one of the reasons he's so successful at what he does.

SLAGEL: Again, in my opinion, the greatest song ever written is "Hallowed Be Thy Name." Not to harp on this, but that is the perfect song written by the perfect band. Everything about that song is perfect. The lead guitar solos are some of the best I've ever heard. The lyrics and the music and the subject matter are amazing. Bruce sounds phenomenal. The playing and the different time changes—incredible. As an ending track, it's like, wow. I remember the first time I heard that record and it ended, I was exhausted because there was just so much going on.

POPOFF: To round things out, point out a few other high points on the record.

SLAGEL: I kind of go back and forth on my second favorite. "The Number of the Beast" is the one you would want to pick because it's the title track and it's a great song, but I do really love "Children of the Damned" too. It's an incredible song with great choruses—and the whole quiet build-up to where it explodes is awesome.

ELLSWORTH: "The Number of the Beast" could be a Broadway play. It's six minutes of Broadway. It's all about presentation and mood. When you think big and succeed, you get big results. But you have to take that chance, go all in and say we're going to make something bigger than us. And if it's bigger than us, it will stand the test of time. Great riff, great vocals, great, moody introduction to the narrative. Top ten over the last forty years with regard to metal.

POTVIN: The songs are all classics except for "Invaders" and "Gangland." "Hallowed Be Thy Name" is probably their best song of all time. I loved the throwaway song, "Total Eclipse," which was the B-Side to "Run to the Hills," and which also is found on some reissues of *The Number of the Beast*. I think it's one of the best songs on that album or from those sessions.

And "Children of the Damned," like "Hallowed," is another showcase. If somebody asks, "What's Iron Maiden?" play "Children of the Damned." If somebody doesn't like "Children of the Damned," they're never going to like Iron Maiden.

ELLSWORTH: "Children of the Damned" was a step up from "Remember Tomorrow." To me, this was the ultimate heavy ballad, with the ringing chords, et cetera. "Remember Tomorrow" was the embryo of this type of song structure and "Children of the Damned" was the evolution. And for the bands that followed in the '80s, this

Opposite:
Eddie the Head stalks the stage, Madison Square Garden, October 2, 1982.

was part of our DNA. "Children of the Damned" set the benchmark for a ballad-esque approach to being heavy without wimping out at the same time.

POPOFF: Maybe it's just because I'm sick of "Hallowed," but I have to say "The Prisoner" and "22 Acacia Avenue" are the two main songs that still draw me back to this record from time to time.

POTVIN: Both classic songs. "The Prisoner" was an Adrian Smith song. It definitely has that more melodic Adrian Smith–style approach to vocal melodies. He probably wrote some of the lyrics to this, just by listening to it. If you listen to "Wasted Years" or "Stranger in a Strange Land," I have a feeling he's involved in the chorus. Can't go wrong with that beat at the beginning—that is a drum hook, straight up. If you're into this kind of music and you don't get going with that, there's just something wrong with you.

A pair of The Beast on the Road tour T-shirts.

It's about the British TV show, and it's Maiden starting to write a lot about things that already exist. Think about Steve Harris's inspiration—he's literally calling the song by the title of the show. Whether it's "The Fugitive" or, you know, "To Tame a Land" was supposed to be called "Dune," but they had some copyright issues with that. "Die with Your Boots On"... the list goes on. "Murders in the Rue Morgue" was a poem and then a film.

SLAGEL: Great subject matter and an amazing signature song. It shows their mastery of the heavy-but-melodic-and-hooky. But even then, you knew it was based on a huge TV show in England. Out of all those British bands—Zeppelin, Sabbath, Deep Purple, Priest—Iron Maiden definitely wore their history on their sleeves the most.

POTVIN: "22 Acacia Avenue," let's not forget, was an Adrian Smith song that he brought over from Urchin. Steve Harris said, "Hey, do you remember that song you used to play with your band? That song called 'Countdown?'" And they turned it into a story about Charlotte the Harlot. Steve is good at that. Like with Bruce's "Bring Your Daughter . . . to the Slaughter." And so "22" is another borrowed song, however slightly.

And is there a song in metal that sounds like "22 Acacia Avenue"? I don't think so. There are a lot of these riffs that you're like, "Yeah, that sounds like Mercyful Fate," or "That sounds like this." That opening riff to "2 Minutes to Midnight" has been done by a hundred bands. "22" is just a fairly straight-ahead riff in E, but I can't think of another song in metal that sounds like "22 Acacia Avenue."

POPOFF: Last question—with this album cover and title, do you remember any religious backlash?

SLAGEL: Of course—there was tons of that back then. I don't know if outside the US there was nearly as much hullabaloo. But, if you read the lyrics, they're just telling stories. This is what drives me nuts about all this—these people are just telling stories. I mean, was Vincent Price a Satanist because he played evil people in all those films? No, he was an actor. These people are storytellers creating art. People take it too literally. It was not so much when it came out, but after they got big. You would go to the shows and there were protesters everywhere. It was all over the media. When they were doing their headline tour back then, Bruce did a five-minute little rap, saying this is all shit, we're not Satanists, we're musicians, leave it alone.

ELLSWORTH: Obviously, this was the music your parents didn't want you listening to— especially if they were devout Catholics. But I don't think it's anything other than being a fantastic heavy metal topic. This could be page one in the heavy metal bible with regard to what we sing about [*laughs*]. You sing about evil. But it's a story about evil, and that's what makes it both expansive and successful. But I guess this was racy for 1982. Metal was about ruffling feathers. It wasn't about finding your niche and going away quietly. That song doesn't mean the guy's a Satanist.

But *The Number of the Beast* survived all that and stood the test of time. When Overkill does festivals with Iron Maiden, I always go out to peek. I like to watch from the perspective of the audience. There's still that energy. It's a show. These guys think big and I love that. If you come in to knock people on their ass, it means so much, especially if you have the tools, and they obviously have the tools. I stand there and have a beer, shake my head, and think, "I can't believe it still appears exactly like the thing I saw back in Westchester."

Piece of Mind

with Blaze
Bayley and
Mike Portnoy

SIDE 1
1. Where Eagles Dare 6:08
(Harris)
2. Revelations 6:51
(Dickinson)
3. Flight of Icarus 3:49
(Smith, Dickinson)
4. Die with Your Boots On 5:22
(Smith, Dickinson, Harris)

SIDE 2
1. The Trooper 4:10
(Harris)
2. Still Life 4:37
(Murray, Harris)
3. Quest for Fire 3:40
(Harris)
4. Sun and Steel 3:25
(Dickinson, Smith)
5. To Tame a Land 7:26
(Harris)

Personnel: Bruce Dickinson—vocals; Dave Murray—
    lead guitars; Adrian Smith—lead guitars; Steve
    Harris—bass guitar; Nicko McBrain—drums
Produced by Martin Birch
Recorded at Compass Point Studios, Nassau, Bahamas
Released May 16, 1983

Not since Led Zeppelin has a drummer put such a stamp on a band as Nicko McBrain, who arrived at Iron Maiden from French band Trust but was more noted for his work with Pat Travers (and Streetwalkers before that). His competence and fluidity only hinted at what was to come.

Whether it was really the arrival of McBrain or other factors, such as the band's inspired ascendance after *The Number of the Beast*, writing sessions at Le Chalet on the island of Jersey, or the relatively languid and relaxed recording sessions at Compass Point in the Bahamas (an indication they were going places), *Piece of Mind* is a creative triumph and the first record of the Maiden sound that exists to this day.

Classics played live throughout the glory years and beyond abound, but even the deep tracks are Iron Maiden gold—"Still Life," "Die with Your Boots On," "Sun and Steel," and "To Tame a Land"—each helping carry the album to gold status within two months, and inevitably platinum after that.

One could almost classify the rumbling and authoritative "Flight of Icarus" as a deep track—even though it was issued as a single, it quickly was overtaken by "The Trooper" as the album's classic, a song that ranks among "Run to the Hills" and "Hallowed Be Thy Name" as the band's biggest and most admired.

Elsewhere, "Quest for Fire" was propped up for pillorying, partly because it smacks a little too much of a class lecture, partly because the movie on which it was based was a recent bomb. This, in contrast, to the slightly older Bible, source material for "Revelations," and the altered quote on the back cover in which the word "pain" was replaced with "brain." That, of course, is

in deference to the cover art featuring a lobotomized Eddie. (The band originally planned to call the album *Food for Thought*.)

Further goading of the religious right took place in "Still Life," on which the band laced in a backward John Bird impression of savage Ugandan dictator Idi Amin, prompted by the backmasking controversies leveled at the likes of AC/DC and Led Zeppelin, not to mention further tsk-tsking of Iron Maiden for titling its previous record *The Number of the Beast*.

But back to Nicko. His distinct and consistent sound, as captured by Martin Birch, along with his trademark fills and groove, unified these disparate songs into a single statement despite the various song structures. McBrain, too, is no less than the performer of distinction on the record's second most famed track, "Where Eagles Dare," which features a crazy drum explosion touched off by a legendary fill, Maiden magnanimously jumping Nicko into the band by allowing him to kick off the album by himself.

The band's latest incarnation in 1983, *left to right*: Nicko McBrain, Steve Harris, Bruce Dickinson, Adrian Smith, Dave Murray.

McBrain (*second right*) in Streetwalkers, in 1975.

MARTIN POPOFF: Mike, right off the bat, I'll join you in calling *Piece of Mind* the band's greatest album. I've got my reasons. What are yours?

MIKE PORTNOY: I just love the songs, plus I think this album, as well as *Powerslave* that follows, are probably the most progressive in terms of instrumentation. On this album, songs like "Revelations" and "To Tame a Land" were very progressive. I remember that '83 was the height of my Rush fanaticism, so to hear Iron Maiden dabbling in these long, extended instrumental sections and epic passages, it reached me.

I remember the day it came out. I was on a high school band trip in Montreal, and I saw it in the record store window—I ran in, bought the cassette, and listened to it on my Walkman for the entire rest of the trip. And being a drummer, I appreciated them starting with Nicko's famous drum fill opening on "Where Eagles Dare," which set the tone for the new drummer in the band. He made his presence felt immediately. I remember wearing out that cassette for months. That's all I listened to.

BLAZE BAYLEY: There's a bit of backstory to that fill, and it makes it even better for me. Up until that time, EMI were allowed to visit the studio and listen to the album before it came out. And when they listened to *Piece of Mind*, they said, "You can't have this drum intro at the beginning of the album." There was a massive row between Iron Maiden and EMI, and it was absolutely diabolical. From then on, EMI were banned from visiting the studio while Iron Maiden was recording. The agreement was, we give you the album, with the artwork we want; you put it out, you have nothing to say about it. Otherwise we walk. And that was it. With *The Number of the Beast*, they had battles over the artwork and nearly walked, so they had to really give EMI an ultimatum. And it was exactly the same with *Piece of Mind*, but with the drums.

It's such a great story, because when I joined the band and we were writing *The X Factor*, you knew these people you're writing with—there is no compromise with anyone outside the creative process. It is all within the band. No one can come up and

The band that never tires, backstage in East Troy, August 1983.

say, "Oh, this is too long; this is too short; we don't like the chorus," or anything like this. Whereas before, in Wolfsbane, we'd often have these ugly compromises with producers. We learned from them, obviously, but it was a great thing as an artist and a writer joining Maiden to know if you came up with an idea and it was good, no one outside the band could say a thing about it. It's going on the record. It's liberating when you can follow your idea through to its conclusion, knowing no one is going to second-guess that.

And, as a massive fan of Iron Maiden back then, I'd seen them, I think, three times at Birmingham Odeon, which is a tiny gig for them. Every band—Metallica, Maiden, Ozzy, Sabbath, Bon Jovi—every major artist at the time went through Birmingham Odeon. It's like a thousand-seater converted cinema.

POPOFF: So I guess we can agree that the main material difference in the band is the arrival of Nicko. What is the significance of this personnel change?
PORTNOY: Before I praise Nicko, I need to credit Clive Burr, because the drumming on *Killers* and *Number* is absolutely amazing. Clive had such great speed and stamina and dexterity. But Nicko brought a real swing to the band. He had the chops and the speed that Clive had, but he added a real swing to the grooves. And it's interesting that both played single bass because, at this time in the early '80s, every metal drummer in the world was going to a double-bass kit.
BAYLEY: I've never worked with Clive, but I can say that Nicko, on his fills and everything, he went in a different direction—Nicko was really big on his fills, which added a lot more excitement. I really enjoyed what Clive did, and I thought he played for the song, but when Nicko joined, his personality came through and his fills gave a very big lift to the melody, lifting the album.

And as a personality, completely crazy, really. He's a very outgoing person, but, also in his way, he's a little bit shy sometimes. I think he has a tendency to bury himself in his drum kit. There were times he would start tuning up his drum kit in rehearsal and start finding little different grooves. And he would just go on, oblivious to everybody for ages and ages. A couple of times, we had really cool jams with Nicko in rehearsals. It was never planned, but we would jam around a few blues chords— me, Dave and Nicko, and Mike Kenney, the keyboardist—and it just sounded great. He's got such a feel.

Also, close up and personal, he's a very loud drummer. In the modern world, with all these superfast, technical death metal drummers, some drum tutors say if you play lighter, you can play faster. Well, with Nicko, there's no playing lighter. He has this

Opposite:
Harris and Dickinson at the Hammersmith Odeon, London, May 26, 1983.

dynamic range that can support so many nuances within the song, but when it's needed, he's full-on. Absolutely loud. To the point he's the loudest drummer I've ever worked with. He hasn't got any more equipment than anybody else. It's still a stick and a drum. So it comes from the man. And that's a huge difference, when you have that energy available to make that drum really sound the way it should.

He started in the pubs and played for years as a teenager, being the drummer for anybody that wanted to get up and jam some blues or any old songs. That's where he started. And I think that experience, plus his love of big band music, those two things really show through. You would never put *Piece of Mind* and big band together, but the connection is Nicko McBrain. And the precision, drawing from the way he holds his sticks, comes from a jazz background, not a rock background. That requires a certain degree of effort. It's much more difficult when you're starting off, but, of course, if you master that technique, it pays off.

PORTNOY: Plus—he plays barefoot! I toured with Maiden many times, and I've sat with him at his kit and he's barefoot. What he does with one bass drum is incredibly fast and syncopated. What he lacks in bass drums he makes up for with his foot. And it reminds me very much of the way John Bonham played. Plus, Nicko is one of those drummers that is a bit ahead of the beat. Clive was as well, so they're very similar in that sense.

But I just love all the fills; they're so tasty. The opening drum fill for "Still Life" that brings the drums into the song after almost a minute and a half of intro is perfect. A couple of them I ripped off, probably a million times since 1983. I love "Where Eagles Dare," "Revelations," "Still Life," "To Tame a Land." He brought a whole new level of energy to the band, which was already on fire from Bruce's arrival on the album. Between Bruce joining for *The Number of the Beast* and Nicko joining on *Piece of Mind*, they finally found the quintessential Maiden lineup.

POPOFF: Almost as big a story as solidifying the lineup is the presence of what many consider to be Maiden's biggest song, "The Trooper." Why is this such a beloved anthem in the Maiden canon?

"The Trooper," the second single to be taken from *Piece of Mind*, released June 1983.

BAYLEY: It's a great song with a great lyric. It's absolutely fantastic, just huge. And I'll tell you why—it's the perfect storm of lyric, melody, and music. When those three things express the same idea, that's when it's a classic. "The Trooper" can be transported to almost any genre as well, with a little bit of effort. I've included "The Trooper" in my acoustic set a couple of times, and it's not slow. We still do it the same speed, full-on, and it just lifts. And the poetry of the lyric is just fantastic. It tells a story and wraps you in itself.

POPOFF: Is it a challenge from a singer's point of view, because you have to sing solo at the beginning?
BAYLEY: No, I don't think it's a challenge from that point. The real challenge is, you listen to it and you see the little bits of melody. It's a very fast lyric, a lot of consonants, and it's not easy to find where you take your breath without leaving an unwanted gap. So you have to get your breath in exactly the right place to give the line everything it needs and find those extra bits of melody and still have the end of

Dickinson serenades Eddie at the Alpine Valley Music Theater, East Troy, Wisconsin, August 6, 1983.

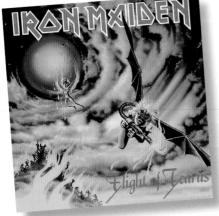

the line not falter. That's always a challenge. It's a thing I learned with Maiden that I've carried into my own music: Find that place where you need to take the breath to get the lyric going, not just where you feel like breathing. Then pace yourself to make sure you don't run out of breath before that line.

PORTNOY: "The Trooper" was the right song at the right time. It's probably my least favorite song of the album, to be honest, maybe just because I've heard it so many times. I like the deeper cuts way more. But "The Trooper" is the one that has stood the test of time and is still a staple in the set. Maybe the sing-along aspect has made it an anthem.

POPOFF: What did you think about artist Derek Riggs giving poor Eddie a lobotomy?

PORTNOY: It's weird—it seemed tied in with their new drummer's name. What came first, the drummer, whose name is Nicko Mc*Brain*, or this concept of Eddie getting a lobotomy?

I found it interesting, Eddie in a straightjacket in a padded room, and the photo on the inner sleeve of them all sitting around eating brain. It was intense. I'm surprised it wasn't more controversial.

I think Riggs needed to go someplace new. The first three covers, he had Eddie in his typical tattered clothing. This was an evolution for Eddie—he's going to new places.

BAYLEY: I just like the whole thing about Eddie being completely crazy. What's nice is there's no religious connotation, whereas *The Number of the Beast* had a certain religious connotation—which begs the question, if you believe there's a devil, then there is also a God. Whereas with *Piece of Mind*, it's one crazy lunatic. To me it's scarier because it looks like if this person, or this thing, ever gets out, we're all in danger. Whereas with *The Number of the Beast*, only the bad people are in danger. If Eddie gets out, he's beyond God and the devil, beyond any religious thing.

POPOFF: What about "Flight of Icarus" as a first single for this album?

PORTNOY: I loved it. I remember seeing the video—back then it was the early days of MTV—and I just flipped out. I would just stand by the TV for hours waiting for them to show it again. It's atypically short compared to the music they were writing at this stage, but it didn't sacrifice anything in its brevity. It was a superstrong song with a great riff and an amazing vocal for Bruce.

POPOFF: How would you contrast Bruce and Paul?
PORTNOY: Paul was punk rock and Bruce was operatic. Paul was like Johnny Rotten and Bruce was like Freddie Mercury.

POPOFF: Blaze, what did Bruce do for you? What did he bring to the record?
BAYLEY: Bruce is definitely an influence on my vocal style. Ronnie James Dio and Bon Scott were early influences, plus David Lee Roth from the early Van Halen records, with his casual, crazy-fun way of singing. And after that, Eric Adams from Manowar, and Bruce with his texture and range.

Bruce's voice was an instrument. He was more than a singer. He seemed the epitome of the machine vocalist of metal, because he could hit those notes regardless of the conditions. When I saw him at Birmingham Odeon, possibly the first time, he had a big box of tissues on stage, and I think he had to go to hospital straight after the show. Yet he sounded fantastic.

POPOFF: How about another favorite track on the album for you?
BAYLEY: I wanted to do "Still Life" with the band, but I never got the opportunity, so, really, we only had "The Trooper." I like the chorus—it's real spooky. "Where Eagles Dare" is just fantastic, great chorus, and it's just brilliant for that to be the opener. The way Bruce sings that is great. I really like the stories of war and battles from that era of Maiden. Being a fan of Richard Burton and the movie *Where Eagles Dare*, I really appreciated it.

But really, "Die with Your Boots On" . . . I remember at eighteen, working my first proper job in a hotel. And "Die with Your Boots On" came on my little radio/cassette player I used to take in on my nightshift, and I couldn't believe there was a song like this. That song changed it for me. This whole thing of being tough as nails, it sort of applied to the band as well. I remember supporting Iron Maiden when I was in Wolfsbane, and they played the song, and it was an incredible feeling. It could be a battle cry or something like that, as you're marching to a battle, where perhaps certain death is your fate.

POPOFF: Mike, you're particularly fond of the ballad, as it were, "Revelations."
PORTNOY: Yes, but I don't look at "Revelations" as mellow. It has its moments of breathing, but I never looked at it as a mellow song. I looked at it as an epic song. And I love that it's the second track of the album. It comes out of "Where Eagles Dare," which is pretty epic in its own right, so it's a one-two punch opening the album.

Opposite:
Steve Harris representing Maiden up top, his football club with his wristbands, and Pete Way with his pants.

The thing I love about "Revelations" is that on that last verse, Bruce sings so many words that he stops in the middle to take this deep breath. You can hear it plain as day. He just stops and takes that big gulp of air, which to me is almost part of the lyric itself [*laughs*]. When I play that song with Metal Allegiance, every time we get to that part, the singer, Mark Osegueda, and I always look at each other and crack up.

"To Tame a Land" is probably my favorite. I got to cover "Revelations" with Metal Allegiance and "To Tame a Land" with Dream Theater. Those two spoke to me in terms of my more progressive leanings, especially at that time when the record came out. But I really love the deep tracks as well, like "Still Life" and "Sun and Steel." These are sleeper tracks that are very underrated and forgotten. I could listen to this album from start to finish, and all nine songs are great.

POPOFF: We haven't talked about Steve Harris. What stamp does he put on the band?

PORTNOY: Steve is one of the greatest bass players of all time, and he was a pioneer. Steve was one of the few lead bass players in metal. He was the engine of Iron Maiden, and his bass playing separated Maiden from all other bands out there. If you listen to the bass in AC/DC or in Priest, those guys are just holding it down like an anchor. Whereas Steve is driving the band. The entire sound of Iron Maiden is based on Steve's bass. It's awesome when you have a bass player like that. There are fewer and fewer players like that these days, which is a shame.

Beyond that, his musical sensibility sets the tone. Although it's Rod Smallwood, too, contributing in other ways. Plus, you have Bruce's constant drive to conquer new lands and somebody like Nicko, who is one of the most fun guys I ever hung out with. You put that combination together, and you put them in a pub with some pints, and that's Iron Maiden.

A poster advertising Iron Maiden's visit to Düsseldorf, Germany, on December 4, 1983, during the final leg of the World Piece Tour, and a World Piece Tour T-shirt.

POPOFF: To what extent does *Piece of Mind* establish the band as champions of their homeland, with these somewhat patriotic songs about war and their flagship position in the NWOBHM? Are they the quintessential British band at this point?

BAYLEY: No. I feel they're this huge band, and they may have come from Britain, but the ownership of that band is international. Every fan in every part of the world where they tour owns a little piece of Iron Maiden. It doesn't matter where you go—from Chile to Argentina to Canada to South Africa to Spain—when Maiden visits, they are your band.

Of course, everybody in the band is British, and the material is written by people who spent their whole lives, or their formative years, in Britain, but it's much bigger than that.

As a former band member, the feeling I got was Iron Maiden belongs to the fans. No fan is more or less important because of their location or the country they're in. And their language is completely irrelevant. Every Iron Maiden fan has the same status. And that is something I've tried to continue with my own music—the emotion of the vocal performance, the melody you've chosen, and the music you've chosen should combine so even if someone can't understand the lyric, they know what the emotion is. You know this is a song of regret or immense sadness or anger or frustration. And that comes largely from my time with Iron Maiden, standing on stage at a hundred shows, singing these incredible songs with their vast, giant melodies and these huge emotional solos and melodic sections. To be in the middle of that and to feel the emotion of the fans and the emotion of the song is incredible. That's why I feel everybody that loves the band is really an integral part of it.

Off the wall—Dickinson and Murray goof around on tour.

5 Powerslave

with
**Blaze Bayley,
Mike Portnoy,
and Nita Strauss**

SIDE 1
1. Aces High 4:31
(Harris)
2. 2 Minutes to Midnight. .6:04
(Smith, Dickinson)
3. Losfer Words (Big 'Orra) 4:12
(Harris)
4. Flash of the Blade. 4:05
(Dickinson)
5. The Duellists. 6:07
(Dickinson)

SIDE 2
1. Back in the Village 5:03
(Smith, Dickinson)
2. Powerslave 7:10
(Dickinson)
3. Rime of the Ancient Mariner 13:45
(Harris)

Personnel: Bruce Dickinson—vocals; Dave Murray—
    lead and rhythm guitars; Adrian Smith—lead and
    rhythm guitars, backing vocals; Steve Harris—
    bass; Nicko McBrain—drums
Produced by Martin Birch
Recorded at Compass Point Studios,
    Nassau, Bahamas
Released September 3, 1984

I've lost count of which flush of success the happy metal-whackers in Maiden are riding at this point, but each one seems to bring a different process, a different way of looking at recordmaking. With *Powerslave*, despite returning to Jersey to write and then continuing to Compass Point to record (a locale that represents serious intentions and sunny distraction at the same time), the band captured the sort of lightning-in-a-bottle spontaneity last heard on *The Number of the Beast* while further developing the sound, arrangements, and member interaction that emerged on *Piece of Mind*.

Remember how back in the NWOBHM days, we threw around the term *OTT*? Well, soon after crinkling back the shrink-wrap and feeling the textured cover beneath (mine was Canadian), my first thought was that *Powerslave* was the "over the top" version of *Piece of Mind*, representing the first such comparison of two Maiden albums.

Recorded during an extended boozy sojourn from February through June 1984, *Powerslave* rocked fast and hard and sod the consequences. "Aces High" threatened to fly off the rails, as did "Flash of the Blade" and "Back in the Village," although on the latter, everybody had to stay mindful of that killer Mensa-mad riff. Even "2 Minutes to Midnight," with its harrowing lyric based on the idea of the doomsday clock, rumbled along jam-like, especially in comparison to songs like "Where Eagles Dare" and "Flight of Icarus" that had the permanence of oak—even as the former skittered, one felt sure everybody would get to the end at the same time.

Closing *Powerslave* is "Rime of the Ancient Mariner," which one could call the

Opposite:
A band portrait taken during the World Slavery Tour's stop in Detroit, Michigan, January 1985.

follow-up both to "Hallowed Be Thy Name" and, more directly, "To Tame a Land," Steve mining literature—in this case, a classic epic poem from 1834 providing the lyrical grist under which Maiden roil—Nicko slide-ruling up a rhythm somewhere between "Powerslave," "Where Eagles Dare," and a traditional Maiden gallop. "Rime" would remain Maiden's longest song until 2015's "Empire of the Clouds," although many fans argue that "Rime" is generally more solid and swift of plot than a dozen other Maiden meanderers in the seven- to ten-minute range. Such is the power of a band at the height of its arsenal. Indeed, "Rime of the Ancient Mariner," the whole 13:45 gulp of it, became a setlist standard and the most popular song from this record, with "Aces High," "2 Minutes to Midnight," and "Powerslave" nipping like ragged dogs at its . . . keels.

Powerslave would set in motion the immense two-year Egyptian-themed World Slavery Tour, which would be instrumental in sending the record to platinum status in the United States, gold in the UK, and double platinum in Canada, meaning *Powerslave* shifted four times as many pancakes per capita in Canada as it did on the band's own turf.

The "Aces High" single, released October 1984, and an "Aces High" T-shirt (*opposite*), as sold on the World Slavery Tour.

MARTIN POPOFF: How would you contrast *Powerslave* and *Piece of Mind*? For me, there's a similarity to Metallica following *Ride the Lightning* with *Master of Puppets*—a continuity but also a band really hitting its stride.
MIKE PORTNOY: I can see that. *Powerslave* is the pinnacle of my love for Iron Maiden. I think for the original classic period of the band, they took everything as far as they could possibly go; to me, this is the most progressive album. A lot of people might think *Seventh Son* is more progressive—and it *is* more conceptual—but *Powerslave* spoke to me more personally. I love the progressive elements, not only in the music, but in the artwork, which they took as far as they could possibly go in terms of detail and grandeur. *Powerslave* opens with two of the best-known songs on the album, the two singles anyway, so there's instant momentum that carries into the deeper tracks, which I absolutely love.
NITA STRAUSS: This was the one album that, when I was playing with The Iron Maidens, we could've done from start to finish. We used to do every single song

CHAPTER 5

on this album in our set, so I had a great appreciation for the lesser-known tracks. I love "The Duellists" and "Flash of the Blade." Of course, "Aces High" and "2 Minutes" are the classics everybody likes to hear, but I like to go into the deeper cuts, the material people don't expect to hear.

As a comparison with *Piece of Mind*, there's a rawness and excitement to *Powerslave*. It's not as polished and as structured, I find. It has more early Iron Maiden excitement to it. And then the evocative Egyptian album cover, with the pharaohs and sphinx and all that, definitely sums up the power and majesty of the album.

BLAZE BAYLEY: That cover and the way it came alive on stage . . . they played the Birmingham Odeon, and I don't know how they fit that stage set in, but they did, and it was absolutely incredible. But there are so many Eddies, or at least Eddie-like figures, and just so much detail. This was the time of vinyl when you could see the details they were putting on album art. But I liked the idea they'd stolen a whole mythology and created their own with Eddie.

POPOFF: As Mike alluded to, the record cracks open with "Aces High" and a momentum is established. Good choice for an album opener?
BAYLEY: "Aces High" is absolutely fantastic. It's poetry, really. For me it evokes the feeling, on the odd occasions I've sung it, of being there before the Battle of Britain. If you've seen the film *Battle of Britain* with Michael Caine, it really feels like "Aces High" could've been the soundtrack.

Churchill is alive and there is a portal to the past and he has reached out to these young men from Iron Maiden who made this song that has been transported back through time. And the fighter pilots are listening to it as they struggle to stay alive against the overwhelming German forces, the Luftwaffe, who are sure to annihilate what is left of our air force and our island. But somehow these brave young men, with incredible courage, hold back the Luftwaffe, stopping a certain invasion of our island!

So it's an incredible song for me and all these emotions and images go through me when I hear it. And the chorus is amazing! I've never spoken to Bruce about singing it, but it sounds so casual and natural I don't think he did anything but say, "Oh, I'll sing this here," and suddenly there's the chorus of "Aces High," as if some kind of spirit entered Bruce and he just came up with this. I don't know the truth of it, but that's what I choose to feel, that there was some spirit reaching out from the past that affected Bruce.

PORTNOY: I just saw the movie *Dunkirk*, and there's a big scene where you hear Winston Churchill's famous speech. Of course, that immediately brings to mind this album and "Aces High." There's a whole Churchill speech that still, to this day, they use when they play "Aces High."

STRAUSS: "Aces High" might not be a conventional single, but it really grabs the listener's attention. It's a snapshot of what Iron Maiden was doing at that time, what they were all about. I think it's appropriate that way, both as a first track and as a single.

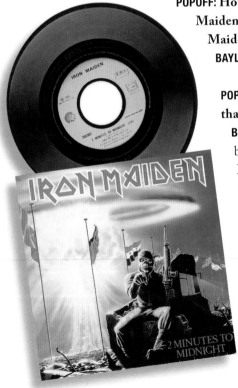

The "2 Minutes to Midnight" single, released August 1984, a month ahead of its parent album.

POPOFF: Hot on its heels comes "2 Minutes to Midnight," my favorite Maiden song of all time, incidentally. And it's a little rock 'n' rollsy for Maiden, right?

BAYLEY: I don't like this word "rock 'n' rollsy."

POPOFF: Okay, but is there something distinct from Steve in the way that Adrian writes?

BAYLEY: I think Adrian comes very much from a melodic background. I always think of Phil Lynott when I think of Adrian. My favorite song from Adrian is "Wasted Years." That's just something that really pulls at the heartstrings. But I always think of him coming from this melodic background. And when you put it in the context of an album, with some of the harsh things and the darkness, then it makes sense. And he's such a good lead player. His solos are really memorable—he's got great tone, and his rhythm playing is so precise. It's just unbelievable.

POPOFF: What about "2 Minutes to Midnight" lyrically?

BAYLEY: Oh, it's horrible. It's a horrible, horrible song. But in the best possible way. The lyrics are horrible, the things they

talk about. But it's great in that it's very simple at the start. It's quite a simple riff [*sings it*]. And then it goes to this horrible place, exploring real terror and hideous things that happen. It never shirks, it never pulls back from that, and it does feel apocalyptic to me. Whenever I sang "2 Minutes to Midnight," it was something that felt, "Oh, this is a bit dangerous to sing." But also, as a heavy metal fan, we take ourselves to the edge, and we like horror and things like this. So it's also something you relish singing. "Kill for gain," you know, just a fantastic song.

PORTNOY: With "2 Minutes to Midnight," I remember thinking it was almost an exact rip-off of two other songs I had heard. One was an Accept song, "Flash Rockin' Man," and one was Mercyful Fate's "Curse of the Pharaohs." But it was a strong single. It was a bit commercial for my tastes. Adrian was starting to put his stamp on the band's singles with that good commercial sense he had. One of my favorite Maiden songs is the one Adrian sings, "Reach Out." It was the B-Side of "Wasted Years," and it's just a great forgotten track and a great example of Adrian's singing ability.

STRAUSS: I agree that "2 Minutes to Midnight" has a dancier, poppier sound versus a sort of aggressive NWOBHM sound, and it's a fun, upbeat song to play. I don't want to say it's joyful, because it's still a pretty aggressive song, and, as Blaze says, it's got quite the apocalyptic lyric.

POPOFF: Tell me about "Back in the Village" and its relationship to *The Prisoner*.
STRAUSS: "Back in the Village" is the first song that comes to mind when I think of challenging guitar parts on *Powerslave*. It's got a pretty complex lead going on in the chorus.

In fact, "Flash of the Blade," "The Duellists," and "Back in the Village"—a lot of the songs on this record have these real interesting hammer-on/pull-off parts that I hadn't heard a lot in music before this. I was born three years after this came out [*laughs*], but looking back at it from an outside perspective, it's cool to see them doing all the complex hammer-on/pull-off harmonizing that was really a hallmark of a later generation of guitar players.

POPOFF: Speaking of "Flash of the Blade," this is related to Bruce's being an amateur fencer at the time, correct?

BAYLEY: Yeah, and he was in the *Sun* newspaper as well—"Bruce Dickinson, Iron Maiden singer, Olympic hopeful." And of course they made it up completely. He was doing an interview with someone and it came out that he liked fencing. It's good to have some kind of activity. And they said, "Well, what standard are you up to?" And he said, "Well, not Olympic standard." And that got turned around and it came out, "Olympic-standard fencer Bruce Dickinson." So he had to live that down for ages.

PORTNOY: Back then we had no internet, so news of what the bands did on their free time was less than what it is these days. But I remember hearing about Bruce's interest in fencing and, maybe, dueling. I guess it was inevitable he would write about it. To me, it brings to mind Stanley Kubrick's movie *Barry Lyndon*. Maybe Bruce had an interest not only in the sport of fencing, but some of the old films that dealt with duelists.

But, to me, "Powerslave" and "Rime of the Ancient Mariner" are the highlights. In 1984, I was really into Rush and more progressive music, so Iron Maiden, with those tracks in particular, was getting pretty much as progressive as they were ever going to be, and it spoke to me.

Dickinson—perhaps not quite suitably attired—offers free fencing lessons in Los Angeles.

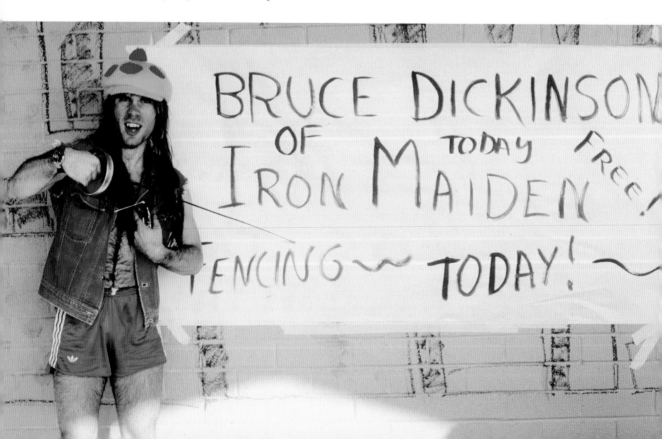

The fact that "Rime" was a thirteen-minute song from a heavy metal band . . . I don't think that existed yet. And that was kind of the blueprint I wanted Dream Theater to be. We formed in 1985, and *Powerslave* came out in 1984. "Rime of the Ancient Mariner" was the perfect example of how you could have heavy riffs and be a metal band but have these very progressive elements and arrangements. It was like putting the writing of Yes and Rush into a heavy metal band. Judas Priest wasn't doing long songs like this, nor was Motörhead, AC/DC, or Twisted Sister. Maiden, around this period, and then Metallica, were the two bands including those progressive elements in the context of heavy metal.

An illustration by Gustave Doré of a scene from "The Rime of the Ancient Mariner," the Samuel Taylor Coleridge poem that inspired the Iron Maiden song of the same name.

POPOFF: Any thoughts on why Steve and Bruce like going to classic literature and film and books for lyrics? Here we've got Samuel Taylor Coleridge, who, of course, Rush had already tapped for inspiration.

BAYLEY: Well, it's a nice way to avoid love. And it's something I do all the time, since my Wolfsbane days, and particularly since being in Maiden. It's a nice way to get out of it. It's so common that people write about love and all the emotions and feelings that, well, for some of us at some point in our lives, are just boring.

It's interesting to think about the Battle of Britain. It's interesting to think about being back in the village and the questions arising from *The Prisoner* TV show. To think about "Powerslave" and slavery and being trapped. And "The Rime of the Ancient Mariner" is a fantastic poem. To take that and put it to music and really express that idea, to me, that's great. So much of what Maiden has done could be a film soundtrack.

STRAUSS: "Rime of the Ancient Mariner" is the most epic of epic songs. We would do "Rime" at probably seventy-five percent of our shows because fans wanted to hear it.

There's not a lot of thirteen-, fourteen-minute songs that fans actually want to see live, and yet "Rime" is definitely a crowd favorite. It's surprising to see what Maiden fans embrace that the general population of music fans wouldn't be into.

But Maiden is a great storyteller. You're not going to see a lot of Iron Maiden songs about breaking up or relationships or partying or your general song concepts. Maiden revisits fables and tells stories—and they'll tell the whole story. They'll talk about history or war or military conflicts, everything from "Afraid to Shoot Strangers" to "Aces High." You really hear a lot of intellect in their songwriting, and, I don't want to say less emotion, because it definitely is emotional, but it's not as personal for the most part. It's about wider and more worldly events.

POPOFF: Any thoughts on the great debate Maiden fans have between the relative benefits or value of the long songs like "Rime" versus the sharp rockers, which are bundled up here on Side 1?
BAYLEY: No. If the song is good, that's all that matters. The main thing is the idea, being truthful and faithful to the idea of the song. If the song takes thirteen minutes

to reveal itself, then that's what it takes. If the song takes four minutes to reveal itself, then that's it. If there is a journey this song has to take you on, and that takes two minutes or thirteen minutes, then that's it.

I think that's the test of a great songwriter, but it also puts you in a different league. When you're in Iron Maiden and bands like Maiden, you're not looking at how long the song is because you're not really trying to achieve a daytime radio hit. That's another side of the music business. The people who can say everything they need to say in three minutes, that's a different skill compared to having a massive idea that takes you on a great journey away from your life and twelve minutes later you're back in reality.

Steve Harris—showing off his monogrammed wristbands in West Ham colors—on stage at the Joe Louis Arena, Detroit, Michigan, January 4, 1985.

POPOFF: As someone who has written with the band and sung old classics written by Steve and Bruce, is there a distinction between the way Steve writes for a vocalist versus Bruce? I've heard it said that, somewhat unsurprisingly, Steve's words can be more of a mouthful, given he's not coming from a singer's point of view.

BAYLEY: I don't think there's better or worse, there's just different. It just comes from a different place. As a vocalist, you're naturally putting the breath into the line. When Steve is writing, he's usually writing a musical phrase then putting in the lyric to go with the melody. It just comes from a different place. There is no way you can have some of these incredible songs that Steve has written over the years without doing it that way. If they were all written by the singer, we wouldn't have "The Duellists" or "Rime" or "Sign of the Cross" or "The Clansman."

POPOFF: "Rime" is the repository of some great twin leads.

STRAUSS: Well, speaking as a guitar player's guitar player, you can never have enough guitars. Of course, Maiden was one of the pioneers of the twin-axe attack, of really utilizing two strong lead players instead of a rhythm guitar player and a lead guitar player—really letting both voices be heard. The skills of both Dave and Adrian really come out and shine, and they don't copy each other—both their personalities show. That's really cool.

POPOFF: How would you demarcate those two guys?

STRAUSS: Dave's playing is more bluesy, classic licks, while Adrian is more the technique stuff, more whammy bar and different phrasing you wouldn't normally expect, although both have pretty unique phrasing as far as the general world of guitar players goes. For me, it was interesting being part of The Iron Maidens because I was never that bluesy player. I would never gravitate to those licks. Getting to immerse myself in a more bluesy, classic style of playing was an interesting experience.

One of the most interesting experiences I had playing in an Iron Maiden tribute band was the ability to go all over the world and have these rabid fans singing the songs, singing every single lyric as well as a lot of the riffs and the solos. They all knew more lyrics than I did, and it was amazing. These people, who might have little to no grasp of English, know all the words to these Iron Maiden songs . . . I think Blaze is absolutely right: it's all about the melody and the structure, the way the guitar and the vocals and the bass all play off each other, and it becomes a universal language—the language of Iron Maiden.

BAYLEY: What people don't realize is how in time and in tune and precise Dave and Adrian are. And live, people may have looked at them back in the day and said, "Well, those guys don't run around much." But when you've been in a rehearsal room with Dave and you hear what he does, it's incredible. I think that's what people don't realize.

A poster advertising the World Slavery Tour's visit to Peoria, Illinois, June 1985, and one of the many band T-shirts sold on the tour.

They make it look easy. But the precision of what they do, and bringing out the feeling of every song every single night, there's no relaxed attitude in Iron Maiden. Every night is, "Right, this is the World Cup final and we have to win." That's the attitude we went on stage with every night, and that's what they still do. For younger guitarists, or maybe people who might not be so keen on Maiden or what they're doing now, I think they don't realize that's the real thing up there. It's the precision and the commitment to excellence that everybody in the band has that's remarkable.

Adrian Smith stretches out at the Poplar Creek Music Theater, Chicago, June 15, 1985.

POPOFF: Any thoughts on the instrumental "Losfer Words"?

PORTNOY: It was good to get another Maiden instrumental because the first album had one, and *Killers* had two. The Iron Maiden instrumental was something I really appreciated, and we didn't get one on *The Number of the Beast* or *Piece of Mind*.

"Losfer Words" is a very forgotten instrumental in their catalog as well. In fact, most of the tracks in the middle of this album I absolutely love. When you think of *Powerslave*, you think of the first two, "Aces High" and "2 Minutes to Midnight," and you think of the last two, "Powerslave" and "Rime of the Ancient Mariner." But there are some good songs in the middle. Those are forgotten gems, and it's kind of like the tracks in the middle of *Piece of Mind* with these strong sleeper tracks.

POPOFF: So *Powerslave* comes out and the band is firmly established, especially after that massive tour. What was your memory of where Maiden sat in the metal hierarchy of the day?

PORTNOY: *Powerslave* was their pinnacle. You couldn't get any bigger or grander. It established them as the biggest heavy metal band in the world. Not in record sales for some reason, although they did well, but in buzz, and probably even concert success. Metallica was coming out, but they were up-and-comers, and it would be many years before Metallica would take over the reins as the biggest heavy metal band in the world. But in 1984, I'd argue that Maiden was the biggest heavy metal band, or at least the most talked about, the one generating the most excitement.

You think of that shift from the '70s—Zeppelin was broken up, Purple was just reuniting in '84 with *Perfect Strangers*, but they were still not on the level of Maiden. This was post-Dio for Sabbath, so they were on a downslide. Within the NWOBHM, Maiden had easily bypassed Motörhead and Saxon. And for a brief instance at this time, they'd even outperformed AC/DC. Sure, there was Priest, Ozzy, and Scorpions, but metal fans, especially at a street level, were more excited about Maiden. I truly believe they went straight to the top, and, for a magic moment there, you could say Iron Maiden was the king of the castle.

The band performed in front of an Egyptian-themed stage set for the World Slavery Tour.

The *Live After Death* LP, recorded during the World Slavery Tour and released in audio and video formats, October 1985.

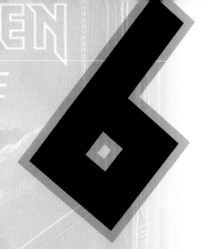

Somewhere in Time

with
Tim Henderson
and
Chris Jericho

SIDE 1
1. Caught Somewhere in Time................7:22
(Harris)
2. Wasted Years............................5:06
(Smith)
3. Sea of Madness.........................5:42
(Smith)
4. Heaven Can Wait........................7:24
(Harris)

SIDE 2
1. The Loneliness of the Long Distance Runner.....6:31
(Harris)
2. Stranger in a Strange Land.................5:43
(Smith)
3. Deja-Vu................................4:55
(Murray, Harris)
4. Alexander the Great......................8:35
(Harris)

Personnel: Bruce Dickinson—vocals; Dave Murray—
    lead and rhythm guitars, guitar synth; Adrian
    Smith—lead and rhythm guitars, guitar synth,
    backing vocals; Steve Harris—bass, bass synth;
    Nicko McBrain—drums
Produced by Martin Birch
Recorded at Compass Point Studios,
    Nassau, Bahamas; Wisseloord Studios,
    Hilversum, Netherlands
Released September 29, 1986

W ith *Somewhere in Time*, Maiden kicks off a second quintessential album pairing, one that would follow the formative *Piece of Mind/Powerslave* duo and precede the rough and drifting *No Prayer for the Dying/Fear of the Dark* one-two.

Somewhere in Time, of course, is inextricably linked with *Seventh Son of a Seventh Son*, marking a period when Maiden struggled with a late-'80s hangover brought on by the exhausting World Slavery Tour—187 shows in 331 days—and the looming dissolution of its metal niche, with Sunset Strip rock booming and thrash, at least creatively if not commercially, blossoming. The tacit suggestion was that new metal flavors were making the old irrelevant.

Maiden wasn't alone: Ozzy, AC/DC, Scorpions, and Priest also struggled. But credit to Steve and the boys, because *Somewhere in Time* would prove a valiant follow-up to the energetic *Powerslave*. Furthermore, it would be rewarded with a platinum disc for its struggles, aided and abetted by the success of the single "Wasted Years," a rare bit of personal human melancholy and an early demonstration of the introspection that would entrench over time, whether or not Steve and Bruce welcomed it.

Somewhere in Time would rise to a respectable No. 11 in the *Billboard* charts, but more importantly over time was that the album went gold in Germany and Brazil and double platinum in Canada, and charted in at least a dozen countries. Fueled on World Slavery, Maiden was becoming the metal ambassador to the world, the new album offering at least a trio of future world anthems (take that, Frank Marino) in the aforementioned "Wasted Years," the screwy sweet-and-sour "Heaven Can Wait,"

and the boldly galloping title track, Nicko and Steve a tour de force cresting the hill and then pouring into the valley.

Notably, Steve penned four tracks alone and Adrian another three, also alone, while "Deja-Vu" was credited to Dave and Steve. As for the absence of the band's usually plucky and participatory vocalist, word was that Bruce was the most knackered of all from the touring. He was also stretching to write outside the box, acoustically even, striving for a Zeppelin-like *masterwerk*. It was a troubling development in retrospect, revealing the seeds were sown for Bruce's discontentment. After four studio albums of which Bruce wasn't particularly proud, he would give up, go away, and write some songs he could stand behind.

Also on the credit front, the Adrian Smith narrative is of some interest, because, arguably, the album's three best songs arrive at his hand. "Wasted Years" is irresistible, irrefutable, soaring, despite being bolted down, Nicko halting and sacrificing groove for a different kind of flavor. "Sea of Madness" is a metal feast, novel for the band both rhythmically and in its note-dense riff. And then "Stranger in a Strange Land,"

"Bruce, you've forgotten something . . ." A promotional portrait of the band from 1987.

launched as the album's second and last single, recalls the weight and majesty of "Flight of Icarus," made all the more multidimensional by independent vocal phrasing. Across all three, melody is at the fore, but each of different, more sophisticated strains than usual.

The "Stranger in a Strange Land" lyric is of quality as well, Smith prompted to write the tale after a conversation with an Arctic explorer who had discovered a frozen body, resulting in these musings on the tragic wanderer's last days. The single charted in the UK at No. 22, following up "Wasted Years," which hit No. 9, pushing the record to its gold status at home, even if Maiden had long transitioned to more of a US and world phenomenon, somewhat forsaken at home. Then again, these guys are anything but homebodies.

MARTIN POPOFF: Set the stage. It's 1986—where are we in Iron Maiden history and in the history of heavy metal, for that matter?

TIM HENDERSON: Maiden was recovering. They had been on their longest run, culminating with *Live After Death*, a very well-received double live album, and they all needed a breather. It's pretty well known that Bruce wasn't represented on this record's writing credits because there was burnout. And there was a transition in the heavy metal community because of "The Big Four" and thrash, which might have had a bit of influence, especially when you listen to "Caught Somewhere in Time." That's brutally heavy.

It also reminds me of why they got Nicko. The first track we heard from him was "Where Eagles Dare." I remember marveling at the drum sound, and then we fast-forward a couple years and, again, it's, "Listen to this drum sound." It's not double bass, but, man, that song could easily have fit onto some death or thrash or speed metal album. Pretty heavy.

The scary thing, too, was this "guitar synthesizer" thing. But as it turned out, it wasn't like a Depeche Mode/New Order/Ultravox thing. Rather, Maiden persuaded everyone you can actually utilize these different sounds on a record in 1986. Also keep in mind that Judas Priest's *Turbo* was released five months before *Somewhere in Time*. And, so, now you have two of the biggest bands in heavy metal utilizing this new technology. But Judas Priest went more the poppy route, Halford admitting

The first single drawn from *Somewhere in Time* was "Wasted Years," released September 1986.

Opposite:
Dickinson on stage at the Philadelphia Spectrum, January 13, 1987.

the idea was to do somewhat of a party album. *Somewhere in Time* was a lot heavier than *Turbo*, start to finish. And good on them—it's brilliant.

POPOFF: Chris, what are your recollections of those times?
CHRIS JERICHO: Well, *Powerslave* is my all-time favorite Maiden record, and a lot of that has to do with what Paul Stanley says: wherever you jump on board as a fan, those songs will always mean more to you. And *Powerslave* was the first Iron Maiden album I bought, and the first tour I saw was in December 1984 with Twisted Sister opening. That's when I really became a Maiden fanatic.

Knowing nothing about the record and not really getting much information, I remember reading in *Circus* that the record was coming out on this day or something. So I'm calling the record store constantly, "Is it out?" I think this was September. "Yeah, it'll be out on Friday." So, Saturday, I take the bus downtown to Records on Wheels in Toronto. I remember walking inside, and the song playing on the PA was "Heaven Can Wait" [*sings chorus*], and I'm thinking, "Is this the new Iron Maiden record?" "Yeah." "Is this the first song?" "No, it's like the fourth song." "Holy shit."

The "Stranger in a Strange Land" single, released November 1986, and a "Stranger" pin.

Dickinson in a more reflective mood in a solo portrait taken later in 1987.

Opposite:
Harris in his West Ham United scarf with Murray outside the EMI offices in New York City, January 1987.

First thing I remember, obviously, is the cover. It was one of the first "clue" album covers—and maybe still the best—with twenty or thirty or forty clues or references to other Maiden songs and other Maiden album covers. Now you can Google them all, but, at the time, I remember making a list with pen and paper. There's the reaper, shadow in the corner. Oh, there's 22 Acacia Avenue, Charlotte the Harlots are playing over here, the West Ham football team's name is over there. So that was cool because one thing about Iron Maiden is, they always had great album covers and great inserts. And the guys are on the back, a cartoon drawing. Bruce is holding a brain. There's some kind of weird, really shitty-looking spaceship. Really cool to see all this stuff.

And then playing the record, it blew me away, but the first thought as a big Maiden fan is that Bruce wrote nothing on it. I always wondered why, and then you hear, years later, the reasons. But they were all Steve or Adrian songs, except the one Dave co-wrote, "Deja-Vu," with Steve. To me, it was like, "Wow, this is all Steve or Adrian, my two favorite guys in the band."

Murray takes a solo during Iron Maiden's latest visit to Madison Square Garden, April 2, 1987.

And then there was always talk about the guitar synth, which, I think, is more prevalent maybe on *Seventh Son*, although I guess it's actual keyboards there. But you don't really hear a lot of it. You just hear the word "synth" as a metalhead and you see a bunch of keyboards. It was just a weird kind of effect they used at times. I thought *Somewhere in Time* was the perfect follow-up to *Powerslave* and close to a perfect album where all the songs are awesome.

POPOFF: Tim, what did you think of the cover?
HENDERSON: It's amazing. It's almost Hollywood-esque, sort of *Blade Runner* meets *Mad Max* and *Star Wars*. And, of course, it touches upon a lot of past. It's like trying to find Waldo. It was just so in-depth and intricate. You practically needed a magnifying glass to figure out what's going on there—and this is when album covers were a foot square.

POPOFF: Would you guys agree with the idea that, of every song on the record, "Wasted Years" has survived and endured the best? What is the magic inherent in that song?
JERICHO: I loved "Wasted Years," and I love the fact it's Adrian Smith's coming-out party. The first single on the new Maiden record is by Adrian Smith?! Like, can you imagine Steve Harris allowing that? That's crazy, right? And it was great. It's got the riff, it's probably one of the most melodic Maiden songs. You could make that into a pop song very easily. You could have Justin Bieber or Lady Gaga singing that song, and it would have the same vibe and hook.

And the fact that they still play it. They played it on the Book of Souls tour. People love it. It's one of the underrated hits. There's "Run to the Hills" and "Aces High" and "2 Minutes to Midnight," blah blah blah, but people tend to forget about "Wasted Years." But I bet when they play it, more people know that song than know "Aces High."

POPOFF: And the lyrics are very personal and delivered in the first person, in fact.
JERICHO: That's one thing that Maiden didn't do a lot of, and I think that's one reason it worked. It was a song about a relationship and being on the road. That's what I always took it as. Because the *Powerslave* tour was two years long and almost killed them, and this song was about traveling so much and doing so much work that you're not even living your life, you're just wasting it. The wasted years.

When you travel around the world, it's great, but it's wasted if you don't enjoy any of it. As a sixteen-year-old kid, what the hell do I know about that sort of shit? But I could still tell it was something different than "Rime of the Ancient Mariner," the albatross seeking his vengeance.

A print ad for the *Somewhere in Time* tour's stop in Richfield, Ohio, in March 1987.

And I know, even from our own experience with Fozzy, that a relationship song is something everyone can relate to. We've had other big songs with word imagery or whatever, but it's the song that everybody can relate to that's the biggest hit. I think that's why "Wasted Years" is so eternal for them. The wasted time, always searching for the wasted years. Everyone can relate to it.

HENDERSON: "Wasted Years" is one of my favorite songs to this day, and it's probably the least synthesized track on that album. It's kind of shocking it didn't really take off at radio. Great chorus lines; every component of that song was constructed for radio. It's such an insult to the Iron Maiden family that great songs like that just didn't resonate. It resonated with the fans, but not with Joe Public.

POPOFF: Many of their contemporaries tried their hand at hair metal, such as Judas Priest. Why didn't Maiden?

HENDERSON: I don't think it was in their hearts. They were never that kind of band. There's no way they were going to soften up, even with the synthesizers, with the rumors of them going down that road being largely unfounded. No, the heaviness is quite clear. These guys did not sell out on *Somewhere in Time*. Things started to get a bit strange after the fact, at least after *Seventh Son*. But, at this point, there was no backlash from the fans at all. It was still primetime Iron Maiden. Speed and thrash were starting to come to fruition, and this record held its own.

POPOFF: Tim, you've worked quite a bit in radio. Is there a connection with the band's lack of those big multiplatinum albums their contemporaries had?

HENDERSON: For sure, it all comes down to radio play. Not to bring up Priest again, but I will [*laughs*]. Those songs, like "Living After Midnight," "You've Got Another Thing Comin'," "Breaking the Law," those could strike a chord. Maiden just went way over people's heads. "Wasted Years" is such an incredible song, but programmers were still afraid of Maiden. It was too dark and too heavy. And it sucks, because all these records should be double and triple platinum in the States. In Canada they did better numbers. We're probably their best territory per capita. But in the States, I always attribute that to the lack of radio play. It floors me that *The Number of the Beast* isn't even double platinum. Sure, they've got a pretty healthy string there of golds and platinums—but not one multiplatinum album—which is just baffling, given how many millions of concert tickets they've sold, not to mention Eddie shirts.

JERICHO: I agree, Maiden never wrote "Living After Midnight" or "Breaking the Law," but who is the big band? I would almost say Maiden is five times bigger than Priest today—maybe even ten times. There's no doubt about it. Priest comes to town, they play the Hard Rock and sell three thousand tickets, and it's great. Maiden still sells fifteen thousand tickets, dude—in the States!

POPOFF: We should touch on a few other songs. Chris, give me a survey of some of the tracks we haven't talked about and your impressions.

JERICHO: "Caught Somewhere in Time" is probably the greatest intro for any Maiden record. "Aces High" is a great intro, and I love "Moonchild," but I think "Caught Somewhere in Time" is great. That was the height of my high school band, called Scimitar; we learned that song about two weeks after the album came out. It was so cool to be able to lock into that. Tremendous tune.

And I really love "The Loneliness of the Long Distance Runner," which is the weirdest . . . it's the most Maiden song title, maybe ever. If any other band would've written a song called "The Loneliness of the Long Distance Runner," you'd be like, "That's the stupidest thing I ever heard." But with Iron Maiden, you're super-intrigued. "Oh, what's that about?" [*laughs*]

Once again, you get into, "What are the movie references on this one?" There's "Alexander the Great"; there's a movie from the '50s. "Somewhere in Time"—that's also a movie with Christopher Reeve. "Stranger in a Strange Land"—that's a book.

A selection of photo passes from the *Somewhere in Time* tour.

"The Loneliness of the Long Distance Runner" is based on a movie from the '60s that came from a short story. So they are lurking everywhere.

And I really dug "Heaven Can Wait" too; I thought that was really great, with the big soccer chant in the middle. And then I thought, kind of keeping the sister album type thing going, where *Powerslave* ends with a history lesson, so does *Somewhere in Time* with "Alexander the Great." It's a little bit forced, but I learned more history from Iron Maiden than I did from history class.

It's a supersolid record. And don't forget, the B-Sides are great—"That Girl," "Reach Out," "Juanita"—there were all these great B-Sides for all the singles. I love that album, and I think it's almost the forgotten album. Nobody really talks too much about *Somewhere in Time*, but it's pretty badass.

HENDERSON: I agree. Not only is it heavy, but there's a ton of depth. It really is one of Iron Maiden's top records, and I totally agree it gets overlooked and possibly is ripe for a rediscovery, just like *Seventh Son* has gotten. "Sea of Madness" is a great tune. "Heaven Can Wait" was on their setlist forever. I love "Stranger in a Strange Land" and "Deja-Vu," which is maybe the most conventional Maiden song on the record, along with the title track.

Harris, Murray, Dickinson, McBrain, and Smith pose with gold discs for *Somewhere in Time*, 1987.

There's probably not a poor song, although maybe "Alexander the Great" started to follow in the grand finale footsteps of "Rime of the Ancient Mariner" and fell short. I think that lost people a little bit; it just didn't have the hooks or anything new—plus, it seemed like they were reaching. It just goes nowhere, and it's eight minutes plus. As I say, it's like they were just dying for another "Rime of the Ancient Mariner," which is not double the length, but another thirty percent. Lyrically it was fine, I guess; I never minded the history lessons. But musically, it just smacked of Steve noodling in the studio and not knowing when to shut it down [laughs].

Not to bring up radio again, but there's a flow much like a well-thought-out radio playlist. You kick off the record with probably the best or certainly most aggressive song and then go poppier with "Wasted Years" and into "Sea of Madness," which is this almost circular and resolving, but still very smart and heavy, song.

They just had so much flow on this record. It was seamless. It almost worked like a concept record, when you just stand back and listen to it. But lyrically, it obviously wasn't one of those albums. One could relate everything on there to the subject of time, but that concept is so vague that most albums could be said to be about time.

But a very listenable album without giving in. There are the hooks in "Stranger in a Strange Land" when you get to the chorus line, and obviously "Heaven Can Wait" has that big soccer stadium chant—they would invite people on stage to do that with them at every show. It's a little goofy sounding to Western ears, but, then again, Maiden is one of those rare bands not for Western audiences only.

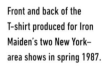

Front and back of the T-shirt produced for Iron Maiden's two New York–area shows in spring 1987.

POPOFF: That's a big thing with Maiden. As I've explored with some other speakers here, it helped make them a band that could appeal to non-English speakers.
JERICHO: We call it "beer stein rock." You sit there at Oktoberfest with a stein of beer, and go, "Oh oh oh." And I'm moving the beer back and forth across my chest like in a rhythmic motion—I mean, that's very much Maiden. And the thing about Maiden that you always loved was they never changed. They were always metal. They were never a rock 'n' roll band. They were just a heavy metal band. They were just Iron Maiden, and that never changed.

POPOFF: To round all the bases, what did you think of the production?

JERICHO: I never noticed anything like that when I was a kid. I was never an audiophile. But the glory years of Maiden are the albums they did with Martin Birch, right?

One thing, though, Steve's bass sound is always so obnoxiously in the front of the mix. But that's what you want from Iron Maiden. It was basically a three-guitar band, even at that time, even though they only had five guys, because Steve's playing is mostly leads. I really liked the sound he had on that record, and the production of it, because I was a bass player. I loved hearing the bass.

With Metallica, you had to almost guess what Cliff Burton was doing because he was always lurking under the surface. You would hear moments of it and see it in the wave, but you could never really get a full glimpse of it. Steve—you never had to worry about it; it was always right in your face.

Plus, Steve played a lot of high notes, and he played with his fingers. And you could always hear that kind of . . . I remember a friend said it sounds like bells, that popping of the strings, plus the galloping, rumbling sound. That's the thing: He plays a lot of chords now. His songs, if you watch him live, he's chording quite a bit. For people who don't play: that basically means he's strumming three or four strings. Back then, he was just doing single notes, and a lot of, like, first string, third string playing with octaves. It was a lot easier to play back then as a kid. You could kind of follow along with Steve Harris. I wouldn't know how the hell to do it now.

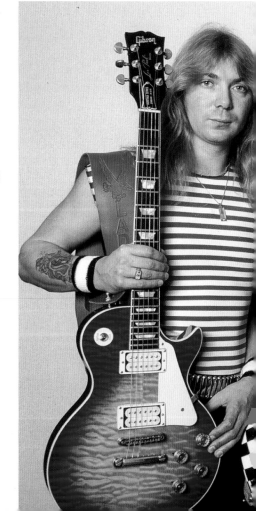

POPOFF: How are you with this idea of the long, involved intros to the songs? It's not overpowering yet on *Somewhere in Time* . . .

HENDERSON: I think they really created a mood. Probably aside from the last song, "Alexander the Great," all the intros are fine.

They set the tone, which was very dark. And believe me, there was a lot of competition out there at the time that was a lot darker than this.

I can't picture those songs without the intros. And then when we get to hear Nicko, the game is on. I think his personality really affected the band by this point, in a positive way, especially after the bonding of that massive tour. The guy is such a joker—free loving, easy living, loose. And his playing, it's almost like some great garage jam. On the title track, Nicko's driving that thing like a freight train. He's a star, no question.

It's quite interesting that Bruce isn't writing here. He was obviously a prolific songwriter. Maybe his head was not where Steve's was, but think about it—even though his presence, lyrically, is not on this record—his voice is just insane. He came to the party knowing he didn't write a single damn song, but if you listen to his voice on "Caught Somewhere in Time," he just soars. It's like the air raid siren times ten.

Left to right: Dave Murray, Steve Harris, Nicko McBrain, Bruce Dickinson, and Adrian Smith, 1988.

Seventh Son of a Seventh Son

with Matt Heafy
and Kirsten
Rosenberg

SIDE 1
1. Moonchild 5:39
(Smith, Dickinson)
2. Infinite Dreams 6:09
(Harris)
3. Can I Play with Madness. 3:31
(Smith, Dickinson, Harris)
4. The Evil That Men Do. 4:33
(Smith, Dickinson, Harris)

SIDE 2
1. Seventh Son of a Seventh Son 9:52
(Harris)
2. The Prophecy 5:06
(Murray, Harris)
3. The Clairvoyant 4:27
(Harris)
4. Only the Good Die Young. 4:41
(Harris, Dickinson)

Personnel: Bruce Dickinson—vocals; Dave Murray—
lead and rhythm guitars; Adrian Smith—lead and
rhythm guitars, synth; Steve Harris—bass, string
synth; Nicko McBrain—drums
Produced by Martin Birch
Recorded at Musicland Studios, Munich
Released April 11, 1988

Just as *Painkiller* is considered pretty much the best Judas Priest album within that fanbase, *Seventh Son* is routinely cited among Maiden fans as the band's best ever. In other words, despite the traditional notion that the band's most beloved albums have to come from among the first five, a youth revolution has gathered, pitchforks in hand, to place *Seventh Son* in that previously impossible-to-penetrate pantheon.

Two things give this record that extra kick: one a myth, one a truth. As for the myth, there is the ossified narrative that *Seventh Son* is much more prog than what preceded it. Not so, really, with much of *Powerslave* and *Somewhere in Time* being just as committed to length, epic flourish, and shifts in tone and tempo—all for little reason (to cite a somewhat snarky definition of progressive rock).

Also regarding the music, there does, however, seem to be a subtle and intriguing shift into the depths of the mind, with melodies more fantastical, moving from the nascent, proto-power metal of the New Wave of British Heavy Metal over to Germany under leaden skies on Helloween night and alighting upon the hilly rise of Italian power metal in all its classical and historical glory.

Even more intriguing is the fact that this is Iron Maiden's first concept album, which, no doubt, stokes the notion that this is a leg-warmers-and-tights version of a progressive rock album. Bruce framed it nicely when he told me that upon hearing Queensrÿche's *Operation: Mindcrime*, he realized it represented the proper way to construct a concept album and that Maiden had, in typical fashion, rushed *Seventh Son* (just ask Derek Riggs, praying

Opposite:
Bruce Dickinson under
the lights at the CNE
Grandstand, Toronto,
on May 20, 1988.

for his paint to dry!), the band cobbling the thing together with a Steve missive here and a Bruce missive there.

Abstract and oblique due to haste though it may be, the story we get is more of a creative triumph than any script handed to us on a plate. Dare I say, *Seventh Son* generated more deep thought and debate than *Operation: Mindcrime* or any number of more deliberate suites of lyrics meant to be linked through plot.

Perhaps this is why the record lives on, despite Iron Maiden having been written off amid the intense flash of hair metal and in the frost and fire of thrash, burning brightly in the middle of its golden era, circa 1986 to 1991. But the modern assessment of the record is a graphic example of history, usually quite rigid, being rewritten. Back in 1988, *Seventh Son* seemed, frankly, an unfocused redux of *Somewhere in Time*; thirty years later, it has been imbued with a mystical sense of power, perhaps underscored by the devilish plot line within, one more diabolical than anything the band would attempt across the rest of its catalog.

Even though it was on the wane, the Iron Maiden machine rolled on, generating considerable ticket and merch sales. Amid barely competitive offerings like *Savage Amusement*, *No Rest for the Wicked*, *Ram It Down*, *Blow Up Your Video*, and *Crazy Nights* and *Hot in the Shade*, *Seventh Son of a Seventh Son* managed No. 12 on the *Billboard* charts and gold certification a couple months after its April 11, 1988, release (although it's still not seen platinum). None of its three singles charted in the United States, although a number of songs became near and dear in the hearts of Maiden fans, especially "Can I Play with Madness" and, to a lesser extent, "The Evil That Men Do," both examples of the impression Bruce can make on your memory bank when he lays into a chorus.

The album's first single, "Can I Play with Madness," released March 1988 and hit No. 3 on the UK chart ahead of the album's release.

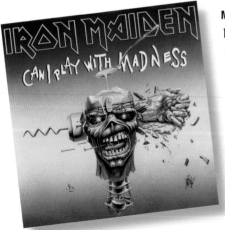

MARTIN POPOFF: To begin, what are the main adjustments the band made with *Seventh Son of a Seventh Son* from *Somewhere in Time*? Where is Maiden in 1988?

KIRSTEN ROSENBERG: Well, *Seventh Son* is the band's first real concept album, and, of course, it deals with mysticism and the occult, which is so metal [*laughs*]. Also, some consider it the last album of Maiden's experimentation phase. Musically speaking, there are keyboards, but they seem to fit with the music and are not prominent. It's one of my favorites. As a singer, I'm drawn to the vocals. I think you could easily say it's one of the best Maiden albums vocally.

POPOFF: Interesting. Why would you say that?

ROSENBERG: Bruce was still singing in a very high register, and the vocal melodies are incredible. The guys are really on fire with this album, despite, I know, sort of the undercurrents where Bruce was already feeling some dissatisfaction and starting to get the itch to move on. And, of note, he had songwriting credits on this album, whereas on *Somewhere in Time* he didn't. There was a bit of controversy about that. But they were on fire, man. They just hit the mark.

POPOFF: Matt, how does *Seventh Son* sit in the catalog for you?

MATT HEAFY: For me, there's always been a big connection with *Seventh Son*. Everything I did was kind of late. I was born in '86 and didn't hear metal until 1998, when I would have been twelve. And I didn't hear Iron Maiden until getting into In Flames, after getting into bands heavily influenced by Iron Maiden. So, backtracking into Iron Maiden, *Seventh Son* seems to be more so the place where all my favorite bands really started getting their influence.

When I'm listening to *Seventh Son*, I can hear not just where bands like In Flames and other melodic death metal bands from Sweden got their ideas, and where I got my ideas, but also some of the black metal bands. Speaking to that influence specifically, Maiden was bringing in the ethereal keyboards and having these longer songs that allowed them to take their time.

The difference between *Seventh Son* and *Somewhere in Time* is that with *Seventh Son*, I feel Maiden expanded even further into the songs. The songs got a little more progressive, even more than *Somewhere in Time* was. I could hear where Opeth got some of their ideas, and where even Emperor and Dimmu Borgir got their ideas. For me, it was really cool to be on this quest of, where did all my favorite bands get it from? And then I start to see it. I mean, I hope I'm not incorrect, but every time I listened to *Seventh Son*, it seems like the root—where everything that built my band, Trivium, came from.

Orson Scott Card's fantasy novel *Seventh Son*. Below that, the conceptual heavy metal album that Bruce thought eclipsed his own offering.

POPOFF: I won't ask you to explain the story of this record in full, but what is the short version? What is this record about?
ROSENBERG: Purportedly, it's based on a fantasy novel written by Orson Scott Card and lays out the story of a seventh son born to a seventh son who has special powers. He's a seer and someone who can heal and is really torn between the powers of good and evil. And good and evil are these real forces battling for his soul. That's a concept referenced directly in "Moonchild," one of my all-time favorite songs. It's very much like a fable, but there's certainly a bit of a parallel with what is going on in the world, to some degree, today. You can turn a blind eye to somebody telling you what's happening—whether it's the science of global warming, where people don't want to heed, or even hear, the warnings and shoot the messenger instead, or somebody's saying, "No, no, no. We just follow this book—the Bible," or whatever it is.

But more specifically, it speaks to this whole concept of somebody with special powers who tries to warn the world of bad things to come, and that we must change our ways, and choose between good or evil. And at the end of the album, my interpretation is that the seventh son is driven mad and, perhaps, kills himself or dies as a result of his own power. And we're sort of back to square one. What has really changed? Nothing.

So it's symbolic that you start with the same music and lyric, those opening lines, and then we come full circle back to those same lines, which are now the closing lines.
HEAFY: Any time a record feels more like a movie or a story, with a beginning, middle, and end—and a record cover that matches—it makes me feel like I'm inside a different world. And I know it's right—right that I'm there and right as a work of art. When it does have an A, B, or C, I just kind of know it. And that's why I keep segueing back to In Flames, who are such a massive influence on making Trivium what it was, and the things I loved about them are the things they got from Maiden. Having these album covers, these worlds. When you look at the cover and listen to the music, these two things pair so well together that it puts you in a headspace of where this world is. When I hear any song off *Seventh Son*, I picture that blue; I picture the ice. And when a cover doesn't match the record inside, I don't see the world in it, and it's not as fun for me.

Opposite:
Seventh Son of a Seventh Son Tour, East Rutherford, New Jersey, July 8, 1988.

But, yes, the reason it feels like a concept—it has a beginning, middle, and an end—even if, personally, I never try to figure out exactly what the singer or the songwriter had in mind. I really like to make my own world of it.

And why I understand *Seventh Son* as a concept, for me, is if you look at that cover, it's a bigger world than some of the other covers. It looks like maybe the aftermath of a global melt or something, or Antarctica. And you can't really tell what era it's in, whether it's past, present, or future, which I like a lot— I think that makes it bigger. I feel like the "blue" Iron Maiden records are the ones I gravitate to—this and *Brave New World* just feel massive to me.

ROSENBERG: It really isn't until the song "Seventh Son of a Seventh Son" that it starts to feel like linear storytelling. Prior to that, the record is more conceptual in that it's dealing with the same themes—the occult, mysticism, reincarnation—but it isn't really telling a story, like, chapter by chapter. The focus isn't really there until at least halfway through the album. Some people say it's a concept album and some people don't—I think it is.

POPOFF: Let's look at some tracks. Kirsten, you mentioned "Moonchild" as one of your favorites . . .

ROSENBERG: Oh God, it's just so fun to sing. It has some great notes in it, great power; it's just very emotive. I really feel the emotion behind it when I sing it. Plus, there's the anthemic chorus, which you could say for the entire album. Every song has an amazing chorus. The choruses are soaring, powerful, really catchy.

There's also "Can I Play with Madness," which is, again, a singer's song. And you can hear their vocal harmonies prominently. That one continues to support the whole concept of the seventh son; now this guy is going to a prophet to get some answers, but he doesn't really like what he hears. It's all part of the story. "Can I Play with Madness" has an oddly upbeat, and even poppy, feel to it, given the dark tone of the content lyrically.

I also like "Infinite Dreams," where someone is dealing with being tormented by their dreams. I'm not sure whether it's dreams or reality, and there's a line in there that supports that. It's not really overt or clear, exactly, who the narrator is. Is it the seventh son trying to come to terms with his powers and his visions? Is he being driven mad by them? As far as the feel of the song goes, there's a lot of emotion and then there's a change in tempo to a sort of march cadence. I just love it. And there's a hell of a scream that almost makes me pass out, right before it goes into the solo middle part [*laughs*].

POPOFF: It's true, many of these songs are defined not so much by the guitar work or the lyrics but by the vocal hooks and the choruses.
HEAFY: I agree. Maiden is the king of making the right metal song. There was a little while when I would try to rebel against having song titles in my choruses, but it just makes sense and it just makes it right. And Iron Maiden is one of the bands that has driven that home. Because, when you have a song title that is the pinnacle of the song, the hook of the song, that's what makes you come back to it.

POPOFF: The title track does that and so does "Moonchild," and, at least for me, that's the first thing that comes to mind when these song titles are mentioned—I sing the chorus in my head.
HEAFY: There are only a couple on this record that they don't do it on—"The Clairvoyant," "The Prophecy," actually "Infinite Dreams" too—which is kinda strange that they don't. But I love that that is an Iron Maiden formula. You know what you're getting, and that's what adds to it. And I think that's why they're such a well-received band internationally, in countries where English isn't the first language. I remember being at their Spain show, where the entire crowd was singing the "fear of the dark"—*and* all the guitar parts. These hooks and titles are something that people who don't speak English primarily can hook onto and understand. And I think that's the best definition of a hook.

POPOFF: Anything more we can add to flesh out the tale?
ROSENBERG: The basis for "Moonchild" was inspired by a ritual that Aleister Crowley used to attain knowledge, and it had a very specific name, and I'm probably mispronouncing it, called "Liber Samekh." And it was somewhat, I guess, inflammatory to Christians, but not to the point where "The Number of the Beast" was, where they overtly reference Satan.

(continued on page 108)

"The Evil That Men Do," the second single from *Seventh Son,* released August 1988. The third single from the album was a live version of "The Clairvoyant," released in November to coincide with the UK leg of the Seventh Son tour.

(continued from page 105)

A poster advertising the band's position at the top of the Monsters of Rock bill ahead of David Lee Roth, Kiss, Guns N' Roses, and more.

Opposite:
Commanding the stage in 1988.

Previous spread:
Iron Maiden in full flow, Brendan Byrne Arena, July 8, 1988.

But, yeah, here you're talking about these sort of occult practices. As far as what it means in the context of the story, the thinking is that it could be the devil, or even the good force, talking to the parents of this seventh son, communicating with them in some form or fashion; like, this is going to happen, don't try to kill yourselves [*laughs*], here's what's coming. So it's communication between the forces of good and evil, and the forces on the parents who are going to bear this seventh son. It gets the ball rolling to some degree.

The title for "The Evil That Men Do" stems from Shakespeare's *Julius Caesar*. Again, there's not an obvious and linear building upon the previous song. You could say it relates to the seventh son, where it's, perhaps, the story about how the seventh son was conceived. I've only sung the song like five hundred times, but I can't recall the lyrics [*laughs*]. There's something about sleeping in the dust with his daughter and the slaughter of innocence. Is it about someone losing their virginity? Is it the conception of the seventh son? What I also get out of it is, it speaks to the foibles of humanity—the dark side.

And then, of course, the title tells you we're getting very literal with this whole story taken from Orson Scott Card. It's the forces choosing between good and evil. And then we move on to "The Prophecy," a favorite on this album. I just love it; it's soaring, lilting, again, great chorus—a singer's song. I really love to belt out those big notes. And this could be interpreted as, now the seventh son is born and he's coming to terms with his abilities and he's trying to warn his village of an impending disaster. No one listens, and, when disaster happens, they blame him. They shoot the messenger, so to speak.

Moving to "The Clairvoyant" now, I interpret this as the seventh son now mature and in control of his powers. But he's also succumbing to his own powers—it's a curse. And perhaps he's driven mad by his visions. And the idea of reincarnation comes up again. And then "Only the Good Die Young" is the recap, the summing up of what this whole story is about. Here's someone trying . . . you can draw parallels

with what's happening in the world today, the battle between foolish belief—what I consider a foolish belief—in religion or religious dogma, in things written a long time ago versus people who have reason and logic and science behind them, saying the planet is warming up, or whatever. People are ignoring the warnings and sticking their heads in the sand. So you still have this eternal battle between good and evil. In the song there are references to bishops and guilt and morality plays and walking on water—definitely digs at religion.

POPOFF: Matt, any musical things you'd like to point out?
HEAFY: Sure, I think the intro to "Moonchild" is important. Because you don't think of a metal record coming in with this kind of folky, almost Tolkien world, sound. It doesn't feel like this fantasy, major-key thing should be an intro for a metal record. But I think it's so appropriate and shows how Iron Maiden can be incredibly theatrical and make it work, and be very storytelling in their music. That song has an intro, where they used an acoustic part, and they could've just extrapolated on that with keys and guitars.

But what I love about this record in general—and what they've always done, but particularly this record—is how the two guitars flow in and out of each other. At times it's about the rhythm sitting there and having this nice, big, open base, where lead guitars can create melodies on top and take other paths, and where the vocal parts are just as interesting as the guitar parts. That's something I love so much about Iron Maiden, that it's melodic both guitar-wise and vocally. But on the guitar front, what's cool is that crisscrossing of rhythm and lead and how they kind of go into each other and coalesce and become all about the dual lead guitars versus just drumbeat and a rhythm. I like that interplay, where they never really sit content with a pattern. It could be rhythm and lead, dual lead, dual melody, solo and rhythm … you're always getting something new.

POPOFF: How would you assess the rhythm section? What is interesting about Steve and Nicko?
ROSENBERG: Nicko's just a monster with the kick drum pedal. I remember people hearing "The Evil That Men Do" and thinking, "Oh my God, he's starting to use double kick"—but it wasn't. It was him still doing it with a single pedal, with something called a cradling technique, where he's rocking with the toe and his heel to make it sound like a double bass drum. So phenomenal. He really shows off his skills on a whole new level.

And Steve—it's funny, our bass player in The Iron Maidens, she is also petite and she's met Steve before, and they've actually put their hands up together and compared hands, and they were pretty close in size. He's got relatively small hands. I don't know how he has the stamina to play triplets like that constantly—the whole galloping thing. You know, there's so little in rock 'n' roll that is totally original, but really, other than hearing that gallop in Heart's "Barracuda," for me as a little kid, it was Maiden that introduced me to the whole galloping concept, and that's all down to Steve and Nicko.

POPOFF: How would you assess Martin Birch's production job on _Seventh Son_?
HEAFY: What I like about Iron Maiden is that it's a different tone or tonality in sort of eras. I do feel that, tone-wise, _Seventh Son_ and _Somewhere in Time_ are semi-similar, and I like that kind of grouping of twos in the early catalog. I like that they brought the keyboards in; that was questioned back when they first started incorporating them on _Somewhere in Time_, as guitar synths, so to speak. But I feel like it adds so much, even though they are pretty conservatively tucked in there. And I like that, on some Iron Maiden records, keyboards will be there, and on some they won't. Some songs have them, some don't. It just adds more to the canvas. They can make the listener feel like they're on a different planet or in a different world.

But again, the big thing with this record, I feel like this is one where they really nailed this idea that people can sing you a riff from a song and you can determine pretty quickly what song it is. That can't be said about too many metal bands. When you think of metal, it's usually like a rhythm guitar part; it's more arithmetic based. With Maiden, it was melody based. Someone can sing you a guitar line of Maiden's and you'll know what song it is. That's such a cool thing, to be able to literally sing a guitar line.

POPOFF: So *Seventh Son of a Seventh Son* gets released into the marketplace in 1988. How is it received? Is Iron Maiden still valid at this point?

ROSENBERG: Certainly, I would say they're still valid, very much so. But at the same time, the winds of change are blowing. And a backlash is beginning against the big metal bands of the '80s as we move into the darker '90s, especially against hair metal bands . . . not that Iron Maiden was one of those. I feel like they had peaked in terms of commercial success, and then there was a slide and decline for quite a while, although glad to say it was temporary.

POPOFF: Many '70s and '80s bands—Kiss, Alice Cooper, even Cheap Trick—tried their hands at hair metal.

ROSENBERG: Right, well [*laughs*], did that help any of those bands? I don't think so. I think it was a risky move for Iron Maiden staying so steadfast, but it totally panned out in the long run. They followed their hearts and literally played to the beat of their own drummer. They added some synths and keyboards, but it's hardly a move away from their roots. Look at them now—they are bigger than ever, headlining major festivals all over the world.

AC/DC charted a similar course. The whole world knows who AC/DC is, and, still, you hear their songs so much on the radio you want to blow your brains out [*laughs*]. And their popularity never waned. Or if it did, it came back one hundred percent.

I remember reading some comments from Bruce, starting to feel that the band needed to change it up to be more relevant with what was happening in the music scene. So, the fact that Maiden didn't, here or on *No Prayer* or *Fear of the Dark*, may have been a point of contention contributing to his departure.

POPOFF: Would you agree with the idea that *Seventh Son* has, in recent years, dramatically moved up on fans' lists of favorite Maiden albums?

ROSENBERG: Yeah, absolutely. We play a lot of songs from this album, and whenever we do, people go nuts. It's a universal favorite. For a certain demographic, *Seventh Son of a Seventh Son* is the pivotal Maiden epiphany.

POPOFF: At the time, the album sold okay but not great. Steve has reflected that, in America, the album was viewed as too European sounding. Is there something to this?

ROSENBERG: I just think times were changing and these epic songs, with all these beautiful twin leads, were going out of fashion. It was all about Ratt and Dokken and Mötley Crüe and Poison. I suppose they were quite British, specifically, with the

whole band being British, and with so many British themes, you could almost call them Anglophiles. Certain musical passages reflect that as well. But I never thought of Maiden as a distinctly British band—to me, they're just a great metal band. But they did rise to fame as part of the NWOBHM, so maybe, in that regard, they're thought of as a British or European band. But it's interesting, Steve's comment maybe speaks more to the changing tides of what was going on musically at the time.

HEAFY: It's amazing you ask that question, because this is something that we, in Trivium, have talked about a lot while doing records. We've had our labels say to us, "Oh, this song sounds too European metal and we don't think the American metal kids will get it." I didn't know about that quote. That is so funny.

Look at the influence this record had on large swaths of European metal, how *Seventh Son* feels like such an integral record to extreme metal bands that built upon it, and not only melodic death metal and black metal, but definitely power metal bands. Power metal bands would not exist without Iron Maiden, and they would probably not exist without this record, in particular. I feel like *Seventh Son of a Seventh Son* is the one where all the subgenres of metal stem from more so even than the classic records.

Maybe those bands would say *The Number of the Beast* or *Piece of Mind* before anything else. But I feel this is the one that inspired them to really bring keyboards into the music, to really bring in storytelling, and the intense ups and downs—juxtapositions of soft and fast or soft and heavy. This is where it all stems from, in my opinion. I could be wrong, but over all these years, since the first time I heard *Seventh Son*, I always thought, this is where melodic death metal comes from. This is where power metal comes from. This is where prog metal comes from.

Murray and Smith performing at Cal Expo, Sacramento, California, June 28, 1990.

No Prayer for the Dying

with
**Rich Davenport,
Tim Henderson,
and Jimmy Kay**

SIDE 1
1. Tailgunner 4:13
(Harris, Dickinson)
2. Holy Smoke 3:47
(Harris, Dickinson)
3. No Prayer for the Dying 4:22
(Harris)
4. Public Enema Number One...................4:03
(Murray, Dickinson)
5. Fates Warning 4:09
(Murray, Harris)

SIDE 2
1. The Assassin 4:16
(Harris)
2. Run Silent Run Deep.......................4:34
(Harris, Dickinson)
3. Hooks in You 4:06
(Smith, Dickinson)
4. Bring Your Daughter . . . to the Slaughter 4:42
(Dickinson)
5. Mother Russia...........................5:30
(Harris)

Personnel: Bruce Dickinson—vocals; Dave Murray—
    guitar; Janick Gers—guitar; Steve Harris—bass;
    Nicko McBrain—drums
Guest Performances: Michael Kenney—keyboards
Produced by Martin Birch
Recorded at Barnyard Studios, Essex, England
Released October 1, 1990

Like many an old-school metal band (Steve and his
blue-jeaned charges, over time, proving themselves
more parochial than some others from the '70s), Iron
Maiden found itself drifting—like the proverbial ancient
mariner—in a sea of brash upstarts and genres as the
'80s lurched to a close. Thrash was exciting and productive,
hair metal was chalking up golds and platinums, and, on the
horizon, a volatile and spontaneous new form of metal called
grunge would roll through and marginalize the lot of older
bands (save for Metallica and, soon to arrive in the public
consciousness, Pantera).

Maiden at least saw the problem, if not the solution.
Mythmaking deems *Somewhere in Time* and *Seventh Son* polished
or too polished. Nonetheless, those records were excessive and
fancy-pants in the band's own rock-scrabble working-class way.
So the brief this time was for Bruce to grow a five o'clock shadow,
show up at Steve's home studio (Barnyard, but using the Rolling
Stones Mobile), and scream his rest-deprived lungs out over
freshly penned material recorded fast 'n' loose.

Problem is, the songs exposed a band spinning its wheels.
Adrian Smith had left the fold to be replaced by Janick Gers, who
had come up the honest way, through an authentic NWOBHM
band called White Spirit, into Gillan for two records, and then
into Bruce's *Tattooed Millionaire* solo album, on which Bruce
bridged classic rock, hair metal, and Maiden
to acceptable effect. But Janick's not writing
here, leaving the song construction mostly to
Steve, with a bit of Dave and lots of Bruce.
We didn't know yet that Janick would write
pretty much like Steve; for now, what was

Opposite:
A solo portrait of
Bruce Dickinson, taken
in the Netherlands,
November 1990.

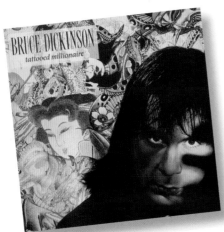

Dickinson's *Tattooed Millionaire* album, released May 1990, five months ahead of Iron Maiden's latest.

missing was the songful sense of Smith, who, like Bruce, was finding Maiden a bit silly.

Ergo, love it or hate it, *No Prayer for the Dying* is pretty much the domain of Steve and Bruce, who, gamely, at least for half or a third of the album, put aside the historical warring—and the TV shows and movies about historical warring—for more immediate societal concerns, with religion coming in for a return needling on highlight "Holy Smoke." The songs are deliberately short as well, a characteristic that fit the admirable brief. It would have been rough sailing indeed if some of the deep tracks like "Fates Warning," "Run Silent Run Deep," "The Assassin," or, at the bottom of the C pile, "Mother Russia," had been allowed to sprawl toward the nine-minute mark.

At the positive end, the aforementioned "Holy Smoke," issued as an advance single, was refreshingly linear, living and breathing on stacked chords as opposed to a riff. "Bring Your Daughter . . . to the Slaughter," previously a Bruce solo track, was similarly straightforward as well as starkly silly. "Hooks in You," with its dangerously accessible melodic chorus, folded in a little of both and a little more *Tattooed Millionaire*, as Maiden tried subtly to participate more universally—less eccentric and vaguely American—while the racing opener, "Tailgunner," was Steve and Bruce offering their unquestioning base another "Aces High."

Maiden isn't particularly a fan of the record, Bruce being most vocal about its shortcomings. This was confirmed by how the album has been ignored in the band's live sets past the No Prayer on the Road tour, save for brief visitations from "Bring Your Daughter . . . to the Slaughter" and "Tailgunner." This also would be the last Maiden record to go gold in the States, with Canada even notching back from steady double platinum support to single platinum, while the UK held steady at gold, aided by the home country's surprise taking to "Bring Your Daughter," which improbably, vaulted to No. 1.

MARTIN POPOFF: Set this up for us. What has Maiden changed, transitioning from *Seventh Son* to *No Prayer for the Dying*?

Opposite:
New boy Janick Gers on stage at London's Wembley Arena, December 17, 1990.

TIM HENDERSON: I love *Seventh Son*, and *No Prayer for the Dying* was certainly a step down. It was just rawer. Adrian's gone, which probably affects that album more than we think, and you've got Janick in there, and how much of a songwriter is he at this point in time, right? He's got no songwriting credits at all, while Adrian even gets one

for "Hooks in You." So it's raw and in your face compared to *Seventh Son*. Plus, it's the odd man out because the songs were a lot shorter. Like, there's not one epic on this thing, which underscores or telegraphs the idea they were looking for a back-to-basics approach.

RICH DAVENPORT: I understand what they were doing. Steve Harris has been quoted as wanting a street-level raw approach, to strip it back down. Toward the end of the '80s, overlapping into the early '90s, production was swamped in reverb, and if it was done badly, it muted so many good hard rock and metal albums. Reverb tends to take the power out of the drums, it takes the edge off the guitars, and it sounds like the band is playing down a mineshaft. It worked for the glossier stuff. Def Leppard pioneered that sound and it's great for them—but for metal, not so much.

I think they made the right move in terms of wanting to be rawer. Steve said they wanted everything to be fresh and to record it quickly. But Steve also said the songs were written quickly, and this is where it didn't work for me. This is where the album fell down. If I had to rate it out of five . . . delivery—four-and-a-half, in terms of the playing and the energy and Bruce's vicious vocals. In terms of material—three.

And that's where doing it quickly can scupper a band. It can work great in terms of spontaneity, but I know things can be underdone because you've not got the time to sit back

Gers in Copenhagen, Denmark, with Gillan in 1982.

CHAPTER 8

and be objective. From my limited experience as a musician, if you write a riff and you play it in the rehearsal room, it can feel great to play. You've got your amp cranked up and you're playing with lots of energy. And then you hear it back a few days later, and you think, "I enjoyed playing it, but it doesn't really hold up." You got caught up in the feel of playing it.

And I suspect there's an element of that on *No Prayer for the Dying*. In fact, Adrian has been quoted as saying that in the band, generally, he thought there was more time needed to finish the songs, basically, and that was one of his reasons for leaving. He didn't find that way of working particularly stimulating. I think he's right.

JIMMY KAY: I think they were trying to create another *Iron Maiden* or *Killers*. You could almost say Bruce was doing his best Paul Di'Anno voice. The narrative is that it's stripped down, but there are still keyboards on, I believe, the last song, "Mother Russia," and on "No Prayer for the Dying"—you can hear the keyboards in the background. Another difference is the emphasis on political, religious, and social aspects. It's quite surprising this far in; they've rarely gone there.

POPOFF: What was your first reaction upon shedding the shrink wrap?

DAVENPORT: When I got this album, I was initially disappointed. I've talked about this, but this thing about playing in a major key didn't always suit them. I bought the "Holy Smoke" single before the album came out, and I thought, "Yuck." The delivery is aggressive. That's fine. The opening lick is a bit like Status Quo, which is different, but it lacks a big chorus. It's got a good verse, but the verse and chorus chords are similar.

I must say I enjoyed the album more going back and listening to it now than I did when I bought it in 1990. But what struck me is, there's some repetition of past riffs and past lyrical themes, which was disappointing. This is down to, perhaps, writing the songs quickly and recording them quickly because you haven't got time to sit back and say, "Wait a minute. That sounds like such and such from three albums back. We need to change that."

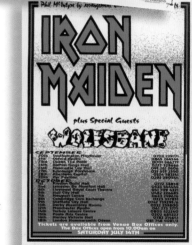

A poster for the Berlin stop on the No Prayer on the Road tour and a print ad for the tour's UK leg.

"Holy Smoke," released September 1990, was the first single to be taken from *No Prayer for the Dying* and the first to feature Gers.

So the opener, "Tailgunner"—bags of energy, bags of aggression—delivery-wise, it's great. The bass line at the beginning, to me, sounds like a faster version of "The Clairvoyant." Lyrically, it's a revisit of "Aces High," really. And I thought, "Oh, are they running out of ideas? I know a tailgunner sits at the back of the plane. He's not the pilot like the guy in 'Aces High,' but it's World War II, he's in a plane, so . . ." [*laughs*].

And then the track straight after that, "Holy Smoke"— I wasn't wild about. And then "No Prayer" I liked, but, again, it reminded me of "Infinite Dreams" straightaway with those Hendrix-y trills on the clean chords under the verse. It's a great song, and, once I got past that, I enjoyed it, but I had to get over this, "Wait a minute, that sounds too close to something they've already done."

HENDERSON: I agree, they were rehashing themes, and a graphic example, as Rich says, is "Tailgunner." Back to the war, right? That's where Steve's head is, almost as a fallback position. It's kind of like a modern-day "Run to the Hills," but instead of cowboys and Indians, we're refighting World War II. And "Holy Smoke"—what sticks out to me is Bruce's vocal. Was he smoking and drinking too much? Maybe he's such a deliberate and fine artist that he served up what the song required rather than some rendition of an air raid siren melody. Maybe he calculated that the whole album just required more forceful in-your-face vocals as a match to Steve's philosophy about what they were doing.

POPOFF: While we're on the topic of "Holy Smoke," this is the band's first single off the record. Good choice?

KAY: I don't know if there are any good choices, but it's a nice little departure. It's refreshing to see them strip it all down and just play straightforward hard rock, almost rock 'n' roll. I really like Bruce's raspy voice. As opposed to the opera, he's in the gutter—which fits the lyric.

This is Iron Maiden's shot at the religious right of the day—the fakers, the money-grubbing TV evangelists. And it's a clever title. And beyond all that, it's an expression of surprise. So it's about the smoke and mirrors these guys create to take your money before the inevitable happens and they end up in jail.

And before that, I love "Tailgunner." It's what Iron Maiden does best, conjuring images of war, not romanticizing it but creating a type of nostalgia, and most

definitely from a British standpoint. It's the guy who sits in the bomber planes in the back, and they're shooting at each other just to protect their planes. And with Bruce involved, there's a nice tie to his aviation hobby.

POPOFF: Besides these two, the only other song from the record that has survived in the memories of anybody, really, beside the most ardent Maiden fans, is "Bring Your Daughter . . . to the Slaughter." What's the story concerning this one?

DAVENPORT: A basic version of it, recorded by Bruce as a solo track, showed up on the soundtrack to *A Nightmare on Elm Street 5: The Dream Child*, which was a strange mix of hard rock at the front end and hip-hop for the second half. Steve had heard it and said he wanted it for Maiden, so they reworked it and embellished it a little bit.

I say that Bruce's version was basic, and it was, arrangement-wise, but it was also tighter and cleaner than Maiden's take, which is recorded, I suppose, in the spirit of the album. Which, let's not forget, they recorded on Steve's property using the Rolling Stones Mobile. I remember Bruce joking they recorded on hay bales or that there was hay everywhere because it was in Steve's barn. Anyway, Maiden made it their own, and it works well.

I saw the band not long after the album came out, Christmas 1990, and in the UK, "Bring Your Daughter" got to No. 1. And what happened was, they gave out flyers, hundreds and thousands of flyers, at shows. I saw them in Ingliston [at the Royal Highland Centre] exhibition near Edinburgh, which is a big venue, and they gave everyone a flyer saying the single's coming out, basically, on Christmas. So they heavily promoted it and, obviously, everybody went out and bought it, and it went straight to No. 1.

As a song, it's something a bit different for Maiden. It's almost AC/DC-ish, with a type of bluesy feel, which works well here. The band makes it their own. For me, a later example of it that doesn't work as well is "From Here to Eternity" on *Fear of the Dark*. That's a similar kind of thing. But again, "Bring Your Daughter" is a good example of a bluesy feel for Maiden enhanced by the album's dirty production values. And I think I'm right in saying it went down really well live.

HENDERSON: It's amusing that it went to No. 1. Not only is it flawed as a single, but 1990 is not exactly the year people associate Maiden as the reigning star of hard rock. I mean, it could have happened, but not with this suite of albums. But, hey, AC/DC made it work and even more fantastically. So did Aerosmith.

But in our world, our bubble, great tune—didn't do a bloody thing in the States or Canada. But "Bring Your Daughter . . . to the Slaughter" is one of my favorites on the record, although "Hooks in You" is another great tune. And the "Bring your daughter . . . to the slaughter" lyric is just a catchy turn of phrase that makes for a hooky chorus line.

I remember trying to pitch for a job at a college radio station in Toronto at the time, and I put that on my demo, and, holy shit, it was like I put a Deicide song or something on there. But I love it, I think it's fun. It *is* fun. You know what it is? It's fuckin' British humor. And to us on these shores, it fell flat. "What are they talking about?! Bring your daughter to the slaughter?! I can't play this for my kid. Give me that record, you're not listening to this."

I don't know, *No Prayer for the Dying* is a strange record, and I don't listen to it very often. And you certainly don't hear any of the songs live. You don't even hear "Bring Your Daughter . . . to the Slaughter" live, although it was used a little bit. But none of these songs are in the setlist. And when you think "Bring Your Daughter" has one of their greatest choruses of all time—you think, why not play it? It's a perfect choice to represent that era, to have the fans think about where Maiden was in 1990 and where rock was in 1990, with all kinds of metal huge but about to get swept aside by grunge. It's a beautiful song, obviously lacking

Iron Maiden's only UK chart-topper, "Bring Your Daughter . . . to the Slaughter," released December 1990.

seriousness or gravitas, but it certainly resonates with the fan base.

KAY: I don't know, I find it a bit forced, like they're wincing as they're trying to sound salacious and relevant in a hair metal world. "Bring Your Daughter" is sort of Iron Maiden dumbed down. I always thought that should be a B-Side rather than an A-Side. I could never guess why people liked that song so much, because it's repetitive, especially in the chorus. I've always twinned it with "Hooks in You." That's something Maiden hasn't really done before, and it's a good thing they're not doing it again. It kind of works and it doesn't. It's cool to see them try something different, but that song's probably another reason people don't like that album as much.

DAVENPORT: "Hooks in You," that's Adrian's last will and testament to the band at that point. That's a good example—"Can I Play with Madness" is another one—of a slightly more commercial song with that major-key style of writing done very well for them. There's also a twin lead section, and it's a strong song overall.

A poster for *A Nightmare on Elm Street 5: The Dream Child*, the soundtrack to which featured an early version of "Bring Your Daughter . . . to the Slaughter."

Janick didn't get to write anything on this album, but he was a very good foil for Dave. And the styles are more similar. I'm sort of paraphrasing a quote from the *Run to the Hills* biography, but the characterization of Dave is as the king of improvisation and soloing off the top of his head, and then Adrian as the hunched figure with a haunted expression working out his solos in advance. And I think you can tell that. You can always tell Dave and Adrian apart, but you could still tell Dave and Janick apart—but they're both Strat players. If I'm being an accurate guitar nerd, I believe Janick uses the bridge pickup for solos and Dave uses the neck pickup more. You can tell them apart, but they're both more aggressive than Adrian.

No disrespect to Adrian—I think he's great—but having heard the Gillan stuff, I think the development in Janick's playing was incredible. I know he had some time off from the business, and then he did Bruce's solo album. He used to get hammered a bit as a Blackmore clone. Well, that's totally gone. There are small hints of Blackmore here and there, but his playing has gotten faster. He's more of a shred

Dave Murray on stage at the Brendan Byrne Arena, East Rutherford, New Jersey, January 21, 1991.

guy now; the speed he was playing at just this year, it's like, wow.

And Dave, by this stage, he's also around that kind of speed as well. Maybe not quite Yngwie Malmsteen speed, but you can tell that the guys—Adrian as well, when he came back—all kept up their chops. As a fan of Janick, I was glad to see the guy doing well on *No Prayer for the Dying*. The fans accepted him, and his playing was superb, even though he didn't get to write.

KAY: When Janick came into the band, I met Dave Murray and Janick. They were doing this promotional tour. Adrian Smith had been in the band for six albums, so this was a big change, but Janick blended in well. What I really love about Maiden is that when Bruce and Adrian both came back in 1999, they kept Janick. That's how loyal they are as an organization. They appreciate anyone who has talent and is hardworking. They just didn't dump Janick for Adrian. And he does a great job. Of course, he was familiar because of being with Bruce on his solo album.

POPOFF: I always thought "Public Enema Number One" was overlooked. It's really heavy, and it seems made for this kind of production and delivery.

DAVENPORT: I think this is where we get to the meat of the album and I enjoy the rest of the album much more. "Public Enema"—that's one of the strongest tracks. It's got the classic Maiden twin guitars, which were lacking in the mid-'90s through to *Brave New World*. And I found that very, very frustrating. They used to be such an integral part of Maiden, and they seemed to be gone. So, anyway, this is one of the last examples. There were a few on *Fear of the Dark*, but this is where we see some of the last examples of the classic Maiden twin guitars.

The chord pattern is great, and Bruce sounds vicious in delivery and lyrics. There's a tempo change in the chorus; it's a very clever arrangement. It goes slower for the "Fall to your knees and pray . . ."—it goes to half time—and then for the

"Get to your feet . . ." bit, it speeds up again, back to the verse tempo. And then there's an interesting guitar figure before the solo, which almost sounds like the same rhythm as "Don't Stand So Close to Me" by The Police—kind of triplets. Overall, I really enjoyed that song.

KAY: It's funny they don't use the word "enemy." Historically, "public enemy number one" was Al Capone, but, here, it's politicians—their greed and how they pull the wool over everyone's eyes and how the world has just hit a breaking point. Everything is falling apart around us and it's probably politicians' fault. So they use the word "enema" to describe politicians.

POPOFF: Take me on a tour of what we might call some of this record's deep tracks.
DAVENPORT: "Fates Warning," again, great intro with the clean chords, a tradition harkening back to "Strange World" and "Remember Tomorrow." And then it rips in with a key change and you get the galloping triplet rhythm. The verse chords are great. The chorus is a bit like "The Clairvoyant." So a bit more repetition yet again. I didn't dislike it, but that stuck in my craw. That's a little more obviously repetitive than the band had been, up to that juncture. But, again, there's a superb twin lead.

Harris, Murray, Dickinson, and Gers, Brendan Byrne Arena, January 21, 1991.

Then we get to "The Assassin," which, again, has a nice atmospheric intro, nice choppy rhythm when the chords come in. There's another cool key change in the descending riff. Where it falls down, again, is the repetitive riff. And I wasn't the only one thinking this. I was listening to the album and I remember buying *Kerrang!* the same week and they said there were echoes of Maiden classics in the songs, so it's not just me. The riff before the chorus, that "You better watch out" bit, sounds like "The Trooper" with the same rhythm and quite a similar descending riff. Catchy but intricate. And then there's a dead stop late in the song, which, again, it's a bit like "The Trooper." It's also something they do in "To Tame a Land."

POPOFF: Is the closer, "Mother Russia," this album's "Quest for Fire"? Do you think the band is just asking for complaints?

KAY: It's got that verse and then it breaks off into this instrumental passage. I think it should've had no singing at all. It should've been like a "Genghis Khan" instrumental. Because there's some great musicianship on there. Then it would have escaped the ridicule it got for the topical lyrics.

DAVENPORT: It's a mixed bag. I like it overall. I remember thinking the lyrics with the "dance of the czars" bit seemed cheesy. Maybe I'm being a nerd, but it jumped out and I was thinking, "Oh, the czars are dancing. Are czars known for dancing?" [*laughs*] But there are some cool riffs. There's a bit where a keyboard part echoes the riffs and the twin leads in the middle, and there's a fast bit with some cool solos. The song's delivered well but parts of it don't work. There's the bit toward the end, with the "dance of the czars" bit, plus the vocals are a bit jerky along with the riff, which I didn't think worked particularly well.

But it seems like a historical epic for the sake of doing a historical epic. And I wasn't particularly old at that time, I was eighteen, but I still was on the ball enough to compare it, much to my dismay, with "Alexander the Great," which closed *Somewhere in Time* with a bit of a droop.

Overall, Steve's lyric is really good, in terms of summing up what was happening in Russia. Because I think this was approximately a year before the breaking up of the Soviet Union, wasn't it? The Berlin Wall's come down in '89 and then, in September '91, there was the big concert with AC/DC and Metallica—the first big show in what was now considered Russia—and then the official dissolution of the Soviet Union in December '91. So, yeah, "Mother Russia" is acceptable, but a bit more time on it would have been time well spent. I think this sums up the album as a whole.

HENDERSON: I don't know if "Mother Russia" is as bad as "Quest for Fire," but it's indicative of the band—or Steve, sole writer on the track—duplicating or running out of ideas. If you are going to tackle this topic, it should've been longer than five and a half minutes. You wanted the album to end on a high, and it just doesn't. They should've cut it off with "Bring Your Daughter . . . to the Slaughter."

Harris, Murray, and Gers at the Knickerbocker Arena, January 1991.

POPOFF: And, so, to summarize?

DAVENPORT: In terms of the delivery, committing it to tape quickly worked well. In terms of writing, not as well. It's a calculated risk, and it's admirable they took it. They could've gone a more comfortable route and repeated *Seventh Son*. Instead, they're recording with minimal studio comforts and keeping the song lengths in check. Other than "Mother Russia," there's no overtly historical epic. So it's a mixed album. If they took more time to develop it, it would have been stronger.

KAY: A lot of the songs sound like something Bruce would do on his solo album more so than on an Iron Maiden album. But the songs are fewer than six minutes, each of them, and they pack a punch. It's underappreciated, I think, in many ways. But I can see why people routinely vote it the least liked Iron Maiden album. Because there are some fillers there, like "Fates Warning," "The Assassin," and "Run Silent Run Deep." But the first four tracks? They knock it out of the park.

As for the production, the band says, in retrospect, they thought it was a bad idea. I don't think the production is as bad as people make it out to be. It's rough and ready. The songwriting was the problem. I think, in more than a few places, the guys just seem grasping for ideas and, more often than not, lacking in terms of clear direction.

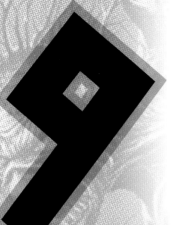

9

Fear of the Dark

with Tim
Henderson,
Sean Kelly, and
Nita Strauss

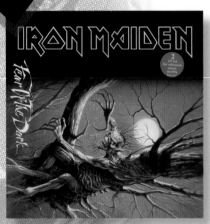

1. Be Quick or Be Dead 3:21
(Dickinson, Gers)
2. From Here to Eternity 3:35
(Harris)
3. Afraid to Shoot Strangers 6:52
(Harris)
4. Fear Is the Key 5:30
(Dickinson, Gers)
5. Childhood's End 4:37
(Harris)
6. Wasting Love 5:46
(Dickinson, Gers)
7. The Fugitive 4:52
(Harris)
8. Chains of Misery 3:33
(Dickinson, Murray)
9. The Apparition 3:53
(Gers, Harris)
10. Judas Be My Guide 3:06
(Dickinson, Murray)
11. Weekend Warrior 5:37
(Harris, Gers)
12. Fear of the Dark 7:16
(Harris)

Personnel: Bruce Dickinson—vocals; Dave Murray—
    guitar; Janick Gers—guitar; Steve Harris—bass;
    Nicko McBrain—drums
Guest Performances: Michael Kenney—keyboards
Produced by Martin Birch and Steve Harris
Recorded at Barnyard Studios, Essex, England
Released May 11, 1992

Grafted unattractively to *No Prayer for the Dying*, like Eddie is grafted to the tree on the front cover, *Fear of the Dark* is a record of minor adjustments where a larger overhaul was called for. First off, the band again recorded at Steve's place—the cramped Barnyard Studios—only now they were using his new permanent gear rather than the Rolling Stones Mobile. Martin Birch, who really, let's face it, hadn't gotten a great sound for the band since *Piece of Mind,* half-fired himself, co-producing the record with Steve rather than receiving full credit. Famously, Birch would retire after this, never to be seen again.

Also on the outs is artist Derek Riggs, passed up for the cover art for the first time. His replacement, Melvyn Grant, kind of pooches his first assignment. The story on the writing credits is that Janick Gers, who arrived in time to play on the last record but not for writing, is now fully ensconced as part of the team, second only to Steve in productivity, writing both with Harris and Dickinson. Again, it's to no discernible effect—as similar as Bruce and Steve can be with a pen, thesaurus, and VHS tape rental, Janick and Steve worked from the same playbook musically. Maiden had lost the versatility they had when Adrian was writing music—and very often in the process knocking off the fun 'n' flash highlight on any given album.

Still, the band cooks up nearly an hour's worth of music and breaks a few eggs in the baking, turning in an AC/DC-style rock 'n' roller ("Weekend Warrior"), an actual power ballad ("Wasting Love"), and a near–hair metal shuffle ("Chains of Misery"), complete with gang vocal chorus. Elsewhere, in the dark creases there's a substantial

Riding high: Iron Maiden prepares to launch *Fear of the Dark* into the world, spring 1992.

amount of Blaze Bayley–telegraphing prog ("Fear Is the Key" and "Childhood's End"), and a fair bit of it Zeppelin-esque.

Nonetheless, the record coughs up one massive everlasting Maiden chestnut in the record-closing title track, its last classic before the break, probably the biggest world anthem since "Rime of the Ancient Mariner," basically the latest song allowed to live from the hallowed original run. There's also "Be Quick or Be Dead," very brisk of tempo for Maiden, and the record's first of three singles.

Credit must also be given to the band's willingness to stretch lyrically. Putting aside how "Wasting Love" and "Weekend Warrior" call for fresh perspectives, "Afraid to Shoot Strangers" finds Steve turning in a smart lyric from the perspective of a soldier in the Gulf War (clumsy title notwithstanding). "Fear Is the Key" finds Bruce tackling the subject of AIDS, having been affected by the death of Freddie Mercury, and pointing out in the song that it takes famous people to die for a critical mass to take notice.

But none of the abovementioned and well-intentioned modest reinventions would be enough for Bruce, who looked around and saw great things being done in

Dickinson steps out into the crowd at the Laugardalshöll in Reykjavík, Iceland, June 1, 1992.

Opposite:
Dickinson and Gers share a moment in Iceland, June 1992.

the name of rock—just not at Barnyard Studios. *Fear of the Dark* would be the last record of Maiden's original run. As proof that the band was running on fumes by this point, the record would be the band's first not to reach gold certification stateside, let alone platinum. So, the '80s essentially ended in 1992 for Iron Maiden, as for pretty much every other metal act.

MARTIN POPOFF: To start, let's contrast this record with *No Prayer for the Dying*. What are the adjustments?

SEAN KELLY: I think the lesson learned here was they really went for this kind of raw, dry thing on *No Prayer for the Dying*, and it was a step too far. It made them sound small at a time when their throne was being challenged. You've got Metallica and Queensrÿche coming up with these amazing-sounding records. Maiden went back to basics and maybe went a step too far. Even though, maybe, it was a little ahead of its time, given grunge, so who knows?

So, with this record, there's a kind of concocted ambience with reverbs and things like that. It sounds somewhat better and just more fleshed out, with the judicious doubling of guitars and places in the mix for melodic lines. It sounds a little more finished to me. Hard to believe, but *No Prayer for the Dying* was engineered and produced by Martin Birch. But I think that was under heavy direction by Steve. I have a feeling that somebody gave Birch a little slap on the wrist and said polish this one up. Also, maybe the compositions lend themselves to that, being a little more polished.

TIM HENDERSON: *No Prayer for the Dying* is a lot more fierce and raw than *Fear of the Dark*. Listen to songs like "Afraid to Shoot Strangers" and "Chains of Misery" and you notice the edges are a bit more rounded off here. It was Steve's first production, so the tone is a lot different. As he told me, he's always been way more involved than people think, but he hasn't taken the credit. But it reminds me of when AC/DC started to take the reins from Mutt Lange.

There's some good depth on this record—there really is—but you can tell it's not a Martin Birch production. It's just more raw and in your face, and Bruce's vocals are not as powerful. As well, Dave told me it was recorded straight to digital, and it was the first time they'd ever used digital.

NITA STRAUSS: I think *Fear of the Dark* is a comparatively more polished record, and it's interesting that Steve Harris is co-producing it. Steve was the visionary of this band, with a clear-cut vision for how he wanted the band to sound, and it's amazing when a founding member gets to do what he wants rather than executing the producer's vision. So it's really cool from a fan's perspective and a musician's perspective, for me, to see the founding member taking and shaping this album.

POPOFF: Before we even hear it, we see it. What did you think of the *Fear of the Dark* cover?

STRAUSS: It's funny to see the new Eddie, because this is the first one by Melvyn Grant. As a newer Maiden fan, I didn't have the attachment to the old Eddie, so it didn't bug me personally. But it was still strange to see, like when you're watching a familiar TV show and they replace one of the actors.

HENDERSON: Rod's quoted as saying he just didn't want to get stuck in a rut. This really sticks out in terms of artwork. It was probably a good decision to start using some outside people. You have one visionary against literally thousands, especially later when we're talking about the birth of the internet and you can reach out to more people and people can reach out easier to you as well. But this album cover's awesome. It's wicked, scary as hell [*laughs*]. Maybe that was part of the downfall. Maybe retail looked at this thing and went, "My God, this is a little bit too mean."

POPOFF: Into the album, we get hit hard with "Be Quick or Be Dead," which was an advance single as well. Good choice?

KELLY: I love it; I think it's great. It's fiery; it's got interesting chord movement. It works for me. It does what I want a Maiden single to do.

STRAUSS: I think it's a strong song. Maiden has a way of picking a song that might not be the most typical one and coming out and showing what they're all about in that moment. I think "Be Quick or Be Dead" definitely did that.

POPOFF: Nita, as a guitarist who was in The Iron Maidens, what did Janick Gers bring to the band on his second Iron Maiden album?

STRAUSS: I am a big Janick fan. I really am. The joy in his playing, his note choices and phrasing, the way he is on stage—that sort of infectious enthusiasm? It really comes across in his playing. You hear this *joie de vivre* in

The album's second single, "From Here to Eternity," was released as a picture disc held in a presentation plinth, June 1992.

Backstage at the 1992 Monsters of Rock festival, which saw Iron Maiden make a return appearance as the headline act.

his playing, and it's fun to listen to. And again, born in 1986, I didn't grow up listening to Iron Maiden. I came to them much later in my life, so I didn't have that, you know, super "Adrian and Dave or nothing" mentality that a lot of diehard Maiden fans have. I started listening to it all at the same time, and, I was like, this is great, two great guitar players: Adrian, a phenomenal player, Janick, a phenomenal player. I think the joy and the enthusiasm he brought to this album made it a lot of fun to listen to.

POPOFF: Did the twin leads change when Janick joined?
STRAUSS: Well, I think the Maiden dual lead is the Maiden dual lead. In my opinion, it didn't change too much. It still had that minor third, harmonized lead that is the classic Maiden sound. But as far as songwriting and song structure and phrasing, I'm trying to think of a less technical way to say it, but it's almost like Dave is the classic guy, Adrian is the technician, and Janick is the fun one. I'm generalizing, but that's how I feel.

POPOFF: Tim, you were in radio. What are your thoughts on "Be Quick or Be Dead" as a single?
HENDERSON: Interesting but regular concept for them across these last two albums, right? Basically, attacking greed and corruption. And begging comparisons to *No Prayer for the Dying* with the same kind of upbeat, in-your-face vibe, from

"Tailgunner" to "Holy Smoke" to "Be Quick or Be Dead." Second single "From Here to Eternity," which they put out a month after the album was launched, stresses chorus more and is more of a typical single. But there are similarities between those first two tracks on each record. But, yeah, they couldn't go with "Fear of the Dark" or "Afraid to Shoot Strangers," which are my two favorites on the record, because they're too long. Then they went with "Wasting Love" as the final single in September. And it kind of makes sense, the order of these. And I'd say they picked the best songs for singles, but they're not my favorite Iron Maiden songs. How often do you listen to "From Here to Eternity" or "Wasting Love"?

POPOFF: True. And I tend to forget that "Wasting Love" was even issued as a single. What did you think of Maiden dabbling in the world of power ballads?
STRAUSS: I believe "Wasting Love" came from Bruce's writing for *Tattooed Millionaire*. Maiden was one of those bands that had always just done Maiden, so I would be skeptical that they did something like "Wasting Love" primarily to cater to a radio audience. But I enjoyed having that break from the triplets and the more typical Maiden stuff—a welcome change from a listener's perspective.
KELLY: I don't think it's as power ballad-y as other bands doing power ballads. This is coming out after *Tattooed Millionaire*, right? I wish hair metal would've been *that* [*laughs*]. That would've been amazing. "Wasting Love" is written by Bruce and Janick, and it's from those sessions—and, to me, that's exactly what it sounds like, like something from that album. And I can also see Steve Harris being totally on board with it, just like he was on board with "Wasted Years." It's like Adrian went, "Oh man, this is too poppy for you." And Steve goes, "What are you talking about?" He loves that stuff. He loves Kim Mitchell and Coney Hatch and UFO—he has an ear for melodic rock. I thought they did a really good job. But certainly, it's not "Every Rose Has Its Thorn." It's definitely still gothic enough, with enough gravitas to warrant being on a Maiden album.
HENDERSON: They were trying to break in America. They did a video for it and everything. I'm not saying it's a terrible song, but it was a last stab at trying to get more legs with this record in the States. That's definitely their first ballad—and yet another song that didn't click on radio! [*laughs*] But no, they didn't really whip out the acoustic guitars very often. And after that, they kind of floundered. Maybe Bruce saw the writing on the wall.

The "Wasting Love" single, released to coincide with the band's Monsters of Rock appearance, August 1992.

POPOFF: Tim, you were sent to England on a press junket to listen to the album. What did this say about hopes for the record?

HENDERSON: It was my very first junket, but it was also tied in with other bands. It was this dark setting, Porchester Hall, and they only played three songs, what would be the three singles. There were a lot of Iron Maiden characters dancing around—right away I met Steve, Janick, and Dave—and media from around the world. But we only got to hear three songs and didn't even get to see the album cover. I had to wait until I got back to Canada. Back in Toronto, I also interviewed the guys again, Janick and Dave this time.

So, hopes were high, I guess. Iron Maiden had always had huge support from Canada, in particular. EMI really worked well with Rod, and, per capita, Canada is one of the strongest territories for them. And Quebec, that's the center of the metal universe in Canada, right? That's where Iron Maiden probably doubled any audience size compared to any of the other provinces by far. They used to say that Quebec accounted for fifty percent of all metal sales in Canada, with a quarter of the population of the US.

Bruce Dickinson giving it his all at Wembley Arena, London, May 17, 1993.

POPOFF: Do you recall how these three songs were received by the English press?
HENDERSON: They were happy. All Englishmen are happy with fellow Englishmen, because they want to get a beer bought for them at the pub. I'm kidding. But none of the Iron Maiden albums have truly been dissed by the British media. I just remember it being a really dark setting, and they were serving drinks.

POPOFF: Another outlier is "Weekend Warrior." Is this another example of Maiden trying to place themselves more in the mainstream of metal, specifically American metal? After all, that's pretty close to a Ted Nugent album title!
HENDERSON: "Weekend Warrior" is a Steve song, but it sounds more like a Bruce song, like *Tattooed Millionaire*. Good, fun tune. But this is really where Maiden started changing from being less serious than they probably should have been.

"Weekend Warrior" is one of my favorite kind of poppy tunes. I'm not saying there are throwaway songs, but there are too many songs on this record. That's the problem. It's nearly an hour. They probably should've trimmed two or three, just to make it a little more palatable. Maybe it's that long because there were so many songwriters. Because if you drop a song—"Hey, that's my only song!" [*laughs*]
KELLY: "Weekend Warrior" is kind of AC/DC-ish. I like the straight-ahead ones. I think Maiden does that so well; I love it when they're covering that ground. I also like "From Here to Eternity" because I like the salacious Bruce lyric. I think it's just kinda funny. And I like that hook—it's got the "Woman from Tokyo" vibe to it. I'm a sucker for that sweet-and-sour thing they do.

Nicko McBrain, poised behind his ever-expanding drum kit during the 1993 tour.

ACHTUNG NEUER TERMIN
Sonntag, 11. April 1993 – 21.00 Uhr
Huxley's Neue Welt

Kartenvorverkauf: KaDeWe **218 10 28**, Hertie-Wilmersdorf **312 87 95**, Wertheim-Steglitz **792 99 43**, Wertheim-Kudamm **882 53 54**, Hertie Blücherplatz **251 63 67** und an allen bekannten Vorverkaufsstellen. Telefonischer Kartenservice **301 99 99** und **312 94 97**.

Ortliche Durchführung: concert concept Veranstaltungs GmbH
Tourneeleitung: Marek Lieberberg Konzertagentur GmbH

POPOFF: How strong are some of the more traditional tracks on the album?

STRAUSS: I'll speak to "Fear of the Dark" first, because more people know it. I get chills now thinking about this experience, being in Brazil and Colombia and all these places, and getting to play "Fear of the Dark." Because when that intro hits, and when the crowd is singing along to the guitar lead, it's an experience like nothing I've ever felt before.

And to get to be a small part of that . . . we were playing in a cover band, playing to 2,500 people a night, if that, at festivals here and there, but to even feel some small part of what Iron Maiden feels when that song kicks in was just really a joy. Playing Iron Maiden songs for a living was one of the most fun times in my life. I've been a professional musician for fifteen years, and those two years I spent with The Iron Maidens were really some of the greatest times—and with the greatest fans, the most hardcore fans I've ever come across. And playing with Alice Cooper, now that says something [*laughs*].

But then "Judas Be My Guide" is criminally underrated. It's catchy, cool, great leads, intriguing lyrically, a fun song to play. The solo has some interesting parts, too, stuff sort of ahead of its time guitar playing–wise, with some of the tapping and some of the phrasing. Generally, Dave does a lot more of the sort of bluesy, single-hand hammer-on/pull-offs, and Adrian would be more of the two-hand stuff, and Janick would do, probably, most of the two-hand stuff, and then adding in the sort of slides at the top with the right hand and all that kind of stuff. It's really interesting.

KELLY: I think Dave and Janick are closer in style than Dave and Adrian. They're both a little more improvisational. They tend to kind of grip it and rip it. Although Dave, compared to Janick, would lend himself to being a little more composed. Also, I've got to say, out of all those guitars, the strongest sonic identity is definitely Dave Murray. Dave Murray puts his hand on a guitar and it sounds like Dave Murray. Some people have it. I sure as hell don't have it. I wish I did, but I don't [*laughs*].

STRAUSS: From a guitar player's perspective, the main thing that stands out in my mind between the Adrian/Dave team and the Janick/Dave team is that Janick/Dave have more of that playful element. It doesn't sound quite as serious, if that makes sense.

KELLY: I guess those twin leads are coming from Wishbone Ash and Thin Lizzy, right? I hear Lizzy in the Celtic melodies and in some of those grooves. It's really like Celtic drums too. I was writing with Johnnie Dee from Honeymoon Suite recently, and he called it "argy-bargy" music. There's lots of threes, lots of sixes, just where the accents lie. And it's such a beautiful sound. In Crash Kelly, I ripped that off all the time. It's such a powerful device.

Opposite:
A poster for the European leg of the Real Live Tour, which Dickinson announced would be his last (for now) with Iron Maiden.

POPOFF: For sure. Sean, what are a couple highlights for you on *Fear of the Dark*?

KELLY: "Afraid to Shoot Strangers" is just a cool perspective on war. This idea of, I don't want to do this, but I have to do this. And obviously, this is someone who reads a lot. One thing I noticed about this record is how Bruce's voice sounds kind of wild. This is the most ragged I've ever heard his voice on record. Where he's either really trying to inject some kind of energy into it, or he's just fried from the road.

And you can't deny "Fear of the Dark." Was it South America that made that such a monster anthem? I know the Finns sang along to it, which was recorded for *A Real Dead One*, so a lot of people heard that. But did it really start to grow out of people singing it in South America? Just to share a little personal anecdote, I went over to South America with Gilby Clarke, and those fans, they sing guitar riffs back to you. Somehow, I almost feel like "Fear of the Dark" is a big part of the reason they're so popular over there. Because those fans sing every riff, every lyric to every Maiden song. On DVDs that came later, you see them doing this.

But that song starts up with a great melody right off the hop; it's melodically very strong, thematically strong. And maybe part of the draw is the horror film thing, the fear thing. It's something simple people can relate to, and it's also not trying to be anything other than being afraid. I don't find this one going deep into metaphor and personal things. It's just like, "Hey man, this is a cool song about being scared." [*laughs*]

The live single version of "Hallowed Be Thy Name," recorded at the Olympic Stadium in Moscow and released October 1993, would be the last to feature Bruce Dickinson until 2000.

HENDERSON: With "Fear of the Dark," it's the mood and the darkness. In your mind, you picture this really menacing Eddie coming out of this tree, and it just works. There's the slow buildup, and then you get punched in the face. It's a beautiful song. Perfect for their setlist, with what is possibly the quintessential Maiden football chant.

But the song I really gravitate to is "Afraid to Shoot Strangers" because, once again, the mood is visceral. I think it's a better song than "Fear of the Dark." Bruce is almost whispering, and it's a rollercoaster of emotions. It strikes me deep in the heart. And then you look at the lyrics, and it's Steve writing about the Gulf War. It's strong.

POPOFF: Given the times, was *Fear of the Dark* doomed before it even got off Steve's property?

STRAUSS: Well, it's hard at any time to do something that is not on the nouveau wave of what's being played. It's very rare that a band can come out with an album in a style of music that is not popular and then chart super high. It was not an easy time to put out *Fear of the Dark*, although it was huge in Europe.

KELLY: I guess it didn't do as well as *No Prayer for the Dying*. It was a gold record here in Canada but not in the States. *No Prayer for the Dying* was the start of the declining fortunes. I moved to Toronto in '91, and it seemed like here they held on a little bit. There were still bands getting signed to major labels that were hair metal or metal. But by the time of Nirvana and Soundgarden, it was pretty clear that was happening and this stuff was in trouble. *Fear of the Dark* would've sounded pretty dated. Even though there is earnestness here, it's a different type of earnestness because it's tongue-in-cheek. Bruce is talking about wiping his kickstart clean and things like that [*laughs*]. It wasn't going to fly.

HENDERSON: The end was near. Things were starting to get dire. There was a lot of competition, tastes were changing, and stuff like this started to sound dated. It was out of fashion, and it just wasn't resonating—even with heavy rock fans. There were still people like you and me that remained fans, but a lot of fans of exactly this kind of music would move on to hair metal and then grunge. And even the fact that radio didn't embrace them at their peak, well, radio wasn't going to touch this fucking thing in 1992.

POPOFF: And then Bruce would leave the band!

KELLY: It's an artist's natural inclination. Familiarity breeds contempt. There was always a power struggle between him and Harris; they were always butting heads. It probably felt good for Bruce to make *Tattooed Millionaire* and have a guy like Janick Gers, who is accomplished, talented, and kind of, "Well, what do you say, Bruce? It's your band." It must have been nice, and you don't forget that feeling, I imagine.

The X Factor

with Chris Jericho and Sean Kelly

1. Sign of the Cross........................11:16
(Harris)
2. Lord of the Flies 5:02
(Gers, Harris)
3. Man on the Edge 4:10
(Bayley, Gers)
4. Fortunes of War..........................7:25
(Harris)
5. Look for the Truth........................5:10
(Bayley, Gers, Harris)
6. The Aftermath...........................6:20
(Bayley, Gers, Harris)
7. Judgement of Heaven.....................5:10
(Harris)
8. Blood on the World's Hands 6:00
(Harris)
9. The Edge of Darkness.....................6:39
(Bayley, Gers, Harris)
10. 2 A.M. 5:37
(Bayley, Gers, Harris)
11. The Unbeliever 8:05
(Bayley, Gers)

Personnel: Blaze Bayley—vocals; Dave Murray—
    guitar; Janick Gers—guitar; Steve Harris—bass;
    Nicko McBrain—drums
Guest Performances: Michael Kenney—keyboards;
    The Xpression Choir—Gregorian chanting
Produced by Steve Harris and Nigel Green
Recorded at Barnyard Studios, Essex, England
Released October 2, 1995

As with Judas Priest's situation with Tim "Ripper" Owens, it took Iron Maiden a long time, a lot of pain, and a ton of rumors to replace its star ex–front man. Both bands went on to produce a couple of ill-received albums until it all blew up again. Further, the Stones hired a guitarist who looked like Keith's night-prowling brother, Priest got a K. K. lookalike in Richie Faulkner, and Maiden hired on a firecracker of a hometown belter who was a ringer for Bruce circa *No Prayer for the Dying*.

I also maintain that, in Blaze Bayley, Maiden hired a very cool dude from a cocksure buzz band. Wolfsbane's 1989 album, *Live Fast, Die Fast*, was produced by Rick Rubin, and the band's 1992 follow-up, *Down Fall the Good Guys*, was produced by Brendan O'Brien, and both were on Def American. Both albums are loaded with magnetism, most of which emanated from the band's light-'em-up lead singer. Between drinks, those guys were going places. They were The Wildhearts before The Wildhearts.

The point is, Blaze Bayley, at that crease in heavy metal history, was a very inspired hire. It became difficult to make it work, but suffice to say, going in, it was a cracking idea.

There were other reasons the making of what was to become *The X Factor* would be hard graft. Steve was going through a divorce, not only with Bruce but with his wife, and the results can be heard in the record's introspective and defeatist lyrics. Harris took it upon himself to produce as well, along with engineer Nigel Green, and, like the last two albums, at the not-ideal Barnyard Studios.

The record was very much Steve's show, so bass is prominent (especially in those interminable intros), as is his writing style, which leans to the lengthy. Janick writes like

Steve, Dave doesn't put up much diversity, and Blaze is adamant he is happy to respect the space of Steve and the other long-time band members, staying in his lane. Ergo, Steve writes three songs while ruminating on his own, Janick writes a lot, and Dave is not in the credits at all, nor is Nicko. Blaze is prominent, but always as part of a trio with Steve and Janick.

In terms of positives, the band was creative enough to write and record fully three extra tracks not included on the album, namely "Justice of the Peace," "Judgement Day," and "I Live My Way," all of which surfaced on singles and elsewhere. And Steve felt confident enough in what turned out to be the first three tracks of the album that they would still be in the set when Bruce returned. Opener "Sign of the Cross," the band's sixth-longest song at 11:18, turned out to be a fan favorite, while "Lord of the Flies" (based on the William Golding book) and "Man on the Edge" (based on the very recent Michael Douglas movie *Falling Down*) would be issued as singles, with Blaze particularly proud of his wordsmithing on the latter.

Add a surprisingly crap cover from the legendary Hugh Syme, man of many great sleeves and pretty well no duffers, as well as the fact that 1995 might have been the very worst year to be putting out a heavy metal record since 1979, and *The X Factor* was doomed from the start.

MARTIN POPOFF: I think with this record we have to back up a bit and set the thing up. What is happening in Maiden's world leading up to the release of *The X Factor*?

CHRIS JERICHO: When you first asked me about this project, my initial reaction was to talk about *Powerslave* and *Seventh Son*—those are my two favorite Maiden records. But then I thought, okay, no one's ever going to talk about *The X Factor*, and that is kind of a sleeper favorite of mine. I think one reason is because nobody likes it, because I'm always a little bit different from the norm, and I'm also the über, über fan. I appreciate what bands are doing even when they make records that aren't up to snuff. And I love *The X Factor* because it's very dark. It almost reminds me of *St. Anger*, where you had a band in flux that had a lot issues and put out a very dark and raw album a lot of fans don't like. I appreciate the reasons it turned out that way.

This year's Maiden: the band's latest lineup, featuring new vocalist Blaze Bayley (*center*), photographed at Steve Harris's Barnyard Studios in Essex, England.

"Man on the Edge," the first single drawn from *The X Factor*, released a few weeks ahead of the album in September 1995.

This all started for me because I was working in Japan exclusively at that point in time in '94 to '95. So when I saw the ad in *Burrn!* magazine for the new Maiden lineup and the new Maiden record, it blew my mind. There was still no internet, so you got your information from magazines. And, obviously, when Bruce left Maiden, it was very organized, he finished up the tour, did the live album, they killed him at the end.

The "Hallowed Be Thy Name" live single sleeve actually had Eddie killing Bruce on the cover, and they did a video with a magician, and he did all these tricks like Dave had his hands cut off so he couldn't play guitar, whatever it was, and, in the end, they killed Bruce. And that was symbolic.

So who are they going to get, right? There were suddenly these rumors, and I always hoped it would be Michael Kiske from Helloween, but Michael said there was no way British Maiden fans would accept a German singer. I kind of agree with that. There was a guy in America, in a Christian rock band called Barren Cross, Mike Lee, who also sounded so much like Bruce, that I thought would be great. Plus, rumor is that Andre Matos from Angra out of Brazil was a finalist.

But then they pick this guy, Blaze Bayley. I had a Wolfsbane album I got at a flea market, and it was cool that it was on American Records. When that *Burrn!* magazine came out and I saw Blaze's picture, he looked like a serial killer. The pointed sideburns, all dressed in black, and he just looked mean and hard and evil.

The X Factor, I always loved that name, and the cover was a kind of realist image of Eddie with the brain-crusher on him, whatever it was. And from the looks standpoint, it seemed they had done everything right. And then when the record came out, it was a different story.

POPOFF: Pick it up there, Sean. What was the story with the music behind the pictures and the package?
SEAN KELLY: Well, it's a dark record coming from a dark place in time for the principal. Steve is going through his divorce, and he also has a bone to pick with Bruce, who has left him high and dry. But if you look at Steve Harris, that guy's never going to quit his band. This is his life's mission. And, already, Bruce was critical of those two records—*Fear of the Dark* and *No Prayer for the Dying*. Steve Harris is not a guy who criticizes this band—he's a big booster. He will always look for the positive angle.

He won't bullshit, but he's always looking
for the positive angle, and he believes
in it.

So all these things happen and there's
probably a sense of betrayal. And it all
leads to this dark album. Martin Birch isn't
involved anymore. You've got Nigel Green,
great engineer, but a new engineer. And you
have a new MO from Steve, who wants to
make this kind of . . . it's funny . . . he also
wanted the drums to sound more ambient.
I wouldn't call this album ambient at all, but
that's what he was going for.

Also, we're in the middle of
Soundgarden and Alice in Chains and the
drudgery and the heavy and the sludgy.
So, I mean, all artists out there making
commercial music are affected by what's
contemporary, sonically—it's hard not to
be. I think that's the framework. People
criticize this record—or at least I feel like

Blaze Bayley at the mic
at Barnyard Studios,
summer 1995.

Opposite:
Steve Harris, flanked by
his bandmates, dips his
toes in the pool at his
Barnyard Studios, 1995.

it's been criticized—for being a dark record. But it seems kind of apropos for the
time, artistically and personally. And I think there are moments that aren't that dark.
I think there are some pretty hooky rockers on here.

You have to go back and place it in context because, on top of all this,
you're dealing with a time when metal is the uncoolest thing you can be doing.
You have a new singer, which is tough, but you also have the principal member of
the band, Steve Harris, going through a terrible time in his life. I think it's like
exorcising demons. I think that's maybe the genesis of the elongated kind of
composition process too. And the Celtic melodies lend themselves to that kind
of mournful quality.

But Blaze, the guy had a boot on his throat right from the beginning. I felt the
same way about "Ripper" in Priest. How do you rise above being the new guy with
these iconic singers you are replacing? On top of that, the world at large thinks your
music is outdated. It's terrible.

Bayley with his previous band, Wolfsbane, and the group's second LP, *Down Fall the Good Guys*, released in 1991.

POPOFF: So you play the record and you hear Blaze for the first time in the context of Maiden. What do you think?

JERICHO: That's the strange part. It's a classic tune now, "Sign of the Cross," but it starts very slow, and there's about two minutes of kind of snare drums and monks chanting, kind of some low-level mumbling. So it didn't really start with a bang. Look at the way *The Number of the Beast* starts, to introduce the new vocalist. The first song is "Invaders" with this crazy-high vocal part, and it's really awesome.

Not so with *The X Factor*. This was the beginning of Maiden doing these ultra-proggy slow starts and slow endings and these ten-, twelve-minute songs. But the biggest thing is, Blaze's range is so much lower than Bruce's. And I picked that up right away—he did not have that high end. He was almost straining a little bit. I remember on the last song, "The Unbeliever," where it goes "all my life." He almost goes "all my [*screams*]," like he almost doesn't make the note. And I'm thinking like, holy shit, this is on record?! If he's not making those notes on a record, what's going to happen live?

And I still had the best of intentions. When everybody gave up on it as a stinker, I took it with me on vacation. I went to Hawaii with the Japanese group I was wrestling with at the time. I was the only English-speaking guy, so while they were doing their stuff and talking, I used to listen to *The X Factor* over and over. And that's where it started to catch on to me.

"Sign of the Cross" is pretty awesome, "Lord of the Flies" is great, "Unbeliever" is great, "Blood on the World's Hands" . . . I started to get it: this is just a really dark, depressing record. If you listen to Pink Floyd *Animals*, there's nothing poppy or radio about that album. You gotta be in a certain mood, maybe even some kind of a weird, dark place. And that's where *The X Factor* lives for me. Whenever I'm feeling a little bit off or angry or a little psycho or just weird, I'll put on *The X Factor*, and I really relate to it. And that's why I like it so much.

It's also one of those things where you have to understand that Steve is still writing melodies for Bruce Dickinson—but he has a singer that's not Bruce. He's got a singer that is more in a Jim Morrison–style range. So he didn't help Blaze at all. Blaze gets caught in the middle. He was singing the songs his boss was giving him to sing, and they weren't in his range.

Listen to *Rock in Rio*, where they do "The Clansman" and they do "Sign of the Cross" live with Bruce singing them and they're brilliant because those songs are meant to be sung by Bruce Dickinson, not Blaze Bayley. Everyone gives Gary Cherone shit, but he was only singing the songs Eddie Van Halen wrote for him, and those songs weren't any good.

There's only so much you can do. Speaking as a singer, you give it your best stab. And that's the thing with Blaze—he just didn't have that range. Even when you hear "The Number of the Beast," he doesn't have anything close to that scream. Because, as you know, that's a hard-ass scream to do, and Blaze wasn't the guy for the job. But they chose him, and they didn't transpose anything or tune down anything or help him out in any way, shape, or form.

KELLY: I describe it like this: You're going from an air raid siren to a car horn. And I don't mean that disparagingly. The tone of Blaze's voice is boxy. And you're dealing with, how do you replace Bruce Dickinson?—who has not only an incredibly wide vocal range but really rich harmonics in his voice. The guy just has tones and overtones that are otherworldly.

Blaze, tons of attitude; he's closer to Di'Anno in my book, and I think he does bring some of that energy. He looked great. He comes in, a little bit punk rock, looks like one of the guys, doesn't come off as pretentious. Tough, good-looking guy. But, man, right off the hop, the first song here, "Sign of the Cross," you've got this wide, wide vocal range to cover. I do think it's a good performance, but, unfortunately, to me, it showed limitation compared to what came before.

The "Lord of the Flies" single, released February 1996 to coincide with the start of the US run of *X Factor* shows.

Steve Harris during the show at the Birch Hill Night Club, February 20, 1996.

It's tough. I think there are better songs on *The X Factor* that show off the sweet spot in his range. Most producers listening to a singer like that would find the sweet spot and then go in and talk about altering keys and stuff like that. I don't think that's how Maiden works. I think Steve Harris comes in with his part and you figure it out. In this situation, that's a negative.

POPOFF: So where does it work? What are some good all-around performances and songs on *The X Factor*?
KELLY: Definitely "Lord of the Flies." I just love the plucky guitar riff, which is one of Janick's. And I love the big melodic chorus. It sounds like something Adrian might've come up with. Weird comparison, but it goes into this Queensrÿche thing, and Maiden was obviously a big influence on Queensrÿche.

Opposite:
Blaze Bayley revs up the crowd at the Birch Hill Night Club in Old Bridge, New Jersey, February 20, 1996.

A poster advertising the band's show at Sneakers in San Antonio, Texas, March 15, 1996.

I also love "Man on the Edge," the first single, even though some of the lyrics are a little cringeworthy. Like "The car is an oven and baking is wild"—that stuck in my head—and not in a good way. It's about the Michael Douglas movie *Falling Down*. But it's cool in that you can hear the Janick Gers in it. Janick does this cool thing in his verses where it sounds kind of happy [*sings it*]. It's this kind of major scale melody that happens over the guitar riff, and then it modulates to something darker and heavier. And when that chorus comes in, the "Falling down/Falling down," it's heavy again. I like the sweet and sour of it. I also thought Blaze sounded really good on it. It reminded me of something off a Rainbow record, like the Graham Bonnet one, *Down to Earth*. Something in the guitar riff is very Blackmore-esque.

JERICHO: I think I'd even just seen *Falling Down*, where he can't even give his kids birthday presents. And that's even one of the lines, ". . . can't even give birthday presents" or whatever. It was a bit too contemporary for me; it wasn't that classic Maiden.

But I agree, I thought "Lord of the Flies" was great. I love the way Blaze sings that song. It's probably the best vocal performance on the record. He's got a really cool low vibrato he was able to use at certain times. But, like I say, I'm being totally glass-is-half-full, and I know why people hate it, but it was Iron Maiden, dammit, and to me it was a new Maiden album and I was gonna like it no matter what. I can't say the same about *Virtual XI*. I thought that one really stunk, but, *The X Factor*, I got it after a while.

Then there are, of course, more songs based on books and movies. "Sign of the Cross" is from the book *The Name of the Rose*. There's a movie with Sean Connery in it.

KELLY: "Sign of the Cross," how I interpreted it, is this idea of, why is there a God there to help me out? Why do I deserve to be sanctified? I don't deserve this. And he talks about having some kind of inner strength, but, really, he's made the choices that have led him to this fate. Once again I think that speaks to the whole idea of questioning your own inner intentions.

But that's a classic Maiden epic. What I noticed about this was the big vocal difference. Bruce has this wide vibrato, and Blaze has a vibrato that tails off at the end. And that's where the car horn comment came from. It's just this midrange-y blast of tone you can hear in this chorus. It's very clean. And I think this is a good example of how Maiden, even though they've got these two guitar players, and they often go into harmony, a lot of times it's just the power of doubling up on one riff in the same register, that sense of ensemble playing, where it's like, no, we're gonna rock this one riff and we're gonna own it. Same thing AC/DC does, where, it's like, this is the part and we're not gonna let our ego get in the way. We're gonna rock this riff.

POPOFF: What would you consider the album's chief flaw?
JERICHO: Well, there comes a part on that record where some of the songs blend together because there are so many long intros. It seems like every song has a big, long intro. "Blood on the World's Hands"—the bass isn't even in tune. It's like he was just noodling or something and they decided to keep it on the record [*laughs*]. When Maiden started moving away from Martin Birch, there was nobody there to say, "Listen guys, you need to cut these songs down. They're way too long," and it's been that way ever since. If you look at every Maiden album since *The X Factor*, that's where it started. These ideas support songs that should be three or four minutes long. I think once Bruce left, Steve took over completely and said, "This is what we're doing; this is the way I want it." And everybody said, "Okay, Steve, you got it, buddy."

POPOFF: Fair enough. Despite that, though, is there anything deep in the album that might be classed as a hidden gem?
KELLY: I'd go with "Judgement of Heaven." The bass riff reminds me of Pete Way, like a UFO-type thing. Faster, but something Pete Way would come up with. And I know he was an influence on Steve. It's this really melodic thing, but it's also a very, very dark lyric, because he's talking about how he's considering ending it. I don't know how close that was to the bone, how true it was, but he's talking about suicide. I like this British stoicism: That's a selfish way. That's for cowards; I'm not going to fuckin' do that [*laughs*].
I'm just going to fucking get over it, stiff upper lip and here we go.

Musically, it's one of these where it could've lifted more in the chorus; there could've been some production choices there that made it lift. One interesting thing, in the middle of this ripping guitar solo, suddenly all the rhythm guitars go away and there's just this one guitar and the bass doing this melodic thing. It's a weird dynamic, but, overall, I still love that tune. I'm sitting here criticizing that, but that's academic.

A ticket for Iron Maiden's show with Helloween in Villarrobledo, Spain, August 13, 1996.

The fact is, I like it when things are different. I hadn't heard that before. I enjoy listening to *Van Halen III* because all of Eddie's fucked-up choices are interesting.

JERICHO: I like "Judgement of Heaven" as well—great chorus. But that's another one that's almost comical, how Blaze's voice doesn't fit that song. Just like you want to hear . . . *And Justice for All* with the bass mixed in, I'd love to hear *The X Factor* with Bruce singing vocals. I think those songs were made for him. But there's a lot of great stuff on that record that people just didn't give a shot because of the time frame or they have a bad taste in their mouth about Blaze Bayley. But Blaze did the best job he could with what he was given. There are some great songs on there that, if you asked me for a list of my hundred favorite Maiden songs, I would list more than a few in the first half.

KELLY: Another one from the dark half, so to speak, is "The Edge of Darkness." I thought that was cool. I like what Steve Harris does. He's doing the Joseph Conrad thing, right? He's kind of like the Coles Notes for headbanger kids. It's like, once he reads the book, he kind of truncates it for you.

And there are cool shots in that typical Maiden fashion that build into these neat bass arpeggios. Nice clean guitars. This one kind of sounds like every Maiden tune. Heavy gallop, Celtic melody. I like that in this solo you can hear Janick Gers doing the really frenetic lead guitar stuff, and then it smoothly goes into Dave Murray picking up the harmony solo, which is nice.

As the X Factor tour drew to a close, Maiden released its first non-album single since 1980's "Women in Uniform." "Virus" was issued in three different formats (two CDs and a twelve-inch), each with different artwork and B-Sides.

POPOFF: Speaking of Janick, Chris, what does Janick Gers mean to you? What does he bring to the band and to *The X Factor*? He's writing two-thirds of the music.

JERICHO: First, I love Janick Gers on stage. Great showman. I think it adds to the whole spectacle of Maiden. Especially when you've got Dave and Adrian, who don't move a lot. I think they beefed up their front line by having him. But I was a fan of Janick because he played on *Tattooed Millionaire*, Bruce's solo album, and did a great job.

Adrian was my favorite member of Iron Maiden besides Steve, and when he left, I was bummed out. I always loved Adrian's songs with Bruce; they were always my favorites. But then Janick came in, and I think he was kind of the unsung hero of *The X Factor*. You're right, he stepped up with the writing, because, when you talk about Steve taking over everything, the only other guy contributing at this point was Janick.

Janick was the one guy with Steve saying, "Hey man, I've got some tunes." Since they lost Bruce and Adrian, who were basically the other songwriting team, Steve was on his own. But Janick really stepped it up on that record and produced some pretty interesting riffs. And still does to this day.

POPOFF: I guess the hard reality is that neither the album nor the resulting tour was exactly embraced by the marketplace.

KELLY: No, and it's a shame because you could just hear that Blaze was going in heart on his sleeve. Obviously, this was a huge opportunity, and there's no doubt in my mind he went in and gave it his all. Some people call the performances on this record lazy or uninspired. I certainly didn't feel that. I think Blaze, for what he had to contend with, did an amazing job.

But here they are, they're losing ground on their record deal, and they're a little desperate. When they came to Toronto, they played a smaller place, The Warehouse, I believe. They weren't playing arenas anymore, and everything was downscaled. Unfortunately, the production choices on *The X Factor* didn't help that perception. In trying to strip it back, they made it sound *stripped back* [*laughs*]. I guess that's what they wanted, but it basically sounded like maybe they didn't have a budget anymore.

I reviewed this record for my university paper, *The Mike*, at St. Michael's College, University of Toronto, and I remember feeling like people were laughing at this record. I wanted this record to be great and I was excited about it, but I also remember the pain of those years, of being a fan. It was like, holy shit, Iron Maiden is really taking a beating.

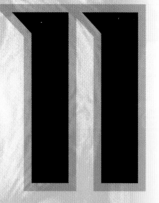

Virtual XI

with
Rich Davenport,
Jimmy Kay, and
Ahmet Zappa

1. Futureal. 3:00
(Harris, Bayley)
2. The Angel and the Gambler 9:51
(Harris)
3. Lightning Strikes Twice .4:49
(Murray, Harris)
4. The Clansman 9:06
(Harris)
5. When Two Worlds Collide 6:13
(Murray, Bayley, Harris)
6. The Educated Fool. 6:46
(Harris)
7. Don't Look to the Eyes of a Stranger 8:11
(Harris)
8. Como Estais Amigos 5:26
(Gers, Bayley)

Personnel: Blaze Bayley—vocals; Dave Murray—
    guitar; Janick Gers—guitar; Steve Harris—bass,
    keyboards; Nicko McBrain—drums
Guest Performances: Michael Kenney—keyboards
Produced by Steve Harris and Nigel Green
Recorded at Barnyard Studios, Essex, England
Released March 23, 1998

Awkward titling, an Eddie that doesn't look like Eddie, shoehorning virtual reality gaming and soccer onto the album cover . . . even before we hear *Virtual XI*, it feels like this is Iron Maiden adrift.

Recorded in March 1998, once again at home, *Virtual XI* would be the band's second and last with Blaze Bayley at the mic. They gave it a valiant go until February of the following year, when it was announced that both Bruce and Adrian would return to the fold. In between, a number of shows were scotched due to Blaze's vocal issues, even though the stated reason was an allergic reaction to pollen. Fact is, Blaze was blowing out his voice. Second fact is, none of it was Blaze's fault. As a fine future solo career and exhaustive tour schedule would attest, Blaze is a consummate front man, but when repeatedly forced to sing outside his natural range, bad things are gonna happen.

With *Virtual XI*, Steve made glancing ties to 1998 being a World Cup year—the album's publicity tour included soccer games—and slightly deeper ties to gaming and virtual reality, through racing second single "Futureal" and the (delayed, as these things often are) release of the *Ed Hunter* video game, which was pretty good stuff for the time.

Aside from the drama of Steve wanting "The Angel and the Gambler" issued as the first single and Rod wanting "Futureal" (Rod was more right, though both were wrong), it seems Steve wasn't challenged enough on the record, even taking over some of the keyboard parts usually handled by his bass tech, Michael Kenney. Most notably, Blaze continued to struggle to sing whatever Steve handed him. Even there the problem wasn't particularly with the vocals, but more so the ragged production and the lack of editing on songs that could have used it, most

Iron Maiden in full
pelt at the Roseland
Ballroom in New York City,
July 7, 1998.

cringingly "The Angel and the Gambler," where Bayley is forced to paint himself into a corner with fans by repeatedly singing, "Don't you think I'm a savior?"

"Futureal" would live on to see Bruce sing it on tour; "The Clansman" would live on even further into Maiden sets, in fact embedding itself into the hearts of Maiden fans. Based on the *Braveheart* movie, the song, according to Steve, is about defending your turf, something he had to do on stage with Blaze against occasional fan hostility, a situation reminiscent of battles Deep Purple waged on behalf of Tommy Bolin.

With "Como Estais Amigos," Blaze touches on the Falklands War, a topic much better handled by Roger Waters, but one that nonetheless seems to have scarred the British psyche. "Don't Look to the Eyes of a Stranger" admirably steps well outside the band's usual, with Steve addressing parents' fears of child abduction, while "The

Educated Fool" finds Harris questioning just how wise he's gotten with age—the idea serving as a metaphor for how capably, or incapably, he's steering the band.

MARTIN POPOFF: To start, how would you describe the contrast between *Virtual XI* and *The X Factor*? What were the subtle adjustments, if any?

RICH DAVENPORT: *Virtual XI* is a more concise album. But first of all, I'm an unapologetic Blaze apologist. I don't think the guy got a fair shake. He was always going to have his work cut out for him. There are always fans who will never accept the band without Bruce. Blaze is a strong vocalist, but he got so much abuse when he was in Maiden, and the simple reason is, he has a lower vocal range than Bruce, so he was always going to struggle live.

Sure, you can do exercises to broaden your range, but that will only take you so far. I mean, Blaze obviously nailed his audition, and I think I remember hearing that he did "The Trooper," which, when he got into the band, he really struggled with live. You can sing something once and nail the performance, especially when you're not tired and your voice isn't fatigued, because it's a muscle after all.

I saw them on the *Virtual XI* tour, and although it was a very Blaze-era-heavy set; he sang the old songs, and I remember him singing those well. But try singing out of your range night after night—that is going to cause damage. I'm not a gambling man, but I would put money on that being why Blaze had problems and why nobody, when they were auditioning him, said, "Look, this guy's got a different vocal range than Bruce, he might struggle." I don't know why nobody flagged that. It may have been a lot fairer on the guy.

JIMMY KAY: One thing Blaze said to me was that, pretty much, his only regret of that whole experience is that, in concert—and it probably applied to the studio as well—he didn't stand up for himself. He didn't stand up for the tuning, for his voice, to fit in his baritone range. Because he was kind of like the new guy. And because he didn't fight for it, it put him in an awkward situation, singing songs out of his range. If you listen to his solo material, he's singing in his range and he sounds fantastic. You can't expect a baritone to sing tenor songs. That is his one regret. He told me that many times.

In typical opera, you have tenors and baritones and basses, right? And in an opera, the tenor is usually the hero. And the baritones are usually either the bad guy or a guy who's confused or darker. He's more sinister. So Blaze brings that darker tone to the band. He's like Bruce Dickinson minus an octave. He's singing operatic, but he just can't sing as high as Bruce.

Opposite:
Janick Gers on stage at the Roseland Ballroom, New York City, July 7, 1998.

POPOFF: Rich, could you expand on what Jimmy said about tuning?

DAVENPORT: Basically, the band could have played the Bruce songs in a lower key live and that would have saved Blaze's voice. Because Blaze does some of these songs with his solo band with the guitars down-tuned, and it's more comfortably in his range. And if you hear his first album after leaving Maiden, *Silicon Messiah*, his vocals are superb. He's more what they call chest voice than Bruce. Every night on tour with Maiden—and they toured hard—he had to force his voice somewhere he would struggle to get unless maybe he worked with a vocal coach. If you want to expand your range, you have to work on these exercises.

But it's a common procedure live. David Coverdale does it. Dio did it, which you can hear on *Holy Diver Live*. Scorpions did it after Klaus's vocal nodes issue in the *Blackout* era. If they'd gone down half a step for Blaze, or a full step to drop-D . . . drop-D would've given them a slightly more contemporary edge at that point, slightly heavier. I can't see Steve Harris entertaining something like that. I may be wrong. But that would've given Blaze more of a fighting chance.

AHMET ZAPPA: It must've been really challenging to step into Bruce's shoes, although I think there are similarities in their musical approaches. Blaze doesn't have the strength of the high notes that Bruce Dickinson has, but he brings a different attitude. But Blaze is also hobbled by the production. Some Maiden records, I love the sound even if they aren't particularly high fidelity because they sound like a time capsule. But *Virtual XI* is not a great-sounding record. It's hard to hear very much vocal clarity from Blaze. I think he's overpowered by some of the guitar work, which is awesome. Still, there are a few tracks on the record where he shines vocally and seems comfortable as the singer of Maiden. But he was under a lot of scrutiny when that record came out. It was new, and I think what is interesting in hindsight is there were a couple songs from that record they played with Bruce: "Futureal" in '99 and "The Clansman," of course, being super-epic and living on well past the record. And I think Blaze had a lot to do with that epic feel, in terms of underscoring those melodies.

DAVENPORT: It's true, the production wasn't great. No disrespect to Steve, but it was what we were saying on *Dance of Death*—that if a band member is producing their own band, there's a danger they will push their own instrument to the fore. In Steve's case, it's hard for them to be objective about the bass being too loud but also about song lengths. I think that's a fault on both albums Steve produced. I understand, at that point, metal was down in general, and Maiden was under siege, and he was the main guy. And him producing it, I understand that's a way of

Opposite:
Steve Harris, Roseland Ballroom, New York City, July 7, 1998.

protecting Maiden, but there were pros and there were definitely cons. And yet, poor Blaze; a fan who comes into the Blaze era is going to hear *X Factor* and *Virtual XI*, and what they don't like about it, chances are, they're gonna blame Blaze for it.

POPOFF: Ahmet, you made reference to epic material that has lived on from this record. I suspect you are referring to "The Clansman."

ZAPPA: Yes, in fact the main thing I like about the record is "The Clansman." I love the melody, I love the guitars, obviously the vocals—it's timeless. It goes to the strong songwriting of the band, and it's got one of the band's best guitar intros ever. They played "Clansman" live until 2003 at least, and it was one of my favorite moments in their shows and a crowd favorite. Overall, I was excited there was a new Maiden album at all when this came out, and I appreciated it for what it was, but I rocked "The Clansman" like nobody's business [*laughs*]. Live, it gets such a reaction when Bruce sings "Freedom!" Who can't relate to the spirit of what they're talking about?

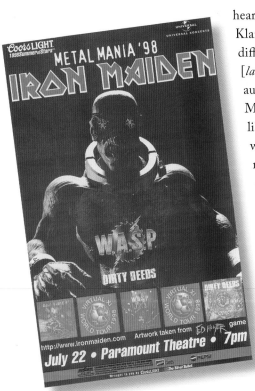

A poster advertising Maiden's scheduled performance at the Paramount Theater in Denver, Colorado, on July 22, 1998—a show that was ultimately canceled because of voice issues affecting Blaze Bayley.

There are a lot of misconceptions, because, when some people hear the word "clansman," they relate it wrongly to the Ku Klux Klan. Fair enough—reading it and reading the lyrics is a lot different than just hearing someone say the name of the song [*laughs*]. Steve, perhaps, missed the sensitivity an American audience would have to calling a song that. Anyway, a lot of Iron Maiden songs are mini-history lessons, which is a huge reason I like Iron Maiden. It's just interesting that when other bands are writing love songs, Maiden talks about moments in time—war, religion, historical politics—and in that song, the struggle to overcome oppression. All I can say is that, live, I can't wait for that "Freedom!" to hit.

KAY: Written by Harris, but you have to credit Blaze's vocal delivery. Of course, 1995, William Wallace, *Braveheart*, Rob Roy, the struggles of the Scottish clan to free themselves from English oppression. I agree, when Blaze sings "Freedom!" it just translates to every oppressed group in the world who wants freedom. And that's why it resonates around the world. If there's anything of Blaze's legacy with Iron Maiden, it's that song—even though he didn't write it, he delivered it. "The Clansman" will carry on—it's one of the best songs Maiden's ever written.

DAVENPORT: It's a Maiden epic, and, as Ahmet points out, they kept it when Bruce rejoined. For me, Maiden in this period hadn't done as well with the longer songs. "Sign of the Cross" works but some of the others on *The X Factor* don't. But this is a longer song that plays to their strengths. You've got the dynamics of the song with the quiet bass, and the "Freedom!" It's them playing to their strengths. But there's a single-note melody in the end, where I would shout, "Twin the bloody solos!" This is a bugbear for me in this era.

POPOFF: Another one that Bruce would sing with the band, and maybe even more of a marquee track at the time, was opening track and second single "Futureal." To my mind, you wanted more of this from Blaze-era Maiden, not least of all because it's Blaze singing in his range.

ZAPPA: I love that song. It all starts with the guitar playing. When it comes to guitar melodies on this record, Maiden was really original in terms of creativity; it doesn't feel like they are retreading song structures from the past catalog. "Futureal" is pretty original in terms of song construction, not rhythm or the sequence of parts, but the melody, the chord changes. They totally stick in my head. I can play that song over and over. I love that they continued to play that with Bruce and the fans went crazy.

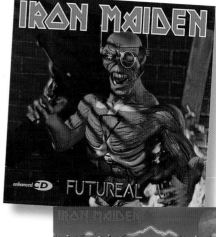

The "Futureal" single was released in two formats in July 1998: a standard seven-inch and an enhanced CD featuring video content.

DAVENPORT: "Futureal" comes blasting in with a fast pace. Again, this is a frustrating thing about this album, which I mentioned previously about the twin leads being missing. There's a single-note melody, a little riff screaming out to have a twin-guitar harmony on it and it would be classic Maiden. Blaze's solo band does it like that and it sounds like classic Maiden [*laughs*]. Why Iron Maiden themselves would miss such an integral part of their own sound is beyond me. Again, this might have something to do with self-producing, whereas a producer might say, "Hang on, you're missing that." To me, that's an example of a band getting so bogged down in self-producing they miss something crucial about their own music. Otherwise the album starts well with "Futureal." Blaze sounds great, but the production isn't great—the bass is too loud and the guitars don't have enough edge.

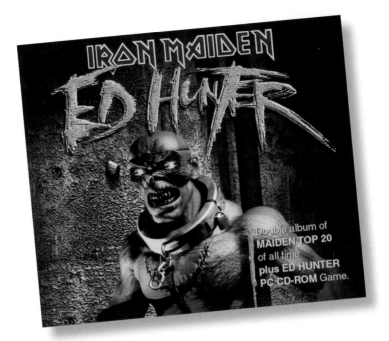

POPOFF: With "Futureal," there's the gaming tie-in, which leads to the release of the *Ed Hunter* video game.

ZAPPA: Clearly Steve and the band, and the way they utilize Eddie . . . I don't think there's another band in history that did this as adeptly. Journey in 1982 had the *Journey Escape* video game, which you could play on an Atari. But Maiden was being futuristic. "Futureal" was kind of forecasting what's happening today. Look at the album cover and that's kind of where we're at. People are placing devices on their faces and playing games with Eddie-like characters they're battling against or playing as. It is interesting that it's actually come to pass. They were looking way into the future.

KAY: I've met Blaze many times, and when I've interviewed him, I could see his gaming console in the background of the interviews. He's a gamer. Back in '98 and into the millennium, there was a fine line being crossed between reality and the virtual. There were a lot of gamers and a lot of addictions happening, a lot of suicides happening from depression. The thin line between reality and gaming, right? The real world and the gaming world. And Blaze was sort of part of that too.

That song is "The Trooper" on steroids. Incidentally, he also told me there were two leftover tracks from *Virtual XI* on *Brave New World*: "Dream of Mirrors" and "Blood Brothers." He didn't get credit for "Dream of Mirrors," and how much he wrote of "Blood Brothers," I don't know. And then there were a few song ideas that went on his first solo album.

DAVENPORT: "Futureal," that's the direction Blaze went with quite a few of the solo albums, starting with *Silicon Messiah*, where it's based on very futuristic concepts.

He writes that stuff really well. But that futuristic thing, Maiden had done it on *Somewhere in Time* to a very prominent degree. "Futureal" is an example of Blaze contributing well to the band.

POPOFF: And how the heck did soccer get mixed in with all of this?
KAY: The sixteenth FIFA World Cup was happening in 1998, and, at the same time, they wanted to release the band's computer game, *Ed Hunter*, which ultimately got delayed to July 1999. On the album cover you see the Eddie figure, you see the boy with a virtual helmet on, and, if you look closely, you can see kids playing soccer in the distance. In the booklet, the band is dressed in soccer uniforms.

POPOFF: I suppose the third biggest track from the record would have to be the debut single, "The Angel and the Gambler." They made a six-minute edit of the thing, down from ten, but I don't know . . . it *still* feels too long!
ZAPPA: Well, at least that's a good Blaze performance. But it's hard to get past that cheap Wurlitzer or Casio or whatever, fake horns keyboard sound [*laughs*]. It's so *not* Maiden. When they're going into the second verse, after the chorus, there's just that *sound* [*laughs*]. Like, what?! What was going on in the studio? You think about the records coming out at that time—Foo Fighters, Everclear, Lenny Kravitz—*Virtual XI* sounds tiny in comparison. Honestly, putting Blaze aside, I think fans were dismissing the album based on production.

"The Angel and the Gambler," released as a picture disc in March 1998, and, at 9:56, the band's longest-ever single.

And, of course, metal was in the dumps, so it's a lose/lose situation. Metallica was charting, but, again, look how huge their productions were on *Load* and *Reload*. Maiden's record wasn't nearly as heavy and as big as Metallica, and this was even with Metallica writing their mellowest two records. There's a certain raw energy there, but who knows what they were thinking? The competition was doing some pretty interesting things, but true to the band's character, I doubt they were even listening.
DAVENPORT: "The Angel and the Gambler," I think, is one of the worst songs they've ever recorded. I bought the single first, and I thought, oh man, this does not bode well. The production's muddy. The keyboard sounds cheap. It sounds

like it's done on a kid's Casio. And the verse is very close to "Lonely Heart" by UFO. It's okay, but it needs a bigger punch for a chorus. And that line, at least on the album's ten-minute version, does not stand up to that much repetition. This is where the sort of arrangement side of a producer would've helped.

KAY: Here's a cool idea. "The Angel and the Gambler" is about the addiction of gambling. And a lot of people think, okay, angel on one side, devil on the other, and we naturally think the devil is telling us, "Keep on gambling," and the angel is saying, "Stop gambling." But I think, in this situation, the angel is not really an angel. He's really the devil. He's the financier of the gambling, otherwise it would've been called "The Angel, the Devil, and the Gambler."

Also, people criticize this song for being too repetitive. The chorus is repeated twenty-two times. And if you want to compare, "Run to the Hills," the chorus is eight times. And you think, why is Harris doing this? And after really listening to the music and the lyrics and seeing the pattern of Steve Harris's writing style, he did it on purpose. Because it's hypnotizing to gamble. It's monotonous. He keeps this addicted gambler questioning, "Should I be doing this or not?" He's very calculated, Steve.

POPOFF: Not sure I buy that one, but okay, let's float it out there [*laughs*]. What are some other interesting wrinkles to the record?

KAY: "Don't Look to the Eyes of a Stranger" is a very cool one—it repeats twenty-three times [*laughs*]. But, again, I think it's calculated by Steve Harris. The song is similar to "Fear of the Dark" because it has a slow sort of spider-crawling beginning, and then it builds and builds. And then it gets really, really fast, because the person is panicking. It's sort of paranoia. That's what the song is about, paranoia. And it ties in with "Killers." I picture yet another victim of the killer from that song off the second album.

"The Educated Fool" is like part one of "Blood Brothers." Steve makes a reference to his father, "I want to meet my father beyond." It's self-reflection. Your whole life you can be book-smart and learn about stuff in the library and on the internet, but, at the end of the day, it's all about life experiences. That's more important than just being told facts or reading things.

A lot of people call this an upbeat album, but I think it's a dark album because there's a lot of natural disasters and a lot of self-reflection. "Lightning Strikes Twice" is about a guy reflecting on something really bad that happened, and he doesn't want it to happen again. "When Two Worlds Collide" is about an asteroid that's gonna hit earth. A natural occurrence, a natural disaster. The scientist is doing the calculation, reflecting on what's going to happen to humanity. It's pretty dark.

ZAPPA: "When Two Worlds Collide," there must've been a lot of fucking Stevie Nicks being played in the house, because that is the "Edge of Seventeen" riff. I didn't connect the dots when it came out, but now, that guitar in the back, I crack up every time. I also like "Lightning Strikes Twice," which probably has Blaze's strongest vocal performance. When I hear that, there's a part of me that feels sad for Blaze, because I don't know that people gave him enough credit for the passion. Due more to production choices, the vocals don't shine as much as they could've.

DAVENPORT: On "Lightning Strikes Twice," Blaze is great in the introduction and the quieter part coming in. That's him singing in his low range and he sounds great. There's a Dio influence. Blaze has said he's influenced by Dio, and like Ronnie, Blaze has the dramatic delivery you need for Maiden. With a sharper, heavier production, it would have had a bigger impact. I saw them live on the Virtual XI World Tour, and the songs had a lot more impact and punch live. There's two seconds of twin lead at the end of Janick's solo, where it overlaps into the single-note melody. But again, they missed a trick. They've missed a classic element of the Maiden sound by not having the twin guitars on there.

Blaze Bayley at Easy Schorre in Halle, Germany, September 28, 1998. The Virtual XI World Tour would prove to be his last with Maiden.

A poster advertising the 1999 Ed Hunter Tour, which saw Bruce Dickinson and Dave Murray return to the fold.

POPOFF: How about "Como Estais Amigos"?

KAY: About the 1982 Falkland Islands war. A tribute to the Argentinean people, especially the soldiers who died in the war. And it was about post-traumatic stress on both sides. Because it was mostly hand-to-hand combat, that war. And that's what made it so traumatic. Even though the numbers weren't outrageous, those who did suffer really suffered.

DAVENPORT: I believe he wrote that after going to Argentina, almost as a postwar conciliatory kind of lyric. It's an example of Blaze putting his stamp on a traditional Maiden theme because it's more of a peacemaking thing after a war. It's building bridges between the English and the Argentineans.

POPOFF: And this would be the last album for Blaze within Maiden.

KAY: Yes, and judging from my conversations with him, Blaze was really shocked when they let him go. They said he wasn't good enough. I mean, that's a pretty hard pill to swallow. He was under the impression he was still in the band and they were going to keep him and he was going to write for what became *Brave New World*. He was preparing for that.

He had no friction with anyone. He's the kind of guy who gets along with everybody. That was his dream job. He had to pinch himself that he was in Iron Maiden; that's what he kept telling me. Did he have one best friend? Probably not, but I know that he worked with Steve Harris very closely on the vocal melodies and on a friendship level.

But, yeah, *Silicon Messiah* had songs that were supposed to be on *Brave New World*. And they were writing "Blood Brothers" and "Dream of Mirrors." He didn't see it coming; he was in positive mode. He also told me things were getting a lot better, things were gelling, things were working. On *The X Factor*, people weren't really accepting Blaze, but this time around he felt more accepted by the band and by the fans. But I don't think he has any regrets. He loves the songs. Would he have done things differently? Other than what I said earlier, about maybe asking that the classic Maiden hits be tuned-down live, I don't think so.

ZAPPA: Remember, after Blaze got hired by Maiden, he had that bad motorcycle accident. I don't know if that affected his voice. After they found him, there was that long stretch before they could proceed. What I'm saying is, Blaze could have been a much different singer and person from his audition through all that happened all the way up through the first album and *Virtual XI*.

It must've been super-interesting times. But Blaze is a very strong singer, and I think the way he took Steve's lyrics and interpreted them and added to them, he definitely made a lot of these tracks his own. It's hard when everyone compares him to Bruce. That couldn't have been easy.

Dickinson feels the power at the Ahoy, Rotterdam, the Netherlands, September 10, 1999.

12 Brave New World

with Matt Heafy and Kirsten Rosenberg

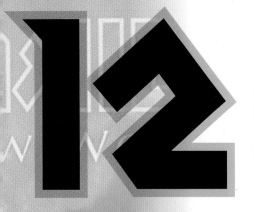

1. The Wicker Man 4:35
(Smith, Harris, Dickinson)
2. Ghost of the Navigator 6:50
(Gers, Dickinson, Harris)
3. Brave New World 6:18
(Murray, Harris, Dickinson)
4. Blood Brothers 7:14
(Harris)
5. The Mercenary 4:42
(Gers, Harris)
6. Dream of Mirrors 9:21
(Gers, Harris)
7. The Fallen Angel 4:00
(Smith, Harris)
8. The Nomad 9:06
(Murray, Harris)
9. Out of the Silent Planet 6:25
(Gers, Dickinson, Harris)
10. The Thin Line Between Love and Hate 8:26
(Murray, Harris)

Personnel: Bruce Dickinson—lead vocals;
    Dave Murray—guitar; Adrian Smith—guitar;
    Janick Gers—guitar; Steve Harris—bass,
    keyboards; Nicko McBrain—drums
Guest Performances: Jeff Bova—orchestration
Produced by Kevin Shirley; co-produced by
    Steve Harris
Recorded at Guillaume Tell Studios, Paris
Released May 29, 2000

Perhaps the lasting beauty of *Brave New World* lies not in its content, almost all of which has faded from view in the avalanche of music Maiden has written since, but in its immediacy. And one might add the idea that it's also a massive notch up on the two Blaze-era albums in the two areas that immediacy affects most: playing and production.

Brave New World is an album of numerous successful compromises. First, Steve capitulates and welcomes Bruce back to the fold, who insists on bringing Adrian. Hard decisions are avoided by not messing with the Murray/Gers team. Yes did this—the band's population explosion stressed people out, and they made a record called *Union* that was panned. With Maiden, the record wouldn't suffer (nor would it soar), but nearly twenty years later, people still seem to rationalize the symmetry of a six-man metal band.

Bruce does worse. He shunts art aside for adoring crowds, coming back to the fold because he's fed up with interviews for—gasp—fanzines, he hates playing clubs, and he's going broke. But he's also just kicked Maiden all over the playground, first with the slammin' *Accident of Birth* and then with *The Chemical Wedding*, both of which find him teamed with guitarist/producer Roy Z and with Adrian contributing moral support more than anything. There are obvious negatives in all of this, but there's also the sense that Bruce returned to Maiden knowing, somewhere in the back of his mind, that as a solo act, without Steve, he's made music that will be respected on par with anything he will ever make with Iron Maiden. In other words, Bruce returns for a victory lap.

Opposite:
A close-up view of Dickinson and Gers at Madison Square Garden, New York City, August 5, 2000.

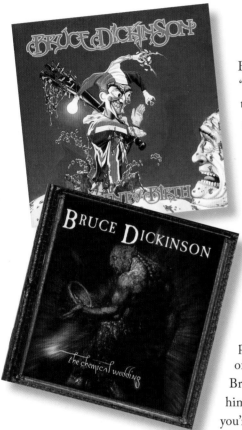

Dickinson's solo albums *Accident of Birth* and *The Chemical Wedding*, released in 1997 and 1998, respectively.

But there's something distressing there: I really do believe Bruce returned for the adulation and the money and for "winning," but deep down, he believed Roy Z was more talented than any of these guys and that he himself was capable of better musical art without them when left to make most of the creative decisions on his own.

But then what happens? Well, Bruce does things largely Steve's way, politely but firmly asking for some tweaks to the way things had been done with Blaze. Maiden gets a producer, but Steve co-produces, and his personality for the lively and spontaneous shines through despite the presence of the equally strong-willed Kevin Shirley, who comes to Maiden with an engineer mindset, not as a diva swooping down with vague ideas. Bruce wanted a producer and they (sort of) got one.

Kevin takes the band to a boom room in Paris and has them play mostly live, sifting through multiple takes and applying a lot of doctoring but having everybody grind the songs out—including Bruce. After the smoke clears, Bruce is taken aback when, preparing himself for the lonely post-playing vocal booth work, he's told, no, you're pretty much done.

A further compromise comes with the writing: the spirit of the Blaze era is maintained across the newly written material (demonstrating Steve's fondness for the mid-'90s Maiden sans Bruce), including songs and partial songs that stem from the *Virtual XI* days, with Blaze's writing on them to boot—most notably "Dream of Mirrors." Bruce is particularly worried about "The Nomad" and, more generally, Steve's current penchant for the "progressive," Bruce having just written much more directly and forcefully but now finding himself in a quagmire of ponderous songs, seven out of ten more than six minutes in length.

So, alas, there are compromises everywhere, but what comes out the other end . . . one might call, by far, the best of the Blaze records—but with Blaze replaced and the sonic picture greatly enhanced. As far as critical reception goes, it matched the sales: *Brave New World* went gold in several territories but not in the United States, and then no further anywhere. In other words, the record was uniformly liked but not loved. More welcome was Maiden's return to world stages with Bruce up front—fans clapping politely for the album and reserving judgment for what would come next.

MARTIN POPOFF: Set this up for us, Kirsten—what are the circumstances in Steve's camp and in Bruce's camp in the lead-up to *Brave New World*?

KIRSTEN ROSENBERG: Well, they're probably doing about the same on their own, in their respective corners. Bruce looks to be having modest success with his solo career. Maiden, at this point, has been playing smaller venues, at least in the US. But the total is greater than the sum of the parts. There's a synergy. Phenomenal people, phenomenal artists . . . pull them apart and it's just not the same.

So I guess they were ready to talk. Time heals all wounds. From what I understand, that initial meeting was all water under the bridge and they were really excited to work together again—and the world was so ready for it. And one of the really great things about this band is, they didn't show Janick the door. We'll have three guitar players—how metal is that?

I think what Bruce brought to the table totally sparked Steve and the rest of the gang to rise to the occasion. It was brilliance from all sides. It wasn't Bruce saving Iron Maiden—it was a coming together, that chemistry that they have. And I agree with you: I'm sure *The Chemical Wedding* was very validating for Bruce and would give him the confidence to present his material and feel like it would be well received.

POPOFF: In a general sense, what is the vibe of the record that resulted from this reunion?

MATT HEAFY: I wouldn't say the band changed their sound in any way, but, for some reason, this record feels like a modern re-approach to Iron Maiden, but in their own way. Not "modern" in the sense they were doing what anyone else was doing, because they really weren't. For me it starts with the record cover. For those who have read *Brave New World*, they imagine that world in their head and they see what's happening in this cover and it brings them into that. I think people always want to be looking ahead. If we look at music right now, everybody's doing this futuristic, spatial, dystopian thing. And Maiden was doing that in 2000, on that record.

POPOFF: How would you assess the production? What does Kevin Shirley bring to the table?

HEAFY: I think Kevin maintained the true sound of Iron Maiden through the sonics of the guitars and the drums and the bass. Those are

The first single from *Brave New World*, "The Wicker Man," released April 2000, and shown here in two formats, the standard seven-inch and a limited picture-disc edition.

the things that still sound and feel like the guys. When it hit, *Brave New World* was a larger-sounding production. I'm not calling the previous ones smaller by any means, but they were quite raw. This one was a little more polished without going into the territory of being overly produced; it still sounded like Steve Harris playing bass. It didn't suddenly sound like this different guy playing with a pick. It still felt like Iron Maiden while bringing a modern production approach, having it come out a bit clearer.

POPOFF: Let's take a little tour of the album. What are a couple highlights for you?
ROSENBERG: Well, "Brave New World," speaking as a singer in a Maiden tribute band. You've got that chorus. If you like to belt out notes, that's really fun to sing. People love to sing along to that, although I only know that from Maiden, because we've not done it live. But the album, what I love, speaking as a singer, the air raid siren has returned. Bruce is back and he's singing these beautiful high-register notes, soaring choruses, big notes, the stuff I, and so many others, love.

The album was very well received critically, and certainly among fans, although I did read a couple sort of negative reviews saying it wasn't anything new. But, for so many of us, it was new—the fact that you've got something very close to the classic lineup back. They captured what made them so great in the past. Was it completely different? Were there scream-o vocals? Hell no. They used what makes Maiden great. You couldn't say it was a big step forward, but I think it was just what needed to be done.

HEAFY: I agree with "Brave New World." I get the same feeling I've always felt with Maiden: they nail the hook; they nail the chorus; it's something you know right away. Soon as I mention "Brave New World" [*sings chorus*], you can sing it on cue. That's why they are who they are. People can instantly recall their songs, by chorus, by guitar line.

POPOFF: Matt, what's another favorite?
HEAFY: In terms of specific songs, "Blood Brothers" has become an anthem that is important as any of their old stuff. And every show I've seen them play this, I see people arm in arm singing. I just saw Iron Maiden in Tampa and Bruce was talking, right before "Blood Brothers," that they do this based on what unites us all. It's sharing the common love of this music that Iron Maiden makes, no matter what kind of lifestyle someone lives, no matter what they're into, what they like, what they dislike.

CHAPTER 12

Iron Maiden transcends it all—political affiliation, religious affiliation—and they provide an outlet from the disconnect, where people are separate. I feel like "Blood Brothers" is an absolutely amazing anthem for bringing everyone together.

POPOFF: The marquee track, first single, as is so often the case with Maiden, is the first song, a short snapper. What is your assessment of "The Wicker Man"?

ROSENBERG: I was reading how Bruce was saying that when he was writing the lyrics for "The Wicker Man," he was really trying to create that live vibe, where people are singing along, people are singing back to him. You've got all the "Whoa, whoa, whoas" in there, and I know, when we do it, I always have the crowd sing that part. The lyrics weren't literally based on the film, whereas I know Bruce, in his solo work, from the *Accident of Birth* sessions, had a non-LP song called "Wicker Man," which more closely followed the story of the film. But I guess this is sort of inspired by the film. There's a radio version of "Wicker Man" that had a different chorus, some different lines in it. Interesting, and apparently that's very rare.

HEAFY: "The Wicker Man" was one of the other most important songs on this record. It's a very energetic song, kicking in with the triple-guitar thing for the first time. I think that was really cool and important. That hook is amazing, and, it's funny, talking about Iron Maiden choruses, the title of the song isn't in the chorus. If memory serves correctly, I think he says it once in the whole song, which is pretty interesting for Bruce.

Backstage at UIC Pavilion, Chicago, October 17, 2000. *Left to right*: Harris, McBrain, Dickinson, Murray, Gers, and Smith.

POPOFF: And what do you think of its suitability as the first single?

HEAFY: I imagine if I were Iron Maiden, with the body of work on that record, you just know that's the one to open with. The way it authoritatively comes in with the guitars, very hooky. And I love the chorus on that song, with the drop to half time, the guitar texture, the non-title lyric. I feel like there aren't too many other Iron Maiden choruses like that. It feels pretty modern, although I don't think they were listening to modern bands to see what they were doing.

ROSENBERG: It's a short song, for starters, if you want to get some radio airplay. It's upbeat, up-tempo, straight-ahead rock with great, catchy sing-along choruses, offering that whole opportunity for crowd sing-along as well as the "Whoa, whoa, whoas" at the end. It's just made for a crowd, for live audiences.

POPOFF: At the other end of the spectrum, were you digging the long songs?

ROSENBERG: I admire their ability to pull it off so well. They're experts at it and it totally works. There's a progressive element for sure, but it's funny: the term "classic" or "old-school metal" is used to describe them, which is completely at odds with "progressive." But they're an anomaly anyway, with their longevity and the fact that they've done it with virtually no radio airplay and very little video. And these long songs make them an anomaly as well. But they work and the fans dig it. They're like multiple little songs combined into one.

POPOFF: You bring up the point about three guitars. Do you recall anything negative said about the six-man configuration? Were any of your friends shocked?

ROSENBERG: You know, I've never actually heard anything negative about it, quite honestly. I know from the perspective of being a tribute band, if you want to play material with the three-guitar lineup, it means an extra body and an extra guitar rig on stages that aren't very big sometimes, so there's a practical implication. But, in a way, it's bizarre how this whole three-guitar lineup seems to be so well received by the fans. Nobody said it was overkill or that it doesn't add anything to the table. And live, I love watching Janick. He's so entertaining. He dazzles me.

HEAFY: I think if anyone can do it, it's them. And it just feels right. I wouldn't want them to go any fewer. I love it—to be able to watch that many dudes, that many amazing musicians—it's great. There aren't that many bands that can have that many people on stage and have it work, but it works for them.

POPOFF: Matt, as a guitar player, what do you think Janick Gers brings to the band?

HEAFY: He's another voice, especially in the leads. That's where you really notice the difference between all three of the dudes who play in the band: their lead style. And live, he's the biggest showman, throwing his guitar around and swinging it behind his back, kind of like goofing around. In the midst of a very serious thing—Iron Maiden making metal—they're having fun, like Janick fighting Eddie and throwing his guitar at him. I've always liked stuff like that.

Regular and enhanced CD editions of the "Out of the Silent Planet" single, released October 2000.

POPOFF: And could you speak to some of the deeper tracks on the album?

HEAFY: Sure, I love "Out of the Silent Planet." Our other guitar player, Corey, that's always been one of his favorites. When I started diving headlong into Iron Maiden, he said, "You gotta check this song out." And what I love about it, it's another one of the really epic, movie-feeling pieces where you listen to it, you picture the cover, you picture what's happening in this world, and you make your own storyline as you go through it. I love that feeling.

I think that's what a lot of Iron Maiden fans, maybe, are sharing, but they don't know how to put their finger on it. When you listen to Iron Maiden, it feels like you're put into this fantasy world, and it allows you to be creative in your own head. Those are the best kinds of bands and the best kinds of songs—ones that make you want to make something. They make you imagine something or make you want to create music or art of your own.

ROSENBERG: I know "Out of the Silent Planet" is supposedly based on the 1956 science-fiction film *Forbidden Planet*, and the title is obviously from C. S. Lewis's book *Out of the Silent Planet*. But I like to think of it as more of an environmental call to action; you know, that if we don't take care of our planet, it's going to die; it's going to become silent. I know Bruce has said it's about aliens that kill their own, destroy their own planet, and now they're coming for ours, which gives it a more science-fiction feel, but I like to draw environmental parallels with that one.

I also love "Ghost of the Navigator," which we do as a band. It's moody, it feels cinematic, and the way it builds in the beginning is very dramatic. It's sort of loosely the story of Homer's *Odyssey*. I love singing it as well.

Another one of my favorites that you don't hear about very much is "The Thin Line Between Love and Hate," which is more or less about karma, says Bruce. You make the choice: there's this thin line between being good and being bad. And it's unusual in that there is a harmony on the entire verse, which is really cool, very different for Maiden, but it works for me. The chorus that sort of takes the song out, it's not really metal, it's just a beautifully sung vocal line that showcases Bruce's voice in a different way. Beautiful song.

POPOFF: What do you know about the origins of the title, *Brave New World*, **and what does that title denote to you?**

ROSENBERG: Well, of course, Aldous Huxley wrote a book called *Brave New World*, but this is not a concept album. I do know Bruce liked that the title created an enigma. It made you think, what is it? What are they talking about? And what I get out of it, the overriding theme, is a dark view of humanity, of society. It adds a dark mood to it, even though a lot of the songs certainly have up-tempo parts.

"Blood Brothers" was apparently written by Steve about the loss of his father, and then on subsequent tours they would dedicate that to Ronnie James Dio after he passed, and on other tours they dedicated it to victims of earthquakes in New Zealand and Japan. But yeah, overall, there's this dark view of humanity and what we're doing to this planet and what we do to each other.

Left:
Aldous Huxley's *Brave New World*, which gave Maiden's twelfth studio album its title, and C. S. Lewis's *Out of the Silent Planet*, which inspired the band's song of the same name.

Below:
A poster advertising the Brave New World tour's stop in Mexico City on January 9, 2001.

POPOFF: I find it interesting that, as time goes on, we tend to forget that Maiden was not instantly big again as soon as Bruce came back. It took a few years. I like this theory that one of our cast, Franc Potvin, talks about, that it was really Ozzfest 2005 that is the turning point.

HEAFY: Funny you would say that. I've never thought about it that way, but we played Ozzfest 2005 with them. Ozzfest 2005 is the notorious Ozzfest where, I don't exactly know who was the main one to blame, people got other bands to egg Iron Maiden. And we were one of the few bands vehemently against that. Like, you should never do this to a band of this legendary stature. And after the egging, every single day of Ozzfest, we would all wear Iron Maiden shirts on stage. We'd end with "The Trooper," and every day, we would have Iron Maiden flags on our stage. It was our big middle finger to everyone still on the tour that did that to Iron Maiden. So I'm glad we got to do that.

POPOFF: Very cool. But what do you think of this idea that having bands like Shadows Fall bringing soloing back and Sum 41 wearing Maiden shirts all sort of helped Maiden's second rise there?

HEAFY: I think it's a great point. I think that would more so be true in America, mainly. You're right, I guess they weren't crushing it right away. Maybe the earliest turning of the tide is when Maiden headlined Rock in Rio, to something like 250,000 people. That was the last night of the Brave New World tour, January 2001.

But you're right, maybe it was that reintroduction of Iron Maiden to the young kids who, maybe, had always been into metal or hardcore. We saw the birth of metalcore and the death of nu-metal, where nu-metal was about how little you can play your instruments and how little you were capable of playing a solo. And then, suddenly, everybody started bringing musicianship back, me and the Trivium guys included.

And people recognized, hey, this band has been around, this band does it better than everybody else, writes the best songs. Because that's how you last. That's not something you could just want and just have the drive for. You need the goods to back it up, and Maiden has always written timeless, incredible songs. You think about "Run to the Hills" and "Trooper"; these have stood the test of time. And for us, hell, we use "Run to the Hills" as our preshow music every single time. Just like how Metallica uses "The Ecstasy of Gold" and Maiden uses that UFO song "Doctor Doctor."

POPOFF: Kirsten, what do you remember about those times?

ROSENBERG: Oh my God, so not guitar rock at all. It was just a dearth, an era where "rock songs" didn't even have guitar solos. It was amazing that nu-metal did as well as it did. But I think Maiden's success speaks to how we all missed lead guitar and melody and guitar-driven rock. But it was totally not what was going on at the time, so kudos to Iron Maiden for following their hearts.

POPOFF: And they've also gained this reputation as the people's band of sorts, right?

HEAFY: Absolutely. It doesn't seem like something unattainable when you think about Iron Maiden. They put on a show like no other, but you can tell these guys are down-to-earth guys, just by the way they perform on stage, which is something you

Opposite, top:
Murray, Dickinson, and Smith during their triumphant appearance at Rock in Rio 2001.

Opposite, bottom:
The Rio fans soak up the sound of Maiden in full flow, January 19, 2001.

Below:
Not surprisingly, given how warmly the band was received, Iron Maiden's headlining set in Rio was subsequently released as a live album, simply titled *Rock in Rio.*

Smith, Dickinson,
and Gers pick up an
Ivor Novello award
for "International
Achievement" at
Grosvenor House Hotel,
London, May 24, 2001.

can't fake, you can't cheat. It is just who you are before you're in that band. That's something that just exudes from everything they do.

I have this belief that the way one does one thing is the way people sort of do everything. And if these guys are down-to-earth awesome people to their friends and family at home, they're going to be that way on stage. They're going to be that way when they interact with their fans. And, yes, we all have ups and downs and good and bad days, but I feel you can't fake that kind of thing, and people just notice.

We didn't get to meet the guys until 2006, when Iron Maiden brought us out on a six-week European headlining tour. That tour was super eye-opening for us, because we expected maybe older audiences. I remember playing in Bergen and Oslo, Norway, and there were like eight-year-olds there and six-year-olds and five-year-olds with their parents, and sixteen-year-olds there with, like, bullet belts and denim vests with patches on them. It's amazing to see that every time Iron Maiden comes back, their fans keep getting younger, while everybody else who was already there stays.

POPOFF: And, having Bruce back, it became unstoppable.

HEAFY: Again, same thing; he's such a nice, humble, normal person. Bruce was the first guy we ever met from the band. We were on a press tour for our second record, *The Crusade*, and were interviewed by Bruce for his BBC radio show, and we were really scared to meet him, very nervous, and he was just so welcoming. As soon as you sit down with him, you think, "Man, he's a normal guy like me," and, like I say, I know that's the message they always want to convey with their band, and you really feel that with Bruce.

I was talking to him about vocals, asking him about his vocal technique, how he warms up and all, and he said to me, toward the end of the conversation, "Matt, I feel like someday you'll have a voice and a vocal range like Ronnie James Dio." And my jaw hit the floor. To hear one of the greatest singers of all time, and one of my absolute heroes, telling me he feels like I'll develop a voice like another one of my heroes, I still get chills thinking about that.

But he's a hero, the master. I feel like he still, to this day, runs around more than singers a third his age. The fact that he finished the new record with a golf ball–size tumor in his mouth, and still sang some of the best stuff he'd ever sang, and immediately went on tour after recovering, sounding better than he's ever sounded, that just shows nothing can stop him, nothing can stop *them*, and it encourages people. Without Bruce and Maiden, and without Ronnie, none of these bands would exist. Metal wouldn't be what it is today.

Bruce Dickinson reaches out at Rock in Rio, January 19, 2001.

13

Dance
of Death

with
**Rich Davenport
and Franc Potvin**

1. Wildest Dreams............................3:52
(Smith, Harris)
2. Rainmaker...............................3:48
(Murray, Harris, Dickinson)
3. No More Lies............................7:21
(Harris)
4. Montségur...............................5:50
(Gers, Harris, Dickinson)
5. Dance of Death..........................8:36
(Gers, Harris)
6. Gates of Tomorrow.......................5:12
(Gers, Harris, Dickinson)
7. New Frontier............................5:04
(McBrain, Smith, Dickinson)
8. Paschendale............................8:27
(Smith, Harris)
9. Face in the Sand........................6:31
(Smith, Harris, Dickinson)
10. Age of Innocence.......................6:10
(Murray, Harris)
11. Journeyman............................7:06
(Smith, Harris, Dickinson)

Personnel: Bruce Dickinson—lead vocals;
   Dave Murray—guitar; Adrian Smith—guitar;
   Janick Gers—guitar; Steve Harris—bass;
   Nicko McBrain—drums
Produced by Kevin Shirley; co-produced by
   Steve Harris
Recorded at SARM Studios (West), London
Released September 2, 2003

If the Blaze records were writing sessions and demos for *Brave New World*, then *Dance of Death* affirms that *Brave New World*, with its extreme entrenchment of Maiden's personality, was no fluke. The follow-up and its sister record, *A Matter of Life and Death*, have become what one might consider the deep muscle tissue of the evolved Eddie of the 2000s—so much the fiber of his being that, despite what Maiden makes from here on out, the die is cast, Maiden is reflected in these records more so than all those divergent short hits of the glory years.

Which, of course, is not to say these songs are more famed than the hits, but, truth be told, it is inspiring how famed and embedded in lore some of these have become, particularly the title track as well as "Paschendale," "No More Lies," and "Montségur." Fresh ideas, soaring choruses, and unexpected proggy playing and arranging can be heard regularly, all captured by Kevin "The Caveman" Shirley and his analog-minded recording. Somehow, in conjunction with similarly minded Steve as co-producer, Shirley creates an indescribably lively, edgy sound palette using measured, medium-level distortion to arrive at a fidelity that is technically high and yet somehow exudes the spirit of a garage or club jam.

If within the Maiden catalog *Dance of Death* is overlooked, I swear it's partially due to its nondescript title and the fact that the follow-up also uses the word "death" (with *A Matter of Life and Death* being even more nondescript in its titling). As well, the cover art is washed out, dull of applied type, in its totality quite dodgy, with the story being that the typically awesome David

Opposite:
A 2003 promotional portrait of Iron Maiden.
Left to right: Adrian Smith, Nicko McBrain, Janick Gers, Bruce Dickinson, Steve Harris, and Dave Murray.

Patchett (Cathedral!) was horrified that the band went with an unfinished version of what he had been trying to produce, to the point Patchett wanted his name removed from the credits.

A picture is worth a thousand words, and with metal considerably derided during the mid-'00s, and Maiden not quite renovated to the extent the brand would be two short years hence, the message was that the enclosed goods would be equally compromised due to budgetary constraints—a view reinforced by the fact the band was trying to balance the pomp of writing with the immediacy of live-recording techniques.

But the music was both traditional and substantial and then studded with mini-events, including first use by Nicko of double bass on "Face in the Sand," and a first writing credit for the drummer on "New Frontier," where McBrain's Christianity is put to practice on a lyric concerning science meddling too intrusively upon the magic

A poster advertising Maiden's appearance at the 2003 Download Festival, sharing top billing with nu-metal act Limp Bizkit.

of human life—indeed many of the album's lyrics revolve around death, and hence there's some semblance of credence to the album's tired title.

There's also Maiden's first and only fully acoustic track in "Journeyman," on which the band slides easily into Celtic music, belying the fact so many of its songs could be rendered this way. An extreme example on this album is the title track, on which it's hard not to picture leprechauns dancing, nervously out of place down on the bayou, crocs and cottonmouths their hungry audience. Try as you might to inject gravitas (as Bruce might on stage, through costuming and his unparalleled knack for thespian delivery), there are parts of this song, however brief, that find even the most ardent Maiden fans chuckling into their green beer in disbelief.

CD and DVD editions of the "Wildest Dreams" single, released September 2003.

MARTIN POPOFF: Second record with Bruce back. How did the guys do?
RICH DAVENPORT: *Dance of Death* was, for me, the album where they had to really prove they could sustain the reunion. I love *Brave New World*, but I've listened to *Dance of Death* more, because it's slightly more aggressive and they sound more fired up. Parts of the album remind me of *Piece of Mind*, which is my favorite alongside *Killers*; to my ears it references that era, and that's a happy thing.

FRANC POTVIN: It was a consolidation of the six-man lineup. *Brave New World* had some Blaze leftovers on it, and I think that record consolidated the style they started with "Afraid to Shoot Strangers" on *Fear of the Dark* and developed during the Blaze years—the long intros and outros and more mid-paced songs. *Dance of Death* continued this. I call it the "Blaze-sounding Bruce era." Who knew what was going to happen with *Brave New World?* And because there are three or four Blaze leftovers on that, *Dance of Death* becomes, for me, the true first album of the new era, once they realized that, hey, this is actually working. It was maybe like *Piece of Mind* once the Bruce Dickinson lineup turned out to work okay.

POPOFF: Did they put their best foot forward with "Wildest Dreams" as the first single?
DAVENPORT: No! The second single, "Rainmaker," I love; "Wildest Dreams," not so much. In fact, I saw Maiden in May 2003, before this album came out, on the Give Me Ed . . . 'Til I'm Dead tour. It was all pretty much greatest hits, but they

premiered "Wildest Dreams," and it actually made me a bit worried for the new album because it didn't click for me. I thought, I wonder if they're going to sustain this on the new album.

POTVIN: I agree. I don't know if "Wildest Dreams" was a good choice for first single, to be honest. I'm not even sure it's a good first track, although it's efficient. It's a Smith/Harris song, which has become a more frequently seen thing in the songwriting department since *Brave New World* and continuing on all the new albums, producing both shorter-type songs and also epics.

"Rainmaker" would have been maybe a better choice. They probably went for "Wildest Dreams" because it's driving. If you look at Maiden, the first single is not always representative of the album. Look at "Holy Smoke," "Can I Play with Madness," "Flight of Icarus." "Be Quick or Be Dead" was definitely not like the rest of *Fear of the Dark*. "Man on the Edge" wasn't like the rest of *The X Factor*. They never really pick a song that is that representative. "Wasted Years," same thing. It doesn't sound like ninety percent of *Somewhere in Time*.

Murray, Harris, and Gers at the Tweeter Center, Chicago, August 10, 2003, midway through the US leg of the Give Me Ed . . . 'Til I'm Dead tour.

Performing "Wildest Dreams" on *Top of the Pops*, September 3, 2003. Two decades earlier, the band had caused a stir by refusing to mime to "Running Free" on the long-running BBC TV show.

Opposite:
Dickinson looms high above McBrain at the Palacio Vistalegre in Madrid, Spain, November 2, 2003.

POPOFF: Rich, what did you like about "Rainmaker"?

DAVENPORT: To me, it's classic Maiden with a commercial edge. In terms of the melody, you get the commercial element from the melody and the chords, rather than from diluting anything. It's aggressive but very melodic. The contrast between those two songs sums up what I like and what I don't like as much about Maiden. I prefer when they're playing in a minor key, as they do here. Most of the classics for me—"Hallowed Be Thy Name" and "The Trooper," to name two—those are minor-key songs, and, when they do that, it sounds darker, moodier.

And with "Rainmaker," in particular, they remembered the twin leads on this album, which they'd lost a lot of in the Blaze era. In fact, they started to downplay those on *Fear of the Dark*. There are some there, but the big songs like "Afraid to Shoot Strangers" and "Fear of the Dark" have the single-note melodies, and, to me, as a fan of classic Maiden, those are crying out for harmony. Poor old Blaze on *Virtual XI* really suffers from not having those. So "Rainmaker" has got them, and it sounds great. There are some single-note melodies at first, and there's a hook line, but after the solo, they remember the twin leads, and they really use the three guitars on that. They're a band that really uses a three-guitar lineup efficiently. So, to me, that song's much more classic Maiden.

The DVD and limited-edition colored vinyl editions of the "Rainmaker" single, released November 2003, featuring artwork taken from the accompanying promo video.

And when they write in a major key, like on "Wildest Dreams," it's really got to be exceptional in terms of the melody for it to work. Now, "Run to the Hills" is like that, "Number of the Beast" is like that, they're both major key, and so is "Murders in the Rue Morgue." Those are more aggressive songs, and the melodies are more exceptional. "Wildest Dreams," the chorus has a nice twist, but it brings chords into the major scale that are from, like, the blues scale, and that gives you less scope to sing over melodically. I think they limit themselves. There are three songs on this album like that—"Wildest Dreams," "Gates of Tomorrow," and "New Frontier"—and, for me, they don't work as well as the earlier songs. That's a bugbear for me with Maiden—I prefer the minor-key stuff.

POTVIN: "Rainmaker" has everything people love about Maiden, including the melodic, emotional guitar lines, and it's got a classic Dave Murray solo in it; Dave is very prevalent in that song. The guy's been in the band since the beginning, so it's cool to see him highlighted a bit. Against the metal that was commercial at the time, this was straight-up '80s redone, but for the new millennium, with Adrian playing in drop-D on this one, something he does from time to time on the new material and on some of the classics live like "Wrathchild," "Fear of the Dark," and "Number of the Beast."

POPOFF: Not a single, but the cream always seems to rise to the top— would you say the song most beloved by fans from *Dance of Death* is "No More Lies"?

DAVENPORT: Sure, that's quite possible. I love "No More Lies." The buildup on the arrangement is great. It's very atmospheric, which is a Maiden trademark. But it builds up and then a chord change arrives in the verse and then the chorus just slams in and it sounds huge.

The structure and the arrangement are excellent. This is where they apply the progressive rock influence in terms of arrangement and song structure. Because, after the first chorus, the whole band plays like an up-tempo, full-blast version of the same chords from the first mellow section. And then later again, one of the guitar figures reprises the intro, and then there's a variation on it.

And then the way they trade solos among the three of them, I can pretty much tell who's who. It's the way southern rockers used to do it; like on "That Smell" by Lynyrd Skynyrd—you can tell which is Steve Gaines versus Allen Collins and Gary Rossington. I'll tell you who else does it: on "Roller" by April Wine, if you see the video for that, they trade solos, the three guitar players along the front. And "She's a Roller," that's a song by Urchin, Adrian's band before Maiden—how's that for a tenuous link? [*laughs*]

I think it was Kerry King who said that the three-guitar thing—because they toured with Maiden on the Metal 2000 tour—oh, it's like Spinal Tap with the three guitar players. But I disagree. I think they make really intelligent use of it. And as the band has said themselves, there's a lot of extra guitar parts as overdubs. So I think it works really well. And that song has a lot of good structure, a lot of variety, and the melodies are strong. I'm not sure what the lyrics are about. Apparently the Last Supper, but it sounds very heartfelt, the sentiment. Overall, that's a strong song, an example of them doing what they do best.

POTVIN: "No More Lies" is a great song, with a chorus that is very different for Maiden. It's essentially a Blaze-era style of song, sung by Bruce Dickinson. The part at 4:38 sounds almost identical to "The Educated Fool" on *Virtual XI*, and the chorus really stands out. The intro is beautiful, the outro ends just the same way, just like they start doing with *The X Factor* or the song "Dance of Death." I would've reworked the middle part. They're kind of playing the same note, like they did in the Blaze era, as opposed to layering the harmonies. But they went for that with the new era. They would play, sometimes, the same line. "Fear of the Dark" was the same way. They don't do harmonies, just single notes in unison, and it does give it a different vibe.

POPOFF: Let's change tack for a bit. What do you think of the record's sonics?

DAVENPORT: I'd say Kevin Shirley serves the songs well. When you read fan comments, Kevin tends to polarize people quite a lot. But I think he captures the energy well. I'd be interested to see what his role as a producer is. The producer's role is not just engineering the sound, it's in saying that section is too long, cut that, rearrange that. I wonder how much input he's allowed, given it's very much Steve's baby.

The *No More Lies* EP, which came packaged with a Maiden sweatband, released March 2004, shortly after the conclusion of the Dance of Death World Tour.

A wide view of the band's
set at the Graspop Metal
Meeting in Dessel,
Belgium, June 26, 2005.

Opposite:
Eddie stalks the stage
at the Graspop Metal
Meeting, which Maiden
headlined as part of its
Eddie Rips Up World Tour.

That's not a criticism of Steve. He seems very protective. And I think that on the albums he produced—*X Factor*, *Virtual XI*—I can understand Maiden was besieged at that point, and you would circle the wagons, bring it in house, and be very protective. But it's difficult for any member of a band—not just Steve, anyone—to be objective about their own work. That's where a producer can come in and say, hang on a minute, maybe that's going on a bit long, cut that section, rearrange that section.

But the albums since Kevin Shirley started producing are better produced in the song management sense than the two Steve did. And I'm one of the rare fans that likes the Blaze albums. But I think he's captured an aggressive sound as well, particularly in terms of the balance between the bass and the three guitars. That's not easy to capture cleanly so you can hear everything.

POTVIN: As a point of trivia, there's a buzzing sound on the finished product that, I think, doesn't sound that great. Basically, what happened is, Kevin Shirley gave a compressed version of the mix to Steve Harris, and Steve listened to it in a car and it was, like, badly compressed. I don't know what kind of dB range it's at, for the bits per second, but apparently Harris liked it. And it had that scratchy sound. The guitars are peaking, and it scratches a little bit.

And Steve liked the fact that it sounded off a little bit, and he said to Kevin Shirley, "This is the version I want to master." And Kevin was like, really? I have the DVD audio version of *Dance of Death*. Remember when DVD audios were a thing for like a year? I have that version in 5.0, and it's not the same master. It's the one that doesn't buzz. Just like Metallica's *Death Magnetic*; apparently there's one version that sounds better, less compressed, the *Garage Band* version. The version I have sounds mint, and it sounds amazing. So that's a little-known fact—it's the unfinished product he wanted.

POPOFF: Back to the songs, "Paschendale" is an odd one, very ambitious. I suppose I've always linked it with "Montségur" for some reason.

DAVENPORT: Again, classic Iron Maiden, "Paschendale." Great progressive structure and arrangement. Huge chorus. There's a section after one of the choruses where there's a breakdown with keys and there's guitar melody. There's almost a walking bass line. That reminds me, Maiden isn't shy about their Wishbone Ash influence. Steve is a very inventive bass player, and his way of playing is a more aggressive way of doing what Wishbone Ash would do, where you would have the harmony guitars with Andy Powell and Ted Turner or Laurie Wisefield, and then you'd have Martin Turner playing something different underneath. Maiden has their own spin on that, and this is a good example of it.

And you've got another huge riff that comes in, where the lyrics are singing about "The human heart is hungry still," that's very anthemic. Then there's an interesting rhythm change with the solos, a different vocal part, another solo, a heavier version of the intro, and then the keyboards on the last chorus sound almost orchestral. It's a longer song, but they're doing the longer songs more efficiently than on *X Factor*. So they've got their mojo back here, where the longer songs are still interesting and they still pack a punch.

POTVIN: "Paschendale" is about World War I. It takes place on a battlefield in Belgium. Canadians can all relate to it, because Canadian forces had a lot to do with that battle.

And this is the beginning of Adrian Smith writing epic songs. It's his first epic song in Iron Maiden. If you look at *A Matter of Life and Death* and *The Final Frontier*, he's written songs you would not expect he'd have a hand in, the longer, more melodic, less concise and poppy songs, versus, say, "The Wicker Man," which is an Adrian Smith song.

It's got the orchestration in the middle, the riff sounds a bit different, it's got a bit of an *X Factor* style—it's everything you want in Maiden. It's got drama, a little quiet part, the guitars are way up in the mix, and they're heavier than what Maiden has done guitar-wise since probably the mid-'80s. In general, the guitars are heavy in the mix on this album.

Also, this is probably the second album where Steve Harris is playing with his new sound, his new bass tone, which is not sounding like a guitar but playing more bass that sounds like a bass. He went back to his real bass tone for *A Matter of Life and Death*, with more high-pitched runs and a clearer, snappier, clicky '80s sound. But for *Dance of Death* and *Brave New World*, Steve toned down the bass and let the

Dickinson leaps into the air at the Tweeter Center in Mansfield, Massachusetts, July 15, 2005—the first night of the band's incident-packed run of Ozzfest performances that summer.

ACACIA AVENUE E.11

three guitars take a front seat. Fans of Iron Maiden all know how much the bass is its own thing in Iron Maiden, so I have mixed feelings about the bass being deeper and further away into the mix and sort of playing more bass-like lines. But, hey, you gotta give him a break. He's on stage two hours headbanging, so maybe he's okay not running up the neck all the time, you know?

POPOFF: Good point [*laughs*]. And what about "Montségur"?

POTVIN: Again you've got your historical lyrics, about Catholicism, where, generally, not being followers of the church, it appeals to metal fans. It's a song about France, and obviously they have a lot of fans there. Bruce Dickinson speaks French to the audience in Quebec and in France, so people can relate on that level as well.

I think it's one of the first songs that really showcases the three guitars fully. You've got this fast, sort of "The Duellists"/"Powerslave"-style attack in the middle. And whether it's two or three guitar layers, you've got the rhythm guitar in the back, but the bass still taking a backseat. So this is when Maiden sounded a little heavier, really utilizing the three guitars and really sounding like there were more than a couple guitars on the album. I think it's just a great track.

DAVENPORT: Another one with a heavy swing rhythm. And they do that very, very well, looking at "Where Eagles Dare," "Losfer Words," "Quest for Fire," that kind of stuff. Strong hook lines, and there's a really good change. The beginning of the song is minor key, and they switch to a major-key version of it after the chorus. That's an example of them using a major key effectively and to their strengths, unlike "Wildest Dreams."

The men of Maiden and manager Rod Smallwood (*third right*) get their hands dirty at the Rock Walk in Hollywood, California, August 19, 2005.

There are twin leads under the chorus, on one of the later choruses, harmony guitars, which is an intelligent use of the three guitars again. Because you've got one guitar playing the chords and the others are playing a high-octave harmony and it adds, like, a countermelody under Bruce's vocal melody that works really, really well. And there are some nice sort of rhythm shifts toward the end.

Lyrically, it's about atrocities perpetrated in the name of religion. It's a good potted history on something I knew little about, but it made me go learn about it. They're an interesting band, because they talk about spiritual things from different angles. There's something critical like this, and then you've got tracks where Steve Harris seems to be sort of soul searching—like on "Sign of the Cross," he seems to be contemplating spiritual matters. And then you've got stuff like "Holy Smoke." They're capable of giving spiritual matters a fair analysis, and they're also capable of being critical. Which is a bit of a rare dichotomy in metal, because it tends to be either "Praise, hail, Satan" or "To hell with the devil." [*laughs*] And that's something interesting about Maiden—they're able to talk to both sides of the equation.

POPOFF: We'd be remiss if we didn't talk about the title track. It's a bit standard, but they've really gone and sold it to us live, and I guess by now we've bought it!
DAVENPORT: Yes, I remember that one live [*laughs*]. I saw them on that tour. The quiet middle section does have a hint of "Stonehenge" by Spinal Tap about it, when it breaks down and gets quiet, and you think, "Oh, how they danced, the little . . ." [*laughs*]. "Stonehenge!" It loses that when it gets heavy and fast, so you get the same melody and it doesn't sound like Spinal Tap. Bruce was doing this whirling dervish dance, spinning around in the middle of the stage, in addition to having belted out the song. And he had this cowl on to represent the shrouded figures in the song. It's like, whoa, this guy's energy level . . . he's leaping about and it's pretty incredible.
POTVIN: If there's one song I keep going back to, if I'm just picking singles for my listening pleasure, it's "Dance of Death." And I agree, live it just exemplifies who they are. Like Kevin Shirley says in the *Flight 666* movie, "This is our style. We write ten-minute-long songs, there's a slow part at the beginning, a slow part at the end, it goes on forever, and we don't give a shit—this is what we do."

"Dance of Death" is Celtic; there's storytelling. It's a side of the band that really started in the Blaze years with songs like "Fortunes of War," "The Edge of Darkness," "The Educated Fool," and "The Clansman." It keeps that tradition and takes it to a more folksy and even less accessible sound. It's the kind of song that

people who don't get the new Maiden, they'll never get those kinds of songs. If you're looking for "2 Minutes to Midnight" or "The Trooper," it's not for them. That's where a lot of older or North American fans kind of lose understanding of the new Maiden, with a song like that. But that's the go-to song for fans like me of the new Maiden era. It's probably the most representative of what Maiden's been doing since 2000.

But you think, why is he talking about the Everglades? What is this guy doing in Florida? You know, is it "Fear of the Dark, The Alligator Version"? It's got that monsters-under-my-bed vibe, like a scary song, but for children. I know it's out in the woods and everything, but with the cult theme, it sort of matches the imagery of the album cover, with the sort of Masonic black-and-white flooring, just like the *Piece of Mind* tour where they had the same flooring that year. Also with that weird kind of computer-made imagery, it's got a sort of Stanley Kubrick *Eyes Wide Shut*–type sexual innuendo. If you look at the booklet, all the guys have ghosts around them and there are people in masks and it's got a bit of a sexual thing to it, which is rare for Maiden.

POPOFF: It all worked out for them, didn't it? After *Dance of Death*, Maiden really took off again.

POTVIN: I would agree with that timeline. The summer of 2003, when they played the Give Me Ed . . . 'Til I'm Dead tour, which is that best-of tour, using the *Brave New World* clothing and adding "Wildest Dreams" as a preview for *Dance of Death*, I think that's when Maiden came back. And I think when bands like Sum 41, and, to a certain extent, Avenged Sevenfold a couple years later and Shadows Fall, started to add guitar solos, that helped.

If you want to pick a later date, Ozzfest 2005, I think, was when Maiden was officially back. They showed all these Ozzfest kids, opening for Sabbath, what they were made of and what "really good" metal was about. But I think 2003 was the beginning of that, and I think bands like Sum 41 gave props to Maiden a lot, wore their T-shirts, mentioned them.

POPOFF: Come to think of it, I remember being backstage in what they called Rod's Room, and Deryck Whibley from Sum 41 was there.

POTVIN: There you go, and I think a lot of their kids, the kids that followed those bands, kind of checked out the T-shirts and realized Maiden's influence on the bands they were listening to. So I really think 2003, especially in North America, is when they got big again, and *Dance of Death* was the album that happened to be there for that trend.

CHAPTER 13

DAVENPORT: Agreed. I saw them on the tour twice at that time, and they were excellent. I was really struck both times, because, by this stage, Bruce would've been, what, mid-forties? And for me, he actually sings better now, more consistently live, on these later albums than he did on *Live After Death*. And the energy level, the power, not just with Bruce, but the whole band, is incredible. And these are long sets.

I remember Bruce did a bit of audience participation where he sang a long note and sort of challenged the audience to do the same. And the lung power on this guy, you know? He held these long, sustained notes, and it was like, man, this guy had obviously kept his chops up when he was out of Maiden. I think whatever differences they had, he and Steve Harris have a similar work ethic, and Bruce had obviously kept up his game with that raft of solo albums.

And the new material sounded great live; they delivered it very, very powerfully. They were keen to say Bruce was back for the long term with *Brave New World*, and I thought they were as good as ever. I got into Maiden when I was nine or ten, so this is like '82, and I've stuck with them all the way through. And I prefer some of the reunion-era albums to some of the '80s ones. *Dance of Death* is one of them. I had that initial bit of fear at Download Festival when they played "Wildest Dreams," but having heard the album and having seen them live, I thought, yeah, they're back right at the top. These guys, they've pulled it off and it's a long-term thing. I'm proud of my boys [*laughs*].

Bruce gives the crowd the thumbs-up during the band's Ozzfest show in Devore, California, August 20, 2005.

IX

A Matter of Life and Death

with
**Franc Potvin and
Ahmet Zappa**

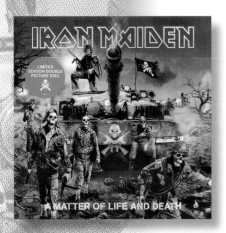

1. Different World 4:17
(Smith, Harris)
2. These Colours Don't Run. 6:52
(Smith, Harris, Dickinson)
3. Brighter Than a Thousand Suns 8:44
(Smith, Harris, Dickinson)
4. The Pilgrim 5:07
(Gers, Harris)
5. The Longest Day 7:48
(Smith, Harris, Dickinson)
6. Out of the Shadows. 5:36
(Dickinson, Harris)
7. The Reincarnation of Benjamin Breeg 7:21
(Murray, Harris)
8. For the Greater Good of God 9:24
(Harris)
9. Lord of Light 7:23
(Smith, Harris, Dickinson)
10. The Legacy 9:20
(Gers, Harris)

Personnel: Bruce Dickinson—lead vocals;
    Dave Murray—lead and rhythm guitars;
    Adrian Smith—lead and rhythm guitars;
    Janick Gers—lead and rhythm guitars;
    Steve Harris—bass, keyboards;
    Nicko McBrain—drums
Produced by Kevin Shirley; co-produced by
    Steve Harris
Recorded at SARM Studios (West), London
Released August 28, 2006

Following the momentous Eddie Rips Up the World tour, Maiden was now back on top, established as a vigorous and vital next-generation classic rock band, a standing that Steve surely welcomed, given his encyclopedic knowledge of and love for '70s rock.

With writing sessions in fall 2005 and recording taking place at SARM Studios (West) in London, the band underwent a long period of preparation and then, as they avow, recording and using mostly first takes. First takes or not, the end result is a record brimming with excitement, aided by the fact that Steve chose not to master it.

Which is a subtlety in the end, because, really, Maiden in this era is defined by the liveliness of performance and Kevin and Steve producing in tandem, the result being this chimera-like flip back and forth in the mind between hearing the polish of high fidelity and hearing the magic of a three-beer basement sound. Really, it's both at the same time, which is sheer genius, because (a) it distinguishes Maiden from what Andy Sneap calls "desktop metal" and (b) it's really good.

As for the songs, Maiden embraced the modern by digitally disseminating three selections in advance of the album's release date. First was the official single, "The Reincarnation of Benjamin Breeg," which offers a wallop of a smart, nonintuitive Maiden riff set against majestic chords. Amusingly, Maiden cooked up a temporary website explaining who this entirely fictional character was, concocting an exciting and mysterious life that fans could further imagine and infer was somehow tied to the equally mysterious biography of Eddie himself.

Opposite:
Bruce Dickinson
during a contemplative
moment in Quebec City,
October 9, 2006.

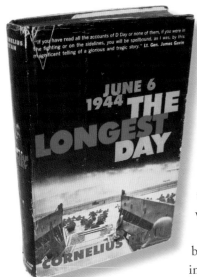

The Longest Day by Cornelius Ryan, which lent its title to a track on *A Matter of Life and Death.*

"Different World," which did a little better at radio (granted, it's the record's shortest track, at 4:17) wasn't quite as impressive, evoking the slacker rock of "The Wicker Man" and "Wildest Dreams." Bruce has called this song a tribute to Thin Lizzy, and indeed the twin leads do tend to that mournful direction, as does the straightforward verse chording, which recalls that band's "Get Out of Here."

Finally, "Brighter Than a Thousand Suns" balanced the hefty bottom-end grind of "Breeg" with the band's prog tendencies, which in the end have always been less prog and rather more "Hallowed Be Thy Name," if you get my drift—more theatrical and epic—a constant tug up the mountain of emotion, producing both exhilaration and exhaustion. That can also describe the band's gutsy decision to play the entire damn album once Maiden hit the road, the boys defending the idea by stating that fans are fans because the band has remained vital; Nicko adding a bit of hyperbole, calling *A Matter of Life and Death* the best album he's made with the band.

But, make no mistake, the album is a barnstormer and was well received by fans and critics. "These Colours Don't Run" joined "The Clansman" and "Blood Brothers" as new-era Maiden world anthems, and "The Pilgrim" (in the running as a possible album title along with *The Legacy*) is a high-energy workout, save for the incongruous Celtic paste-on.

And with that, Maiden was prepared to go to war once again with its most war-like album ever, fighting the establishment on stages the world over, fighting for old-school metal and the tradition of live musicianship and showmanship. In the "different world" of 2006, another war was on—that between downloads (free and paid, the large-scale shift to streaming yet to happen) and physical sales. But Maiden managed to affirm and mirror its pan-world touring business model by quickly amassing a million in physical sales through little piles moved across a couple dozen countries, with India even sending the record to No. 4, that far-flung territory responding with a hearty guns up to the latest salvo from heavy metal's most celebrated globe-trekking ambassadors.

MARTIN POPOFF: Let's start by setting the scene with respect to Maiden's place in the metal world at this point. Records aren't selling and nobody expects them to, but in terms of live profile, Maiden is experiencing a remarkable renaissance.
FRANC POTVIN: Yes, with *A Matter of Life and Death*, we're talking about an album cycle that finds Maiden back at the top. They've got a younger audience back. Keep

in mind, metal had a big resurgence in North America—I really believe—with Ozzfest 2005. I'm talking about guitar solos and not just guttural vocals all the time. Maiden opening for Sabbath, minus the egging incident in San Bernardino, I think went really well for them in gaining fans and people thinking, "Oh man, these guys are actually really good." I mean, they're still youthful, even now, but twelve years ago, nobody thought these guys were nearing their fifties at the time and kicking a lot of young bands' asses, just like they do now.

But *A Matter of Life and Death* features more dissonant textures for some of the guitar tones. I think they really took the long songs concept and sort of threw away most of the stock three-, four-minute songs, except maybe the first song, and maybe there's like a ballad-y song in the middle. It's Maiden at the top of their game commercially, at least in concert, and I think inspiration-wise. Even Adrian is writing more epic songs.

But with, say, the war-related "The Longest Day," there are some new tones, kind of like a modern Tool quality in terms of a dissonance. Also, it definitely has

Murray, Smith, and Harris at the Colisée Pepsi, Quebec City, Canada, October 9, 2006.

a little bit of a Bruce Dickinson solo quality, meaning *Chemical Wedding*–style or *Tyranny of Souls*–style Bruce. Not *Tattooed Millionaire* or *Balls to Picasso*. And Steve Harris goes back to more of his traditional signature bass style and tone. I think Bruce's vocal performance is better on *A Matter of Life and Death* because I believe he may have recorded *Dance of Death* with a cold. His voice sounds a little strained on *Dance of Death*.

POPOFF: One narrative about the record is that it is unmastered. What does that do for the sonics of *A Matter of Life and Death*?
AHMET ZAPPA: Well, I think it's a bold choice, first of all. I'm listening to a remastered version, which I think is interesting, since, yes, they didn't master it to begin with. It feels like a live performance to me. You can really hear them playing—all the good and the bad. You can hear their fingers across the strings. It's a cool record because they're trying to capture what they sound like live, because, after all, most of those live Maiden records are so much bigger-sounding than most of the studio records.

POPOFF: What more can you tell me about what it means not to master this thing?
ZAPPA: Well, it's what they laid down on tape. You can do certain things when you master it. You can change the compression, you can bring certain aspects of it up. They were probably really stoked on leaving it the way it sounded in the room, leaving it raw. "We're going to get it where we want it, and we don't want anybody messing with it." Because, at that point, if you send it to someone who masters the record, they put their own kind of sweetener on it, and that goes for song to song as well, so you get variations. In this case, fortunately, they got a good-sounding record. I went back and A/B'd the productions of the last five, all the Kevin Shirleys, and this is a hard-hitting, good-sounding Maiden record.
POTVIN: From what I gather, everybody kinda sat down and said, "This is the best album we've ever done." A lot of bands do that, but I think they were really, really convinced this was the case with this one. And they just thought—like Steve being quirky and saying, hey, let's use a noisy copy as the final product with *Dance of Death*—you know what, let's not master it. And I mean, the ride cymbal sounds like it's literally right next to you. If you listen to the ride on the first song, it sounds like it's right there. There's no compression. I love it. I wish more albums weren't mastered, to be honest.

The album's first single, "The Reincarnation of Benjamin Breeg," released August 2006.

Opposite:
Janick Gers hits the high notes, Quebec City, October 9, 2006.

POPOFF: **What did you think of the record's first single, "The Reincarnation of Benjamin Breeg"? Strange title, but it sure got people talking, right?**

POTVIN: Yes, an odd single all around, because Maiden always went with the shorter songs, like "The Wicker Man." First one off *Dance of Death*, "Wildest Dreams." This one's got the slow intro and outro, and so it's like they released a non-single, in a way. And it doesn't really have a chorus. It's got the great Dave Murray melody we all love, and it's got the introspective lyrics.

Which is interesting because, when Bruce left the band, he said he wasn't quite capable of singing about more personal things. And this song is pretty introspective, although filtered through the character of Benjamin Breeg, who one could interpret as Eddie . . . Eddie being essentially a reincarnation of Benjamin Breeg.

CD and picture-disc editions of the "Different World" single, released November 2006.

Opposite:
Dickinson on stage at Eddfest on the grounds of Bangalore Palace, March 16, 2007—Maiden's first-ever show in India.

But I'd say it's Maiden going back to what they started with *The X Factor*, both with musical structure and Steve's soul-searching lyrics. If you look at a song like "The Unbeliever" on *The X Factor*, it's got more of Steve Harris's sort of inner thoughts.

Musically, it's got a nice, robust driving riff, and then they threw in *The X Factor* new-era intro and outro. But it's definitely not a typical single. I don't think they would have won over a Creed or Nickelback fan with that song. It's just saying, "We do this, we take our time. Come along with us for the ride if you want."

ZAPPA: I particularly like the way that song is set against the previous song, "Out of the Shadows," which is a monster-sounding song in terms of the licks and everything, including production. If they got beat up for their downscaled production in the Blaze era, certainly by 2006 they've rectified everything. So, after coming out of "Out of the Shadows," they have this cool-down moment that's only temporary, and within thirty seconds, Bruce does what Bruce needs to do, which is invite you in and give you his history, in the guise of this enigmatic character. He makes you feel like you are inside the story, using this voice like the angel of darkness, and then suddenly he rocks your mind out of your skull [*laughs*].

As for whether a seven-minute song like this, especially where a bunch of it is this quiet intro, can get played on radio, hell, all sorts of Maiden gets played on the radio stations I listen to—on satellite. But sure, terrestrial radio isn't going to deal with these way-out structures, this much guitar playing, long solos. Maiden isn't adhering to a radio-play format. Why do you think they're inspired to write? They're being totally true to themselves and maintaining their originality. They're just into what they're doing, and being played on radio is a distant afterthought by this point.

POPOFF: Franc, what are your thoughts on "Out of the Shadows?"

POTVIN: That one, to me, is almost like a Bruce solo song . . . also almost like a modern "Prodigal Son." It would be similar to the acoustic song on *Dance of Death*, but with guitars. Is it good? Yes. Is it very Maiden-esque? No. It would have totally fit on *The Chemical Wedding* or *Tyranny of Souls*. I think it complements the album well in the middle. It gives the listener a bit of a break from the epic kind of involved war lyrics; it fits in well for what it is.

Elsewhere you've got "Lord of Light," with a little intro as in "Benjamin Breeg." Minor, kind of dissonant sounding. And you've got that pure Adrian Smith–type, almost like "22 Acacia Avenue"–style riff, and the song just kind of sits on the speed. It's about Satan, apparently, who has been referred to as the Lord of Light.

Then, after that, closing the album is "The Legacy," one of my favorite modern Maiden songs. It's almost got a Sabbath-with-Dio vibe. And that's a Janick Gers intro, which is very similar to "The Book of Souls," which is almost like the follow-up to "Legacy." And it's also got the driving "Powerslave"-style beat. So it's a mix of "Powerslave" with the Blaze era, but with Bruce's range and sensibility. I think it's one of the best songs of the last fifteen years.

Bruce Dickinson reaches for the skies at Madison Square Garden, New York City, June 15, 2008.

POPOFF: Franc brings up the preponderance of war lyrics, which ties in nicely with the cover. Ahmet, what are your thoughts on *A Matter of Life and Death*'s cover art?

ZAPPA: I like it, but I'm a big comic book fan. It's by Tim Bradstreet. It evokes the feeling that Eddie is sort of communing with the army of the undead. You're right, it's very Maiden in that they have so many lyrics about war. It's funny, when I look at each cover, I'm always thinking what is unique about this one? Or more specifically, what power does Eddie have? Like, what's he doing now? In terms of famous horror heroes or icons, he's like a cross between some of the greats. He's as powerful as a Freddy Krueger or he possesses the powers of Wishmaster. It's like Eddie has all these unique abilities, which I don't know that they ever really discuss.

But I think the imagery implies he can do some pretty heavy stuff. He could be a hero or a villain. Or he's like an antihero in that one day he could be fighting . . . the songs, ultimately, are about oppression. It's like Eddie is the guy who's gonna fix things but punish the people for fucking up in the first place. And this album cover is like, "Okay, you all fucked up now." Because wherever he is going into battle right now, no one's gonna fuckin' survive. It's like, now that they've conjured up Eddie, you're fucked.

Also, I really like that simple Eddie-with-guns logo, which has a sort of pirate vibe. I think that's a logo they could use more often. I would imagine that a lot of military men and women geek out on that logo. I really think that could potentially get used a lot more than it does.

The stage set for the Somewhere Back in Time World Tour was one of the most extravagant of the band's career, with hieroglyphs, mummies, and, of course, the latest incarnation of Eddie.

A poster advertising Iron Maiden's return to the Graspop festival in Belgium during summer 2008.

POTVIN: Eddie with the tank, it's not as computer animated–looking as *Dance of Death*. Eddie is very small, too, just like on *Dance of Death*. He's not the most prevalent or most prominent figure. Even on *Brave New World*, he was in the sky. So they were kind of going for a subtle Eddie, it seems, three albums in a row. And later they went all out with the 1950s, almost comic-looking *Final Frontier* Eddie, which barely looks like Eddie. So I guess they haven't had a classic Eddie since this album. *A Matter of Life and Death*, half the album is about the war so it makes sense.

POPOFF: How about we continue a bit of a tour of the record? What are some other highlights?

POTVIN: Well, "Brighter Than a Thousand Suns" is definitely a standout track, with this almost "Maiden for the new millennium" sound, using a chord progression they've never really used before. It's odd in that Adrian wrote that with Steve, with lyrics by Bruce.

The first song, "Different World," is more straightforward like "The Wicker Man." It's got Bruce singing in a lower register, with Adrian doing the backing vocals. Lyrically, it's got one of those optimistic "me against the world, forget about your problems and everything is going to be okay" sentiments. I don't want to go as far as to say it's as punk-esque as the first two albums, but it is a little, perhaps, melodic punk. Is it my favorite song? No, but I think it's a great opener.

ZAPPA: I love the vocal melody and the vocal performance on "These Colours Don't Run." I don't know if Bruce is ever, like, punching in or punching out or whether he knows the songs and sings them a couple of times and then he's done. But he's so fucking on it here. And then I hear him live, and I can't believe his vocal range and how in tune he is. But that's what I like about this record, which you can hear on this song, that the vocals sound so live and *alive*. It's like you're there in the studio, hearing these guys perform live takes just for you. Versus, when you go to a stadium, you kind of feel the energy from the crowd at the show or on the live record.

Another one that stands out, and maybe not in a good way [*laughs*], is "The Pilgrim," particularly the beginning where I can picture in my head a leprechaun battle. On this record, Steve pulled in, I think, greater doses of folk music inspiration. "The Pilgrim" could probably have been played on flutes and lutes. Some of the inspiration for the music is very old-world British, like old pub music. Maiden is like the heavy metal version of the Chieftains, who my dad played with, by the way.

I can see in my head immediately evil leprechauns biting into people and ripping them to shreds. It's like ancient heavy metal that comes from the deepest, darkest forest. Iron Maiden is the band Sauron would book for his son's bar mitzvah. Or if Emperor Palpatine hired someone to play at his kid's wedding . . . get fucking Iron Maiden.

By the way, the drums on "The Pilgrim," I think about those from a song-sampling perspective. I don't know why people don't sample those drums at the intro. Those are big. Plus they're setting a vibe and then they rock you hard. I love that there's half-time shit that precedes the full-speed verse. The half time and the double time . . . nothing gets you going harder than Iron Maiden with their song structures.

Poster and T-shirt from the Somewhere Back in Time World Tour, which ran from February 2008 to April 2009.

POTVIN: "The Pilgrim" is kind of stock, although I hate to use that word. It's like this record's "Montségur" or "The Alchemist" from *The Final Frontier*. It's another Janick Gers song, and, it's funny because Gers ends up writing what a lot of people would say are more of the classic-sounding songs. He tends to write some of the epics with Steve. But you can hear his style, which is also in "Be Quick or Be Dead," "Man on the Edge," "The Alchemist," and "Montségur." It's generally fast and straightforward, with a chugging riff, yet it will have some kind of twin-guitar attack in it. But is "The Pilgrim" a standout in the repertoire? Not necessarily. I think it's a good solid track. If I tried to compare what it does for the record to a song off *Brave New World*, I'd say it functions like "The Mercenary."

ZAPPA: I really have to reemphasize the overall sound of this record, the sort of old-school analog vibe, yet with good, solid tones. I think that makes them a classic rock 'n' roll outfit. If I could level any criticism at a lot of people making records for a long time, if you're using the latest and greatest all the time, you can get a high level of sonic clarity, but some of those records are bound to feel "of the time" or dated.

Even with Maiden, maybe some of the records don't sound great, but with these guys, regardless of what the records sound like, they've always been consistent with how great their live shows have been. This record, or any of them, is like a moment in time. But when they go out and play live, they are connecting with hundreds of thousands of people every tour. Which is mind-boggling, that they still get those audiences.

And particularly mind-boggling when you consider how this kind of music is not being played on terrestrial radio, but then you have some current show-stopping radio act and that artist is never, ever going to play to the same amount of people that Maiden play to.

But these post-reunion records all have that visceral live feel anyway. This one was recorded at SARM (West) in London, but they've also recorded in Paris. The main thing is, of course, now they aren't recording at Steve's house, which is a good move [*laughs*]. Not surprisingly, they got a better sound.

I mean, Steve as the main songwriter, having a studio in your house, what is more convenient than that? But there's good and bad that goes with that. Sure, Steve would be comfortable there, but I kind of get where Bruce is coming from. It was a smart decision to use real studios again because I think we got better records. Changing the location and the vibe, it's like an equalizer where everybody has to get there and do their part at their time. Rather than being very relaxed about being at your house.

POPOFF: Of course, the result, this time anyway, is a record they felt so good about, they played the whole thing live, start to finish!
POTVIN: They were so confident at that time, they decided, you know what? We're playing the whole album live back-to-back, without a single classic until an hour into the show. They'd never done that before, and they've never done it again.

ZAPPA: I would imagine as a band, you make this new record and you're very proud of it. And the industry around you is trying to steer a course where you have this "legacy" material, but, of course, you as a band want to keep it fresh and go out there and sell some copies of your new record and have people really get into what you're feeling now at this point in your career.

I think it's cool. If you make a new record and you're proud of it, you spend the time doing it, it's your decision. Sure, I think some people were a little miffed they weren't getting their "hits" and having to hear this entire record. But I don't see anything wrong with that. They're going out there and supporting the new record. And I think the people who appreciated that, obviously, were rewarded. For the people who are such loyal fans, I think it made some brand-new crowd-pleasers of some of these songs by gamely going out and playing them. I think that's really smart.

Put it in perspective. No matter what, that's a big tour they're always putting on. Their shows are not rinky-dink events. It's like the best of both worlds. They've mastered just plugging in and playing their hearts out, rocking so hard, but you still get the spectacle. Who doesn't love it when Eddie hits the stage? Even though there are six guys up there playing, I would say the first band member is Eddie. I don't know how that happened! Over the years, somehow, it's turned out as if they're all working for Eddie.

So, yeah, at its core, the best way to experience Maiden is going to one of their shows. And that is actually quite unique. Because that's not always the norm these days. A lot of people right now are super-processed on record and they can't actually put on a show. If you go to a Maiden show, you are going to be completely satisfied. The level of musicianship— they take that seriously and they put on an amazing show. Bruce is running around like a fucking madman. I don't even know how he has the fucking energy.

And in the ultimate analysis, here's the thing: They put out a record like *A Matter of Life and Death*. They give you that, but then they over-deliver. They put out a record that is awesome, and then they over-deliver live. That right there is a big part of the magic of Iron Maiden.

Iron Maiden: Flight 666 documents the first leg of the Somewhere Back in Time World Tour. It was given a limited theatrical release before being issued on DVD and Blu-ray, May 2009.

15 The Final Frontier

with Jimmy Kay
and Sean Kelly

1. Satellite 15 ... The Final Frontier 8:40
(Smith, Harris)
2. El Dorado..........................6:49
(Smith, Harris, Dickinson)
3. Mother of Mercy 5:20
(Smith, Harris)
4. Coming Home 5:52
(Smith, Harris, Dickinson)
5. The Alchemist.......................4:29
(Gers, Harris, Dickinson)
6. Isle of Avalon 9:06
(Smith, Harris)
7. Starblind............................7:48
(Smith, Harris, Dickinson)
8. The Talisman.........................9:03
(Gers, Harris)
9. The Man Who Would be King.............8:28
(Murray, Harris)
10. When the Wild Wind Blows............10:59
(Harris)

Personnel: Bruce Dickinson—vocals;
   Dave Murray—guitars; Adrian Smith—guitars;
   Janick Gers—guitars; Steve Harris—bass,
   keyboards; Nicko McBrain—drums
Produced by Kevin Shirley; co-produced by
   Steve Harris
Recorded at Compass Point Studios, Nassau,
   Bahamas; The Cave Studios, Malibu, California
Released August 13, 2010

Following the methodology of *A Matter of Life and Death*, *The Final Frontier* finds Steve involved in every track, in collaboration with others on all but one, adding music, lyrics, and arranging the work of others, as Adrian has indicated in interviews. The band also continues with the familiar by working with Kevin Shirley and going in with very little writing done.

As a twist, the band returned to Compass Point in the Bahamas, recording locale of classic Maiden albums long past, as well as legendary albums by AC/DC and Judas Priest. But after a month in the Bahamas, production moved to The Cave in Malibu, California, Kevin's lair, where most of the vocals were tracked; Bruce then left to Shirley and Harris the task of assembling what would be the band's longest record to date (only to be eclipsed by the follow-up).

The first that fans heard from the album was quasi-single "El Dorado," issued two months in advance of the album. Disseminated as a free download, "El Dorado" was arguably the most inspired and classic Maiden single since "Flight of Icarus," groovy beyond words as Nicko slinks down into the pocket and drives home the grinding riff and Steve's noisy gallop, punctuating often with his signature short bar-ending fills.

The first fans saw of the album was Maiden's best album cover since *Live After Death* (although there have been some incredible singles sleeves), with Melvyn Grant pulling out all the stops and setting the stage for the *Somewhere in Time*–like vibe of the two-pronged opener "Satellite 15 . . . The Final Frontier."

Elsewhere, "Coming Home" might just be the greatest ballad Maiden ever conjured, balancing heavy and light with the sturdiest of melodic shifts as well as its most Lizzy-esque, and yet proggy, twin lead. Later, the journey that is "Starblind" supports the lightly applied aerospace theme as well as the record's novel rhythms and high-quality riffs, while "The Talisman" finds the band utilizing its gallop in a comfortable, dependable manner, further demonstrating that the transitions between verse, pre-chorus, and chorus all over this record are logical and seamless in serving some of the band's easiest-drinking long excursions.

However, "When the Wild Wind Blows," rated highly by fans, to my mind, is overrated, rehashing ideas from the Blaze-era albums and *Brave New World*, albeit improving substantially with the shift to what is almost a new song—texturally sophisticated and melodically new for Maiden—at the halfway point.

"El Dorado," the first single taken from *The Final Frontier*, released June 2010.

Whether it's the heavy contribution of Adrian Smith, Maiden's most civilized use of keyboards, or Nicko McBrain, relentless, on fire, and doing what he does best and captured live by Shirley, *The Final Frontier* is a further step beyond the two preceding albums. And those records already quietly bettered *Brave New World*, which still gets all the press due as the album on which Bruce returned after an eight-year absence.

A poster advertising one of the first Final Frontier shows at the Cynthia Woods Mitchell Pavilion in Woodlands, Texas, June 11, 2010.

Performed live at various points were "When the Wild Wind Blows," "El Dorado," "Satellite 15 . . . The Final Frontier," "The Talisman," and "Coming Home." Reinforcing the idea these were the songs of which the band was most proud, "When the Wild Wind Blows," "El Dorado" (Grammy winner for Best Metal Performance!), and "Coming Home" would earn spots on the twenty-three-track *From Fear to Eternity* compilation issued the following year. Over time, it has clearly come to pass that "Coming Home" is the gift that keeps giving, the emotionally connecting gem from this record, although "El Dorado" takes care of business on the other end, headbanging band and fan alike back to the magic of the New Wave of British Heavy Metal.

Portraits of Gers,
Smith, and Harris at the
Cisco Ottawa Bluesfest,
July 6, 2010.

A poster for the 2010 Sonisphere Festival, with Maiden—as ever—at the top of the bill.

Two further singles were taken from *The Final Frontier*: "Satellite 15 . . . The Final Frontier" and "Coming Home," released August and October 2010, respectively.

MARTIN POPOFF: Let's start with the sequencing of this record, because an interesting thing takes place there, correct?

SEAN KELLY: For sure, there's a clear division between the front half and the back half. The first half, aside from the kind of weird intro with "Satellite 15," you've got "Final Frontier," "El Dorado," "Mother of Mercy," "Coming Home," and "The Alchemist," which all are kind of digestible, short, punchy tunes. And then the back end is where you have to put in the commitment [*laughs*]. My favorites are definitely the front-half songs. I know people really enjoy the more progressive stuff, and I do, too, but I come from a punchier, early hard-rock background.

JIMMY KAY: Yes, and in that respect, it strikes me as a combination of *Brave New World* and *A Matter of Life and Death*, where *Matter of Life and Death* was more the epic nine-, ten-minute songs, where everything would start slow and go into a mid-pace groove, and then go faster, and then slow again. But *Brave New World* is more straightforward, or at least it makes more of an impression with the shorter songs, and so the first half of this record reminds me more of *Brave New World*. Also, there are a lot fewer guitar harmonies than on most Iron Maiden albums.

POPOFF: The album cover is quite striking.

KAY: Being a science fiction fan, I love it. This is Melvyn Grant and not Derek Riggs, and he gives the thing a *Predator/Alien* feel. And I feel it ties in with what is, at least, a loose concept of the album, which is journeys, and the journey to the New World, being lost in space, and even what happens in the second-to-last song, "The Man Who Would be King," where he's on a donkey going through the desert. There are all these journeys that tie in. I don't know if they did it consciously, but there's a theme there.

POPOFF: I suppose it ties in most with the intro situation, "Satellite 15 . . . The Final Frontier." Were you surprised how this record begins?

KELLY: Yes, "Satellite 15" is a weird one. It's not Nicko playing at the top—that's an Adrian Smith demo they just kind of lifted off his computer. The beginning is four and a half minutes of this mechanical thing, which is so not Maiden. And Bruce is singing way back in the production—which goes with the lyrics, right? The whole "lost in space" motif. But it's such a relief when you get to Nicko's playing, his sense of time, and the straightforwardness of the chording. I love it; it's so powerful. It makes me appreciate the front half because it sounds so good when they kick into the straight-ahead groove.

KAY: The first song is called "Satellite 15" because it's their fifteenth album, but beyond that, yes, it ties in with the cover and the title track. I think it would have been better to separate the tracks. Because you always have to fast-forward like four minutes to get to "The Final Frontier." There are just so many intros that people can listen to. But it's a cool intro. It's basically about an astronaut—he's off course, he's lost, he's heading toward the sun, he's lived a great life, and he's reflecting, wishing he could say goodbye to his family. That's pretty much it. The music really captures that feeling of dizziness and confusion, what the guy's feeling as his little ship is knocked off course. That's the feeling you're supposed to get, and they achieve that. Everything is planned.

By the way, lot of people thought that *The Final Frontier* would be the final album by Iron Maiden. Bruce was kind of feeding everyone that info. And everyone panicked. But it turned out to be more like feeding the media, creating controversy. "The Final Frontier" is Iron Maiden at their best—straightforward, melodic, verse-chorus-verse. I love it because it's similar to *Killers*, where you have "The Ides of March" going into "Wrathchild." And, oddly, there are no guitar harmonics. It's just straightforward rock 'n' roll, more like stacked chords than a riff.

Maiden's own jet, *Ed Force One*, comes in to land at Domodedovo International Airport, Moscow, Russia, February 10, 2011.

POPOFF: Following "The Final Frontier" is the album's one and only single, "El Dorado." Pretty heavy for a single, but, then again, they used to go with some pretty fast songs.
KELLY: For sure, but this one's really thick in terms of tones too. There's a classic kind of Maiden gallop, but it's framed differently. You're right, it comes off heavier than most of this type, sort of Montrose-meets-Maiden or something. And you can tell when Bruce gets in on the lyrics. There's a commitment. He sings with a different attitude than when he's singing the kind of Harris epics. It's almost like a Shakespearean actor taking it on. But when he sings the stuff I know he had a hand in, or I believe he had a hand in, he's completely and utterly believable. He's one of those guys you can just see needling politicians or priests, kind of digging at people.

POPOFF: This lyric was inspired by the late-2008 market crash and 2009 recession, the collapse of the housing bubble, and a pretty big drop in the stock market.
KELLY: Yes, but as usual, he rounds it off and makes it universal. He's taking on Wall Street swindlers and snake oil salesmen. I just love the sneer he has when he has a bone to pick [*laughs*]. "You'll be wanting a contract/You'll be waiting a while" [*laughs*], and all that stuff about the illusion, the greed, lust, envy, pride, the smoke and mirrors. It's the illusion of the ship is sailing, get on quick; you've got to buy into this thing I'm selling you or you're going to miss out on the opportunity. Which is very telling of that time, economically. People were investing in these dreams without any kind of research, just kind of hoping for something, even though maybe it goes against their better judgment.

Russian fans get ready to rock at the Olympiyskiy Sports Complex, Moscow, February 11, 2011.

KAY: I think it's kind of genius, the way Dickinson tells the story, using the mythical city of gold. He's taking the perspective of the con man trying to recruit people on this boat to the city of gold that doesn't exist. It's a metaphor of today, how financial advisors try to take us down this path of gold that doesn't exist, this fantasy, or of politicians trying to pull the wool over everyone's eyes. So, from a lyrical standpoint, Dickinson does a great job of telling the tale, and that's what Dickinson does best.

People miss this, but there's a nice nod to Marillion, a line that says, "I'm the jester with no tears/And I'm playing on your fears." Dickinson—I don't know if he's a huge Marillion fan—but I definitely think it was a deliberate reference.

"El Dorado" is my favorite song of the album. It starts off like the beginning of a concert, and it ends with the same huge bashing windup, like the very end of a concert. And the middle is just incredible. You have the ending of the song, as it were, kicking things off and then into the track itself, into the thumping bass, into a nice sort of "Evil That Men Do" kind of vibe, and then a big chorus. I love the guitar work. If you listen to it on headphones, the guitars are in different places, all three of them.

KELLY: Yeah, agreed, killer track, but my favorite is "Coming Home." To me, they just nail it, that heart-on-sleeve thing that Maiden does really well, often on the reunion albums. Amazing riff, this kind of harmonized, descending classic rock riff, along with the huge drive-home chorus. "Coming home" . . . I can't figure out if it's just about him flying a plane or if it has a loose connection to the space concept. But I can see Bruce as a pilot, that feeling of coming home and seeing the runway lights.

It's a stadium anthem. You can feel everybody singing along. The best versions of these songs, by the way, are on that *En Vivo!* live album. I went back just to watch who did the solos, and I realized as I'm listening, oh man, these are the ultimate recordings of this stuff. I even find it sonically heftier than the album.

KAY: Here you have the great lyrics of Dickinson, the melody of Smith, and, of course, the strong songwriting of Harris. The beauty of this song is that it sort of summarizes that whole *Flight 666* experience, as they were flying *Ed Force One* from country to country, all together on this plane. And this is how brilliant Dickinson is. He doesn't use the word "airplane"—he uses the word "thunderbird," a native word, and the lyrics touch down on the idea that, from the sky, everything is unified and ancient, almost. He doesn't say England, he says "Albion's land." But beyond that philosophical contemplation throughout the song, it just conjures all these images of this wonderful flight experience.

Captain Bruce Dickinson disembarks in Bali, February 18, 2011.

POPOFF: Sean, as a guitarist and instructor, and having examined the *En Vivo!* video, what did you notice in terms of the distinction between these three guitarists?

KELLY: It's kind of like dog owners and their dogs: eventually it's hard to demarcate one from the other. I think that happened as time went on. But going back, the clear distinction between Adrian Smith and Dave Murray was that Adrian is a little more lyrical, composed, kind of played more to the chord changes. Some would say more melodic. I might argue against that, but he definitely plays more of an "inside" style.

Dave Murray has this really bluesy sound—very fast, very agile. And then Janick is just completely off the chain. I doubt very much that guy can play the same thing twice if you paid him. But he obviously has got a great vocabulary and a lot of facility. But it just sounds reckless. Which is exciting—I mean that in the best way.

During the time you had Dave and Janick playing together, but no Adrian, they're both playing Strats. It got a little hard to separate, but really you could still tell. Because Dave took on a little more of Adrian's role, more of the melodic thing. I hate to do those generalizations, because it's not that Janick isn't melodic, but he's more on the edge. A little more like Jeff Beck than Clapton, to draw a parallel.

POPOFF: Did you notice anything interesting in terms of who was doing the solos?

KELLY: No, it just kind of highlighted the stylistic differences. But the one thing I did notice on *Final Frontier* is that Adrian seems to be incorporating more old-school influences. I think he went back and revisited, like, Stevie Ray Vaughan and maybe some Gary Moore; there seems to be more classic rock in his playing.

Also, because there are three guitars, it gets a little cloudy in terms of frequency. In the frequency spectrum, you kind of have to carve out your sonic identity. I noticed he was playing a Les Paul, which kind of separated him from the two Strat players. And even Dave Murray's Strat is equipped with humbuckers in the neck and the bridge position, whereas I think Janick was more of a single-coil pickup player. So I just notice the sonic differences. That's how they were able to distinguish and find their places in a very dense mix. Three guitars, man, that's a tough thing to mix. There's a lot of harmonics.

I did read that Adrian actually came up with new parts to play. So Janick kept Adrian's old parts, and Adrian learned new parts to complement. That was on the older material when played live. But then what happens with Maiden is, whoever brings in the composition tends to take the lion's share of the main riff and will even

(continued on page 226)

Opposite:
Eddie and Janick trade blows at the Soundwave Music Festival at Olympic Park, Sydney, February 27, 2011.

Next spread:
Dickinson climbs the stage at the Soundwave Music Festival, February 27, 2011.

DUPLICATE

IRON MAIDEN
PRESENTED BY LIVE NATION
THE O2, LONDON
DOORS 18:30
FRIDAY 5TH AUGUST 2011

(continued from page 223)

overdub themselves. So even though there are three guitar players, if there's any overdubbing, the same player will overdub on the part they wrote. And that makes sense because it just tightens things up. Otherwise you can get a little loosey-goosey with articulation.

POPOFF: Interesting. Back to *The Final Frontier*, anyone want to venture an opinion on some of the longer and more progressive songs here, songs toward the back half?

KAY: "The Talisman" is a great song. If I were to put a time stamp on it, I'd say it takes place between the sixteenth and the seventeenth centuries. It's a story of persecution, most probably religious persecution, as these refugees head west. You're not quite sure who this group is, but you know they're leaving in many ships, which Bruce oddly just numbers as "tenfold."

But it's a large group of people leaving their country for a better world, families sailing to the new world, escaping persecution. I get goosebumps when I read his lyrics because it hits home for a lot of us immigrants. I'm the son of immigrants; my parents came on a boat from Greece. But this is more primitive, because people are dying from scurvy and harsh conditions and Mother Nature in the form of storms. And the main character, strangely enough, probably dies as they near their destination, and yet the wording is subtle enough there's a chance he's survived, but just barely.

In terms of music, it's another great song because, really, Steve Harris always creates a musical vibe. The beginning of the song has that acoustic guitar. As they're boarding the ships, it has that folky, acoustic intro, and the vocals sort of follow the rhythm of the acoustic guitar. Then as the song progresses, it gets rougher and rougher as the seas get harsher. The reality of being in those harsh environmental conditions hits, and the music plays on the atmosphere of what's happening on the stormy ocean.

KELLY: Even though I prefer the front end, the more compact kind of things, I love "Isle of Avalon." It has this beautiful Adrian Smith guitar figure that reminds me very much of classical guitar. It's simple but just very melodic, very thematic. And each of these components builds on the other. It's an element Maiden has, because they don't use a lot of different devices. It's kind of like an acoustic arpeggiated intro that is either Steve Harris playing it on the bass or a clean guitar and/or an acoustic guitar.

And then there's usually a heavier element brought in, like a heavy kind of straight-ahead stomp or gallop, and usually when that gallop happens, there's a kind of Celtic motif. Honestly, when I was listening, I would go back and forth, and say, yeah, it's variations on a theme. But all it does is drive home the narrative. They're just ways of getting from part to part. And here they did that beautifully.

KAY: For sure, that's another one—brilliant song. The song is about the Celtic myth of the island of Avalon, a magical place where immortals dwell and the departed spirits prepared to go to the other world. It's the myth that tells that Avalon is a place where the magic sword of Excalibur was forged and where King Arthur went to recover from his mortal wounds. And it's another journey, right? Steve's lyrics are pretty oblique. Maybe it's just a description of that area or that mythical place. Listen to the middle section carefully. At 5:18 to 5:37, it sounds like Rush, like something jazzy from *Grace Under Pressure*. The guitar tone is so Alex Lifeson in the *Signals* and *Grace Under Pressure* era, with the flanger effect on it. And it's sort of a Geddy Lee bass too.

POPOFF: There's one late on the album that's hard to figure out, but it's a pretty cool, up-tempo rocker once it gets going, and that's "The Man Who Would be King."

KELLY: I'm not sure what's going on there either [*laughs*], but musically that one has an amazing example of how Maiden would throw these sonic energizers into these epics. Because Steve obviously has a story to tell. And some time over the course of the story, you have to extend sections of the same musical progression. But, man, this one has almost a *Jesus Christ Superstar* feel that kicks in. And, actually, that's the one Dave Murray credit on the album. It's got this beautiful kind of melodic midsection and stuff like that; it's like going to a musical or a play, where there's this moment of levity

From Fear to Eternity, Maiden's latest "best of" compilation, released in June 2011 following the conclusion of The Final Frontier World Tour.

or magic that makes all the stuff that came before it worthwhile and make sense. And that's not easy listening. You then go back to appreciate the music that came before it because of this one thing that just brightens and brings light.

KAY: I agree—the lyrics there, I really don't know what's happening [*laughs*]. It's about a man—he's riding on a donkey; he killed somebody. This is an eye for an eye, so it's either self-defense or payback. He had no choice. Why would he be king? I don't know. It doesn't really tell us much. Again, this is a track that would've fit well on *A Matter of Life and Death*. To my ears, it's maybe the weakest track on the album—it kind of lost me.

Also a bit cryptic, come to think of it, is "Mother of Mercy." It's similar to "Afraid to Shoot Strangers," speaking from the perspective of a soldier questioning war and everything he's done. The mother of mercy is probably the Madonna or Mother Mary. Yet he goes back and forth from the mother of mercy to the angel of death. We don't really know who the mother of mercy is, right?

POPOFF: Any thoughts on the last song on the record? "When the Wild Wind Blows," to my mind, is incredibly Blaze era.
KELLY: Sure, I buy that. "When the Wild Wind Blows" is my favorite of the epics because it sounds like folk music, like true Celtic folk music. Which I think they did a lot of. They're coming from a British folk tradition, really.
KAY: "When the Wild Wind Blows" is a Harris composition based on a pretty celebrated British animated film from 1986, but with a major plot difference at the end. An aging couple, they're watching the news, and the news is saying the apocalypse is coming. And, as old people, you panic and you're very dogmatic, right? And it's in their heads, so for two weeks, they're preparing a bomb shelter and they're getting their food together. And then the news comes back on and says, "Well, it's not as bad as we thought; it was just an earthquake." But they manage to have had their poisoned tea and commit suicide because they believed the first reports. It's just a bizarre story. The nuclear attack doesn't materialize, but they kill themselves because the TV was telling them the end is near.

POPOFF: Yes, that film seems to have had a powerful effect on British people, in particular. Any closing thoughts? We didn't really talk about the production.
KELLY: A lot of people bash Kevin Shirley—at least a lot of people I know. I'm a fan, because I think what he does is, he tries to capture the energy of the moment, the performance energy. When you go for that intention, things like sonic isolation and technically perfect vocals become secondary concerns. Because you're trying to get something early on, right? You can hear that in the guitar parts, you can hear that in the vocal parts, and, yeah, it's weird. It's a bit of a noisy album—but good noisy. It's not superclean. But these records have an energy I think produces a timelessness. It just takes a little bit of adjusting.

POPOFF: How significant is it that they went back to Compass Point in the Bahamas?
KELLY: Apparently everything was exactly the same as it was when they were there thirty years past—same carpet, same broken door. But I'm not sure it matters much.

Technically, when you have a room that is somewhat sonically treated, because of the nature of how you record, which is on digital audio workstations, like, say, Pro Tools, fidelity can be universally pretty good. So I think that was more of an inspiration thing.

And I do know they never recorded with a click track. I would never, ever want to hear Nicko McBrain on a click track. It's just not the way he plays. And it's also not the way they arrange parts. Because these guys don't demo their tunes. They're going in and Steve Harris is there with a bass guitar, going, "Alright, I wrote this song, here's the first part." In total it's eleven minutes, and he's got it all in his head. But if he went through and tried to show that all at once, you'd forget what you did at the beginning. They would record chunks, which I think Kevin Shirley was saying provided a challenge, because with no click track, you have to punch in with the same type of feel and the same tempo.

But what's cool about Maiden, you hear and watch something like "The Trooper," when they count themselves in . . . most bands count in to set the tempo of the song—"One, two, three, four." With Maiden, counting is just a way to start [*laughs*]. It has nothing to do with the tempo of the tune. I remember seeing them do "Rime of the Ancient Mariner" and there's like this fifteen-second pause, and then suddenly all the guitars come in on a pitch-black stage. How do you do that?! You do that by being a band for years and years [*laughs*].

Iron Maiden on stage at the Estadio Nacional in Santiago, Chile, on October 2, 2013, midway through the band's lengthy—and lucrative—Maiden England tour, which ran from 2012 to 2014.

16

The Book of Souls

with Matt Heafy,
Chris Jericho,
and Franc Potvin

DISC 1
1. If Eternity Should Fail......................8:28
(Dickinson)
2. Speed of Light............................5:01
(Smith, Dickinson)
3. The Great Unknown......................6:37
(Smith, Harris)
4. The Red and the Black 13:33
(Harris)
5. When the River Runs Deep.................5:52
(Smith, Harris)
6. The Book of Souls........................10:27
(Gers, Harris)

DISC 2
1. Death or Glory...........................5:13
(Smith, Dickinson)
2. Shadows of the Valley.....................7:32
(Gers, Harris)
3. Tears of a Clown 4:59
(Smith, Harris)
4. The Man of Sorrows 6:28
(Murray, Harris)
5. Empire of the Clouds 18:01
(Dickinson)

Personnel: Bruce Dickinson—lead vocals, piano;
Dave Murray—guitars; Adrian Smith—guitars;
Janick Gers—guitars; Steve Harris—bass,
keyboards; Nicko McBrain—drums

A s if obstinately doubling down, Iron Maiden goes long here, as in two discs—all the better to linger on the lonely contemplation of death heard all over the album, beginning in epic fashion with "If Eternity Should Fail," which sets the tableau for a record during which Bruce wrestled with oral cancer and the troubling questions beyond.

"Speed of Light," the record's second volley (one that deftly ties in with the Maya-themed cover art), catapults the listener through the galaxy. But is the destination the afterlife or oblivion? Suddenly, *The Book of Souls* presents us with two action-packed visions for Maiden, both lyrically and musically. And both songs are from Bruce, the first of which he wrote alone and the second (the advance debut single), co-written with Adrian, cowbell included.

The stage is set with the vibe of the debut album thirty-five years ago and rock 'n' rolling like "2 Minutes to Midnight." Both "If Eternity Should Fail" and "Speed of Light" serve as microcosms of a record that would continue to zig and zag through everything devoted fans expect from Maiden—along with many bonus surprises to spark chatter. This takes place over the expanse of the band's longest record, at ninety-two minutes, necessarily a double, although that designation means less than it might have in the '70s and '80s, doesn't it?

Symbolic of the record's echoes of *Brave New World*'s Bruce-ness, the band returned to the same French studio used on that record, laying down the tracks with the spontaneity typical of the Kevin Shirley

Opposite:
Bruce Dickinson wielding a
Union Jack at the Barclays
Center in Brooklyn, New
York, July 22, 2017.

Guest Performances: Michael Kenney—keyboards; Jeff Bova—orchestration
Produced by Kevin Shirley; co-produced by Steve Harris
Recorded at Guillaume Tell Studios, Paris
Released September 4, 2015

playbook, but laying them down fresh from the writing, much of which took place in the studio.

All the while, the musical sprawl is tightened by the universal eloquence of the lyrics—often featuring Steve writing out of personal strife and contemplation of death. The resulting cohesiveness of the lyrics across the album is yet another example of Maiden's two band leaders being able to write from one pen, only now they've written a timeless novel, a book of souls rather than an approximation of a history text comprising encyclopedia-type entries.

To be sure, there is the semi-topical, addressing war ("Death or Glory," specifically about World War I aerial battle) and ancient gods (the title track), as well as "Tears of a Clown," about the shocking suicide of comedian Robin Williams. It's an incredibly brave topic for Maiden to tackle; then again, life is the serious business addressed all over *The Book of Souls*, very deftly represented as unfathomably large or completely insignificant. Immortality or mortality—Bruce and Steve wrestle with what awaits, placing themselves on the razor's edge of answers but wisely not arriving at the cut and dried.

Gers, Dickinson, and Smith show off their haul at the Nordoff Robbins O2 Silver Clef Awards, Grosvenor House Hotel, London, July 3, 2015.

The most topical and ultimately dominating discussion for a number of reasons is "Empire of the Clouds," the band's longest song ever, which one has to, essentially, call a power ballad in terms of musical structure, with a slow build to rock that still relates back to the first seven minutes, in contrast to many other long Maiden songs that, without much effort, could be busted into two or three songs. It's a gorgeous and gradual build to rocking out, and it's stuffed with some of Maiden's most tasteful guitar battling ever.

Lyrically, Bruce addresses the fate of the British airship R.101, which crashed in France, killing forty-eight of the fifty-four aboard. This story line was prompted by Bruce's reading of *To Ride the Storm*, a lengthy and detailed treatise on the crash. Bruce's musings about the wider significance led him to frame it as a story of "ambition and dreams."

All told, it's an interesting and almost material way to end a record grappling with life after death, Bruce perhaps suggesting that what we strive to accomplish here on Earth is all we can really do to affect our own immortality. With that message, and the skillful telling and additional layered implications within, and with the panorama of the slow-burning music behind it, "Empire of the Clouds" is poignant and lingering like the longest of goodbyes.

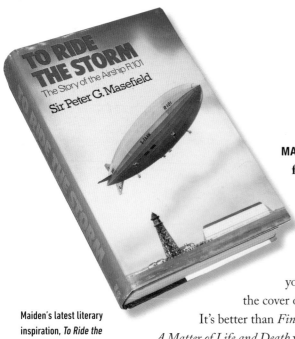

Maiden's latest literary inspiration, *To Ride the Storm: The Story of the Airship R.101*, by Sir Peter G. Masefield.

MARTIN POPOFF: Let's start with this: What were your very first impressions of *The Book of Souls*?

CHRIS JERICHO: Well, I've always been influenced by the album covers. That changes over time, but that's the generation we came up in, Martin. You'd go into the record store and you would flip through the racks and you'd see a couple of different album covers and you'd choose which one you wanted to buy. As soon as I saw the cover of *The Book of Souls*, I thought, "Oh my gosh, that's classic." It's better than *Final Frontier*, which is cheesy, and *A Matter of Life and Death* was kind of stupid, and *Dance of Death* was dumb, but this was a killer album cover that just pops. Okay, what's it about? Oh, it's a Mayan thing, but the pyramids kind of suggest Egypt, which takes you back to *Powerslave*.

MATT HEAFY: That cover is really a step up for them, and, what's cool, I was talking about being a fan of the big world covers—this one is the most minimalistic and modern cover, in a sense, because it's just Eddie—it's just this Mayan Eddie. And they've returned to their classic logo, although it's sort of revamped and modern. I feel like they just reinvented themselves again with this record, and the cover art says that—it looks amazing, and it feels like a rebrand.

POPOFF: Another logical entry into the album is the first single, which came out two or three weeks before the album. I love "Speed of Light," but "El Dorado" was a killer advance single too. Is there the risk of building up expectations too much? What did you guys think of "Speed of Light"?

JERICHO: I thought it had one of the greatest little melody lines, great solo, great vocals. Adrian is their hit writer; he's their hook writer. When I saw them play in Las Vegas, I told him that, I said, "You're the best musician on the stage," and, of course, he's superhumble, and he wouldn't say that, but he's such a great player. That's when Maiden started going down, not when Bruce left but when Adrian left. And when he came back, he was their secret weapon. So he did write the most successful songs on the record.

HEAFY: "Speed of Light" has a very "Wicker Man" feel. If I were a member of Iron Maiden on this record, releasing a single, sure, "Speed of Light" was the perfect single to release, but I think I might've said "The Red and the Black" first if I were them, or "Death or Glory." That would've been my personal choice. But I just love that song. "If Eternity Should Fail" too; the intro to that song reminds me of the way "Seventh Son" kicks in.

This record, for me, doesn't borrow from their past; they didn't go back and try to borrow by any means. And yet still it reminds me of *Seventh Son*, *Powerslave*, *Number of the Beast*, and *Piece of Mind,* when I listen to this record [*laughs*]. That's why I love it so much. I feel like it's the best record they've released since *Brave New World*. It's so damn good.

The "Speed of Light" single, released August 2015.

Below:
Dickinson and Gers in Shanghai, China, during The Book of Souls World Tour, April 26, 2016.

POPOFF: Franc, yet another way into the album—and it's the longest record they've ever made—is the opening track. Tell me about "If Eternity Should Fail."
FRANC POTVIN: That's actually a Bruce solo song that was demoed with Roy Z. Bruce wrote this and a few other songs for what was supposed to be his new album, right before The Book of Souls World Tour started. Apparently Maiden just relearned

the song the way it is. And it's the first song that Maiden played in drop-D tuning completely, not just Adrian Smith. But Steve said, I love that song for Maiden, and that's going to be the ultimate song. And it indirectly influenced the direction of the album.

It's my favorite on the album. It sounds like a Bruce Dickinson solo song because it *was* a Bruce Dickinson solo song—and that's not a conspiracy; there are interviews with Bruce talking about it. But, yes, just like *Final Frontier*, this album opens with more of a mid-paced song. It's not "Aces High" or "Caught Somewhere in Time," it's a slower-paced song with beautiful harmonies. Lyrically, it's Bruce being introspective, and I like the spoken-word thing at the end where it merges into the next song.

JERICHO: First time I heard that, I thought, "Oh my gosh, dude, this is Iron Maiden." It starts with this weird two minutes of, like, Bruce by himself, and just goes from slow and heavy to fast. I instantly fell in love with that record. It's my favorite post-reunion album, and I think if they do go out, I think they went out on their best reunion album, or, if not, their second best.

POTVIN: I also have to mention "The Great Unknown" because I'm a huge fan of the Blaze Bayley style of songs, which a lot of people won't admit to, or know that the current style with Bruce, with the long intros and all that, is, as we said earlier, completely this style they developed with Blaze. Blaze's voice and how good or bad he was, that's a different debate. Production-wise, those albums didn't sound good. Steve Harris produced them, and I think one of the conditions for Bruce to come back into the band was that Steve would not produce *Brave New World*. But going back to this album, "The Great Unknown" has that haunting Blaze-era sound. And it doesn't sound like any other song. Maiden is great at having their own style and copying themselves without a single chorus sounding like the next chorus. There's almost not a single chorus in Maiden that is a copy of another one on sixteen albums.

POPOFF: On the subject of production, how you would compare *The Book of Souls* to *The Final Frontier*?

POTVIN: I've never really had that conversation with other fans, but I think the production is much better on the new one. *Final Frontier* has a bit of a compressed sound to it. The drums and guitars sound kind of muddy, and I think the ride cymbal sounds a little off at times. But there are great songs on *Final Frontier* too.

HEAFY: Sonically, it's definitely in a much better place, in my opinion. I feel like, overall, the record breathes a lot more. It feels a lot more organic sounding, like their older stuff. To me, it sounds the way *Piece of Mind* and *Number of the Beast* did, but

maybe a little bit louder than the classic records. It seems to pull back on the ethereal feel, which is something I loved on *Seventh Son* and *Brave New World*. It's back to painting that picture of the world. I picture that Aztec or Maya vibe, which is always a fun part about Iron Maiden, seeing what kind of world they're gonna be in next. That excites all the comic book geeks and fantasy nerds and video game freaks like me. It makes you picture all these things that you want to picture when you listen to awesome epic metal like this.

POPOFF: What did you think of the band addressing the suicide of Robin Williams? To me it was quite jarring.

A Book of Souls World Tour T-shirt and poster advertising Maiden's appearance at the Resurrection Fest in Viveiro, Spain, July 9, 2016.

Opposite:
Dickinson looks out into the audience at the Mediolanum Forum, July 22, 2016.

HEAFY: I love "Tears of a Clown." The fact that Steve wrote about Robin Williams is obviously something you wouldn't expect Iron Maiden to do, but it's just such a great, touching thing.

JERICHO: "Tears of a Clown" is almost like a kind of winsome ballad. I thought they did a great job on that. It proved there's still a lot in the tank because it's not the same old thing. Like I love AC/DC, maybe my all-time favorite band. But if you listen to *Rock or Bust*, it's the same as *Black Ice* and the one before, ad infinitum. Maiden didn't have that. *The Book of Souls* is different from *Final Frontier*, which is different from *Brave New World*. I think there's no way they're not going to do another record. You can tell they have a lot of creative juice left in the tank just by what they came out with on *The Book of Souls*.

POTVIN: Good song. Is it a great song? No. Had it not been about Robin Williams, maybe people would have paid less attention to it. Because it's one of those songs they start to write around the *Fear of the Dark* or even *No Prayer* era, where they are more like rocking songs as opposed to metal songs. Yeah, it's a good song, but, look, they cut it off the setlist in the second run, right? It could have been on a Bruce album, maybe *Balls to Picasso*. Good song, nothing special, but I like the lead work;

Dave plays with more of a bluesy and quiet tone than usual, while Adrian's solo is full of emotion.

POPOFF: I think we can all agree that at the great end of things is "Empire of the Clouds."
JERICHO: Bruce did my podcast, and he told me he found a piano at a church bake sale or something, and he bought it, went home, and started messing around on it, and he said, "I'll write a twenty-minute song on it; might as well, see what happens." [*laughs*] To me, that's a true artist. Although I bet you Bruce didn't really sit down and say, "I'm gonna write a twenty-minute song"—it just came out that way. I'm sure he was a little nervous to present it to Steve—"Hey man, I've got this eighteen-minute song about the RAF and zeppelin blimp-type shit."
HEAFY: I am absolutely in love with "Empire of the Clouds." That's a song that I'll sit and listen to with headphones, close my eyes, and picture the world that Bruce is singing about. I love the story. I didn't at first—when I first saw that song title and first listened to the lyrics—because I thought it would be about a futuristic world again. I pictured the *Brave New World* landscape. But then I read about, and he's writing about a historical event. Very inspiring song.

Four- and six-string warriors lined up at the Paleo Festival in Nyon, Switzerland, July 20, 2016.

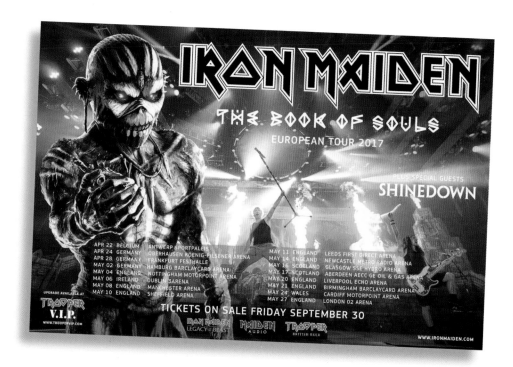

A poster advertising Maiden's run of European shows, spring 2017.

POTVIN: "Empire of the Clouds," the first song with piano. It's got a little of "Hallowed Be Thy Name" to it. It also reminds me of Trans-Siberian Orchestra. Let's not forget, when Bruce wrote that song, he knew his tumor was cancerous, and there's a month remaining on the recording of the album. And from what I remember him saying, he didn't tell the band and chose to finish the album, because there was a chance he would never sing again.

People didn't know, but that could've been his swan song. There's a part of him that thought that "Maybe this is the last song I'll ever write in my life." And he was a fan of the R.101, the zeppelin that crashed in France, on not its maiden voyage, but its maiden voyage overseas . . . no pun intended. Apparently he had a little model of it when he was a kid, so it's kind of funny he never wrote about it until their sixteenth album. Aviation means so much to him and his family, so it's fitting that "Empire of the Clouds" could've been his swan song had the surgery not gone right or had the cancer attacked more furiously. The band I don't think knew they were potentially playing on Bruce's last song ever. When you know that backstory, then you kind of go back in time and it's a little bit creepy, a little bit eerie.

POPOFF: Any other tracks you want to comment on? The title track is pretty special.
POTVIN: Yes, and the overall theme of "The Book of Souls," even as Bruce explains it live, it's about a civilization that disappears. Who knows what's going to happen to our current civilization the way things are going? Great empires, as we know, fail, and no one knows what happened to them.

JERICHO: Yes, well, you've got Bruce's two crazy prog songs, and also "The Red and the Black" by Steve was a great tune, although it's probably four minutes too long, but that's Maiden. I agree, another highlight is "The Book of Souls," because that is so Zeppelin-ish and heavy [*sings it*]. They don't do a lot of songs like that, with that real Sabbath- or Zeppelin-type stomp [*sings the rhythm*]. I thought that was a great song in a style you didn't hear much from them. When did Maiden ever give us that slow, heavy tune? It showed, again, that Maiden could still expand their horizons and step outside their box.

There's a lot of diversity on the record, and, once again, everybody came through. Adrian's on fire with the songs he wrote. Bruce is, Steve is, even Janick. There are a couple stinkers on there, but not many. If the album is ninety minutes, seventy minutes are awesome. I think at this stage of the game, that's more than you can ask for.

The only thing I wish is, they would have somebody produce them. But I don't think anybody . . . why would they ever allow someone else to tell them what to do at this stage? If they did, I think there's still a classic Maiden album in them. And not a classic later-years record, but a classic *Number of the Beast*–type of record.

If someone could do that and say, "Listen, this song needs to be a little bit shorter." But I don't know if they want to put themselves in that position, much like Kiss doesn't want to do it anymore. A lot of bands just don't want to have anybody telling them what to do even though that might lead to a better record. I think that's the only problem with Maiden today. But they're so huge, what do they care?

The Book of Souls: Live Chapter, recorded at concerts across the globe during 2016–2017 and released in various audio and video formats, November 2017.

HEAFY: I agree that "The Red and the Black" has one of the catchiest guitar parts on the album, where they're back to the idea of supercatchy guitar, twin melodies, and supercatchy vocal parts. And I think, on this record, Bruce hit some of the highest notes he's hit in a long time, for example, the beginning of "Speed of Light"—about as high as he's been since, probably, *Powerslave* era. It's freaking fantastic.

For me, this one feels as good as anything they've done in the past. When I heard *The Book of Souls*, I felt like this was rediscovering *Powerslave* all over again. It feels like it could've been done somewhere between *Powerslave* and *Somewhere in Time*.

POPOFF: Franc, I like some of the connections you make between some of these songs and previous material. I guess you are somewhat in disagreement that the record is particularly out of the box for them?

POTVIN: Yes, although I love the album, I think, on *The Book of Souls*, they rehash a fair bit of old riffs. You could argue that some of the riffs on "The Book of Souls" sound like parts of "Losfer Words" on *Powerslave*. But, of course, when Janick Gers wrote it, Steve said, "Hey, that sounds like 'Losfer Words.'" Janick was like, "Sorry, I don't remember that song." He didn't play on it—probably never listened to it.

"The Red and the Black" brings on that sort of European chanting. It was, I think, custom-built for stadium crowds. It has this beautiful long melodic interlude in "The Clansman" style. A lot of people want to forget about the Blaze albums, but they forget how much of their new style was formed in that era. And it's amazing that somebody like Smith kept it going; you don't expect that from him.

There's a rehash of "Wasted Years" on it, which is "Shadows of the Valley." Let's face it, you put on the song, you think it's "Wasted Years" for the first twenty seconds. That's kind of weird to me, because it's a Janick Gers song. It ends up working because they are allowed to copy themselves, and they've done it many, many times. Again, that one has that Blaze Bayley aura to it.

"Death or Glory" is a stock song about war. It's a good song but nothing special. I'm not even sure why there's so much emphasis put on it, because I don't think it's that good. In the '80s, it would've been a B-Side. If I had to cut four songs off the album and not make it a double album, it definitely would have been a B-Side. "Tears of a Clown," same thing. Even "Shadow" could've been a B-Side, but I think it's better, more real Maiden. I know it sounds kind of silly to say that, but it's more like their deeper, more melodic style.

But my main critique of the album, if I may, is its lack of bass lines. The bass is back to taking a backseat and sounding like a real bass. By that I mean Steve is playing mostly low notes. There are too many holes. There are lots empty spaces that could've used some bass lines that we all love from Steve Harris. But, for some reason, he's decided he doesn't do that anymore. I mean, he does, like, a classic Steve Harris bass line in the middle of "If Eternity Should Fail," right before the chorus starts again, after the middle part. He does it a little bit in the first single, "Speed of Light."

So there could be more Steve Harris on this album. And apparently one of the reasons there wasn't is that he had to attend to personal family things. Apparently this is the first album where a lot of it was developed without Steve being one hundred percent around. He was not there as much as he normally is. And the guitars are definitely louder.

POPOFF: What do your knowledgeable Maiden-fan friends think about the album?

POTVIN: A lot of people seem to like it. And a lot of people, funnily enough, consider it a return to form for Maiden, where half of it really sounds like the style that started on *The X Factor*. I mean, I'm not saying that because I love that album a lot or because I played a show with Blaze. I'm just saying that because it's a fact. And I believe that, if people pay attention to it, they'll hear what I hear.

POPOFF: If this turns out to be the last Iron Maiden album, how would you say it ended for them? Did they go out on a high note?

JERICHO: Sure, but they still have so much left in the tank. Just the fact that Bruce wrote two or three of the best songs on the record . . . he really came back into the fray, which, for the last few years, I kinda thought he was in the background. But he started the record and he closed the record with an eight-minute song and with an eighteen-minute song that kicks ass. Who would do that? Everybody expects Steve to carry the load, but I always like it better when the other guys do, and I almost felt like this record was Bruce's spotlight album, and a perfect place and time to have that.

POTVIN: If *The Book of Souls* was to be the last album, it would have been a great ending to an amazing career. I think it represents a creative triumph for the six-man lineup, but it's probably the album of the last five, of the ones with three guitar players, that has revisited their mid-'80s sound the most. And by mid-'80s I mean "Where Eagles Dare," "The Duellists," you know, that kind of Nicko-on-the-ride-cymbal sound.

I always thought of *The Book of Souls* as a mix of *Powerslave* and *The X Factor*, with a bunch of all the stuff they've done since 2000 mixed in. I think most fans seem to love it. I've heard different opinions, but I think those are probably people who have read the reviews saying this is a return to form, when it's really a continuation of what they've done the last seventeen years, so maybe they were expecting another *Piece of Mind* or something.

It's pretty amazing they can write at this level. Some people may claim it's not quite at the level of their mid-'80s glory, but it's quite amazing still. Metallica does a pretty good job these days, but very few classic bands, other than Metallica and Maiden, can write at a level very close to where they used to write.

HEAFY: Bruce runs around twice as much as I do on stage. And he sounds way better than I do and better than all our peers in all the modern bands. Maiden needs to keep going, to keep making records, to keep boarding the plane. I don't know any other way to put it—the world still needs them.

17

Senjutsu

with Rich
Davenport,
Marty Friedman,
and Kirsten
Rosenberg

1. Senjutsu 8:20
(Smith, Harris)
2. Stratego. 4:59
(Gers, Harris)
3. The Writing on the Wall. 6:13
(Smith, Dickinson)
4. Lost in a Lost World 9:31
(Harris)
5. Days of Future Past. 4:03
(Smith, Dickinson)
6. The Time Machine. 7:09
(Gers, Harris)

DISC 2
1. Darkest Hour. 7:20
(Smith, Dickinson)
2. Death of the Celts 10:20
(Harris)
3. The Parchment 12:39
(Harris)
4. Hell on Earth. 11:19
(Harris)

Personnel: Bruce Dickinson—vocals; Dave Murray—
guitars; Adrian Smith—guitars; Janick Gers—guitars;
Steve Harris—bass, keyboards; Nicko McBrain—drums
Produced by Kevin Shirley
Recorded at Guillaume Tell Studios, Paris
Released September 3, 2021

Impressively, amid the scourge of a worldwide creepy-crawly pandemic, Iron Maiden defied the odds and their own musings about the end of the band and issued a sprawling work of inside-baseball Iron Maiden-ness called *Senjutsu*. The whole Land of the Rising Sun imagery had been a storied trope of the New Wave of British Heavy Metal, but Iron Maiden, leaders of that glorious time in the early '80s, had, for the most part, steered clear of it, with their most significant gesture being the *Maiden Japan* EP.

This cultural touchstone was ripe for celebrating, which we get with the title of the new album (discussed in our, well, discussion), as well as the impressive artwork for the record, all richly black and red as opposed to lurid, lime-green, and baked in saturated primary colors. The samurai warrior theme would carry through to Steve and Bruce's melancholy, ruminative lyrics about all manner of territorial conflict, writ timeless like so many tales baked to parchment (on an album that contains a song called "The Parchment").

Fans' first taste of the new record would come with advance single "The Writing on the Wall," a resolutely unshowy and plodding song which had detractors calling it Maiden's "Wanted Dead or Alive." But the innovative video elucidated the song, revealed the thought behind it, and indeed the dark contemplation that Bruce and Steve seemed to be struggling with throughout the course of this strident record. The clip was nominated for the 2021 UK Music Video Awards in the animation category, but more importantly, Maiden proved themselves a band continuing to seek out interesting collaborations and move forward as a multimedia force.

Opposite:
"There goes the siren that warns of the air raid." Bruce and the boys deliver another eternally youthful rendition of "Aces High."

On May 16, 2022, Julien's Auctions conducted an auction preview of Kurt Cobain's personally drawn 1985 Iron Maiden *Killers* skateboard deck artwork at the Hard Rock Café in New York, New York. The board was bought by skate legend Tony Hawk, who has used it as the basis for merchandise sold to raise awareness of mental health and to help build skateparks in underserved communities.

Longtime producer Kevin Shirley was back, producing Iron Maiden's seventeenth album, recording the band at their familiar (and comfortable) French haunt. And as loud as the Internet chatter was over "The Writing on the Wall," it was just as loud, once the album dropped, over Kevin Shirley's continued lording over the board. Debate went wild over Maiden's continuing legacy of sort of working-class analog sounds, with Kevin aligning fully with Steve's vision, one that is also in a mind meld—with Bruce lyrically, Nicko at the drums, and all three guitarists in the band, who grow more alike—and like Steve—every day. As I'm prone to point out, if Iron Maiden hired Andy Sneap and made blindingly perfect albums like Accept, Saxon, or Judas Priest, we'd be complaining about the band having the humanity sucked out of them.

No, it's perhaps best that Iron Maiden, despite being a six-man conglomeration, sound like The Who and rattle at the joints like The Who. This they do so meaningfully, intentionally, and convincingly, that, again as I've often spouted, they still sound very much like that band that ruthlessly dominated the NWOBHM, putting out a classic album in each of the five years of that golden time for metal.

Sure, Sepultura had done the Kodo drum thing with their *Against* album, but now it was Nicko's turn, with the band proposing a very unexpected opening title track, all swirling and tribal and over eight minutes long. Next came fast-tracker "Stratego," followed by "The Writing on the Wall," "Lost in a Lost World," and "Days of Future Past," with the anthemic but unsettlingly contemplative choruses piling up. I suppose melancholy is the word, as if Bruce and Steve had become overwhelmed with how much of a mess the world was in, and how much psychic trauma lives on from battles of the past, both real and mythical. Closing disc one of this eighty-two–minute, two-CD monster is "The Time Machine," a chromatic, ebbing-and-flowing progressive masterpiece with lyrics that could have been written in the 1300s, somewhere in North Africa, originally in a language now lost.

Strength to strength, over on disc two we have "Darkest Hour," only eighty years back in terms of inspiration but penned fully timeless, oblique, and universal, as if found, again, etched into parchment.

The words are placed upon a pageant of a mournful ballad, arguably Maiden's best of a scant and cherished few, with guitar soloing risen to the challenge, drenched in soul like David Gilmour.

Then it's the boss planting his flag, demonstrating who is the victor in all the battles inside the band (well, Bruce) and with the business. He's the sole author of the last three songs, each over ten minutes long, and none delivering any sorts of bells and whistles. Two of them are exquisitely wartime British of melody, with the middle one taking us back to "Rime of the Ancient Mariner" and "Powerslave." As I turn the deeper discussion over to our trio of troopers, if this is the way Steve Harris chooses to retire Iron Maiden as the most globally beloved heavy metal band of all time, he has done it utterly on his own terms.

MARTIN POPOFF: For openers, what is Iron Maiden's mandate on *Senjutsu*? Why do they do what they do and what is the appeal to the band's clearly large fanbase?
MARTY FRIEDMAN: I've come to the conclusion that Iron Maiden is the type of band that has a formula that the fans love very much and can't break away from. And I think it's all on Bruce, his talent, charisma, and his tackling of the lyrics that makes the whole thing work. Is that a pretty fair assessment? I mean, I noticed that the vocals are fantastic. I have no idea what he's talking about, but the people, the fans of Iron Maiden, they understand those lyrics and those themes and motifs, various warrior and conflict motifs, I guess. Their fans relate to it in such a deep way that it keeps Iron Maiden right at the top. I mean, it's them and Metallica, really, who are the only two at that level. And I'm completely convinced that it's Bruce Dickinson's talent that has put them there.
RICH DAVENPORT: I thought they pushed the envelope a little more on this one. I enjoy *The Book of Souls*, but with this one, I'd say it's an album that demands your attention more. It rewards you by presenting the trademark elements of Maiden's style in different contexts in terms of the arrangements and in terms of the rhythms and the Celtic melodies and the twin leads. There's a lot of familiar Iron Maiden traits, but the way they're assembled is more imaginative.
KIRSTEN ROSENBERG: I agree; it's not an easy first listen. I wouldn't call it radio-friendly or casual listening. But that's Iron Maiden, and God bless them. Thematically, they are as intense as ever. I read a funny quote from Bruce, where he said that they wrote about the usual shit grumpy old men complain about, about the crap state of the world, basically. There's war and doom of all kinds—it's very dark.

Bruce calls for a co-pilot at the Tons of Rock festival at the Ekebergsletta field in Oslo, Norway, on June 23, 2022. The show took place during the second half of the four-year *Legacy of the Beast World Tour.*

POPOFF: As the vocalist in the Iron Maidens, how would you assess Bruce's performance on the record?

ROSENBERG: It's a bit different than on previous records. First of all, there's no improvising. There's no yelping or oohing and aahing, nothing like that. But he sounds amazing. His delivery is controlled, measured, almost stately. And there are some beautiful extended notes. But yeah, none of that improvisational, off-the-cuff, kind of wild rock/metal-style vocalizing. You don't hear the air raid siren so much on this record. Maybe that's intentioned, but we are talking about someone who was sixty-three at the time. So it's an older voice plus one that has recovered from throat cancer. I would imagine going for some of those super-high notes is more of a challenge, or maybe he's just bored of that. All those guys were evolving. But it's a different approach. Also, a lot of the vocals are in two-part harmony; it's him harmonizing with himself and it works. It fits with the music, which is dark, moody, and cinematic, soundtrack-like in places. So it's fitting that his delivery is somber and serious.

DAVENPORT: Especially since he's recovered from cancer, I think Bruce has done an incredible job. I don't think the cancer has taken a toll on his voice. Iron Maiden strike me very much like The Who, in the context of Roger Daltrey doing tours in

between Who tours. One was called the *Use It or Lose It Tour*, and there's a parallel here. Maiden did a lot of touring, with this rough pattern of new album tour followed by a legacy tour. I would imagine that's a factor in sustaining his voice at the level it's at.

POPOFF: I thought the album art was a nice change, with the understated red-and-black palette.
DAVENPORT: Yes, it's superb and grabs your attention. And the samurai theme is a perfect fit to Eddie's menacing character and personality. I read that the artist said he intentionally didn't go for the obvious elements of the samurai uniform style because he wanted to show more body, rather than cover him up. So yeah, it's one of those where I opened up that packaging and thought, man, I would buy a T-shirt of that inside [gatefold] Eddie as well as the front—both of them—and it really struck me that at my age, that's saying something about the quality of the illustration.
ROSENBERG: I love the art, although this is going to sound blasphemous as an Iron Maiden fan, but I'm not particularly drawn to monster and zombie imagery. But Eddie as a samurai totally works.

The team minus Janick. Dave Murray and Adrian Smith delivering a twin lead on the *Legacy of the Beast World Tour*.

POPOFF: Okay, well, into the album and Maiden hit us with one of their more nontraditional openers.

DAVENPORT: Yeah, "Senjutsu" eases the album in nicely, shall we say. There [are] the single-stroke war drums, the ringing chords and the rumbling bass. The guitar riff is quite simple and the vocal stays with it. I love the way it builds. There's a more melodic section that comes after. The vocal melody initially stays close to the riff and then counters it, which is quite an interesting and intelligent use of song arrangement.

FRIEDMAN: There's no literal or specific Japanese meaning to "Senjutsu," but it refers to the techniques and artistry of war. I thought the song sounded great at the beginning, but it was about seven minutes too long for me [*laughs*]. I mean, it just drones on one chord, but apparently whatever Bruce is saying in there is blowing people's minds and so it's working. So it's a good sounding track but it's basically just one chord. And it's nothing that I haven't heard twenty years ago from Iron Maiden or from Iron Maiden clones. Again, this is not a bad thing. I would love to be in a band that's like that, where you can just be yourself. That's all you have to be. You don't have to keep growing, you don't have to keep trying new things, you know what the fans like and you know how to deliver it. There's a sort of ultimate happiness in that.

CHAPTER 17

ROSENBERG: Of course it's a great opener, and it's a great opener live, which I've had the privilege to witness. You've got the Kodo drums, which set the tone. There's another funny quote from Bruce, because lyrically the song is about people defending their wall from northern invaders. And I read where Bruce asked Steve, who came up with the concept, whether he was deep into *Game of Thrones* at this time, which Steve denies. But yes, it roars out of the gates. As for the title, loosely translated, it's the art of war. But the word also embodies trickery or even magical tools or abilities. So it gets kind of mystical.

POPOFF: Next, we have "Stratego," a nice, tight, five minutes of up-tempo Maiden gallop.
ROSENBERG: Yes, love the gallop. Lyrically, it sounds like it's written from the perspective of a warrior. Then again, "Stratego" is also a military chess kind of board game. It's part of a great one-two-three-punch to open the album, and that's what they did live too, when I saw them.
DAVENPORT: Nice beat from Nicko, with punchy, rapid-fire bass drums, smart chord changes, sinister, unsettling vibe to the guitar melody. It's not twinned. There's a low, aggressive vocal from Bruce. There's a different hook line that comes in after the chorus. As for Steve's bass, and what Kevin Shirley does for him, it's a full, contemporary rendering of his traditional sound. It's so pronounced with Steve that I can see it being a bit of a love/hate thing for some people. I just take it for granted as part of the Maiden aesthetic. I think the bass is in a much better place since they've been working with Kevin Shirley, than it was on the two albums that Steve produced. It didn't strike me as obtrusive on this one.
ROSENBERG: I don't notice much difference in terms of production. Kevin's been at the helm for the past few albums, and he does a great mix. He's down for all the complexities. From what I've read, it takes a long time to record these songs. There's a lot of moving parts here.

POPOFF: "The Writing on the Wall" was an advance single, which, unsurprisingly, attracted much chatter on the Internet, with a lot of fans calling it a southern rock song!
DAVENPORT: Some parts of it I love and some parts of it, I'm not sure. Perhaps a bold choice for a single because it's not the most immediate track on the album. The introduction is at quite a gradual pace, like you say, with a sort of spaghetti western kind of southern rock–sounding riff at the beginning, quite bluesy, which is very unusual for

Maiden, followed by a more typical Maiden riff. But the chorus kind of makes up for that. I can see why it perhaps didn't grab people and was a little contentious.

Man, new Iron Maiden music always breaks the Internet, as they say [*laughs*]. I mean, you get your Di'Anno fans and other factions. By dint of the fact they're such a huge band and because they've been going for so long, it can inspire really strong opinions. With a band of this stature, there's always going to be negativity. And then you'll get people who love everything or people who prefer certain eras. It can get quite fiery.

ROSENBERG: Kudos to them with their marketing and the whole Belshazzar's Feast reference. I was like, "what?! What is that?" I actually had to look that up. It's a biblical story that influenced "The Writing on the Wall." At the music end, this one takes a few listens, but lyrically, I love it. There's an apocalyptic *Mad Max* kind of vision there. And I love anything that reminds us about how we're totally destroying the planet. So yeah, I'm going to call this an environmental song.

FRIEDMAN: I heard that acoustic intro and remember thinking, well, this is different. And then they threw the acoustic thing completely away and went straight into the song. So I didn't really know the purpose of that. Sometimes I listen to them and I think they're making these seven-minute songs just to make them long. Sometimes with long songs, you feel these huge peaks and valleys and big shifts in excitement, where there'll be a big build-up to a climax and then drop you off a cliff—Opeth does that sometimes. But sometimes when I listen to Iron Maiden, I feel like they're just tacking on these riffs from a cassette. It's like, "Okay, we've got six, seven minutes, now we're done," kind of thing. And that was the case with a few songs on this, although "The Writing on the Wall" is only a bit over six minutes.

But that intro, and this debate over the classic rock vibe of the song, the fans get really impassioned over stuff like that. Those things stand out. To me, they've got their trademark and they're killing it. But if you read the YouTube comments, it's people saying that this has touched their soul in ways I've never experienced. Or that the second verse brought them to tears, and things like that. This is because they're doing what they do and they're the only ones who can do it that way. I definitely respect that.

POPOFF: Speaking of long songs, next is "Lost in a Lost World," the first of four sole Steve Harris credits.

DAVENPORT: Yes, this is one I really like. It's got a synth-y texture at the beginning and acoustic guitars. There's a film soundtrack vibe, it's initially simple but effective and there's a good vocal melody. You've got these ghostly, distant choral voices doing the backing vocals, and then it switches to an aggressive triplet sort of riff, but the beat flows really well. Steve and Nicko are a great rhythm section here, with an emphasis on displaced beats but then a switch into a big four/four rhythm section. That's a rhythmic trick they've used before, but "Lost in a Lost World" offers a fresh angle. Plus, the solos are really good; they're not pointless showboating.

ROSENBERG: Steve's lyrics are about the plight of the Native American Indians, their genocide, basically, which is a theme they've explored in the past. Musically, the song follows the Maiden patterning of long mellow intro and long mellow outro, with a mid-paced full-band rock track in the middle. That notion has served them, clearly, because they've always written what they want to write and say what they want to say, and how they want to say it. And yet, really, aren't they bigger than ever? Of course, we think of Iron Maiden in their heyday—well, quote unquote, heyday—but they're bigger than ever, in terms of their fanbase and headlining festival after festival after festival. Yeah, it is different. I'm dating myself terribly here, but I grew up with the *Powerslave* album. Do I miss some of that? Yeah, I do. I long for a bit more variation of tempo. Because it seems like much of the music now is midtempo, along with the slow builds and slow fades.

POPOFF: On cue, here comes a shorter one, with "Days of Future Past" clocking in at four minutes. It's funny, though, I find the chords kind of rootsy and traditional, along with some added hair on the guitar tone.

DAVENPORT: Yeah, those are some heavy chords at the beginning. Bruce goes to a higher, more aggressive vocal melody, and then there's a majestic half-time tempo chorus, which is typical Maiden. Towards the end of it, Bruce gets some incredibly high vocals in. It's familiar and perhaps overly so in this case, but there's plenty going on.

ROSENBERG: This one's kind of based on *Constantine*, which was a graphic novel, and a movie with Keanu Reeves. And of course, I like the theme because it's also about a narcissistic and vengeful God. There's a great line in there: "Waiting for the judgment, but the judgment never ends."

POPOFF: "The Time Machine" is my favorite on the album, given its proggy riff, as well as Nicko's sort of swaying, swinging beat.

DAVENPORT: Yeah, definitely. The riff at the beginning is quite unusual for them. Plus, there are acoustic and electric guitars put together. Quite an intriguing atmosphere they conjure, and quite a theatrical delivery from Bruce, where he's both in unison and in harmony with the riff. And you're right, there's some unusual rhythms going on from Nicko and Steve, which work really well. They're pushing themselves.

ROSENBERG: Exactly, I'd call this proggy too, and it's got lyrics that are quite eerie, and a departure from the war and battle and bloodshed stuff, yet still with plenty of gloom and doom [*laughs*].

POPOFF: Over to disc two, I'm surprised to say that "Darkest Hour" is my second-favorite track on the album, because it's a ballad, and a somewhat bluesy one at that.

DAVENPORT: Yes, very well done. The slow tempo of this reminded me a bit of "Children of the Damned," but not too close. Very good bridge and a huge chorus, not obvious again, with the way the chorus flows melodically. Plus, it stays on one resolute rhythm, and there's some awesome soloing with kind of a Wishbone Ash feel, which I know is one of the band's influences. Somehow, they keep it lively despite that tempo and it doesn't outstay its welcome.

ROSENBERG: This one's a nice a salute to Winston Churchill. It opens with the sound of waves crashing on the beach, which of course hearkens back to D-Day, or at least it does for me. It's another theme they've touched on before, with things like "Aces High."

POPOFF: And then we're into this trio of long songs all credited solely to Steve, beginning with "Death of the Celts."

DAVENPORT: Right, and this was one of the long intros I don't think works. It's too similar to "The Clansman" for me, especially in view of the adjacent lyrical theme. It picks up in tempo, although it's still sort of relaxed, almost swinging. There's a Thin Lizzy "Black Rose" feel to the Celtic melodies and the trading of licks. This is one where it's overly familiar, or it feels like a revisitation, the same way that "Tailgunner" went over the same ground as "Aces High." I just found that a bit of a weak move, with Maiden being derivative of their own stuff.

ROSENBERG: Right, here's where you just sit down and get whatever you're drinking handy and be prepared to dig in [*laughs*]. And I agree with Rich: that's a theme we've explored in the past.

POPOFF: And Marty, what are your views on Kevin Shirley's production values?

FRIEDMAN: I think they're dated, but it's obviously intentional. Iron Maiden is not the type of band that's going to say, "What's the latest technology? Let's try to adapt it into our music and forge new ways to reinvent the wheel." They do what they are good at doing. They know the sound they're going for. And I don't see them spending a lot of energy trying to keep up with the times. It's not like they have a track with autotune vocals and then one with the latest guitar techniques or effects.

Like I said, I think the sound is dated, but the production is not about sonic things. The production is probably, in my opinion, about allowing Bruce Dickinson to come forward and emote these lyrics that are quite complex, in my opinion, and make

regular people feel like they're enjoying it. Somebody said this the other day and it was the most brilliant thing ever. I don't want you to take this the wrong way, but when I think of stuff like this, it's created in such a way that it makes normal people feel like they're listening to something very deep and they understand it. When they hear these words—which, yes, on this song are Steve's—they're really feeling depth. They're like, "this is poetic. Tears are coming to my eyes and I'm getting goosebumps."

And Bruce and Steve are doing this both with some very difficult subject matter. And so I think Kevin Shirley's production is designed to make sure that Bruce is heard and clearly heard, and to make sure that the content projects the way he's intending to say it and that it's understandable. He's keeping his eye on the ball; he's keeping the eye on where the action is. But sonically, sure, I mean, it sounds like it could have been done twenty years ago, easily.

POPOFF: Okay, next is "The Parchment." What are your thoughts on this one?

DAVENPORT: Right, so here we get kind of ominous Eastern synth textures and a slow chug at the beginning, with a diminished kind of Phrygian scale used on the riff. There's lots of space in the note choices, and eastern touches in the rhythm as well. Again, we're into familiar territory, with both the lyrics and the music taking me back to *Powerslave*.

Janick Gers in his role
as top Maiden merch
salesman, in front
of *Senjutsu*-themed
pagoda structure.

ROSENBERG: Yes, an Egyptian feel to this one, and there's a reference to Parthian in there, which relates the song to an ancient Iranian empire. Again, slow intro, hypnotic in the middle, lots of musical themes, evocative of something like "To Tame a Land." But it totally changes and doesn't end so-called "Egyptian" [*laughs*]. It goes off on different musical and guitar explorations. I think everyone was spot-on on this record, but even as a vocalist. I was really enjoying a lot of these guitar solos—there are a lot of them and they are very well-done. Although back to Bruce's vocals, at the end of "The Parchment," I love his last vocal note in that song. That's the highlight of the album for me. It's very long and it's not high but it's beautiful. It just kind of descends or cascades. It's long and it cascades down—lovely.

POPOFF: Last track is "Hell on Earth," and Maiden bring back the spirited—albeit recurringly Celtic—gallop.
DAVENPORT: Yes, I like the way the guitars and the synths play together. The beginning has a proggier kind of vibe, with complex chord changes and rhythms and it all flows.

Another one with a Wishbone Ash influence. The tempo changes are really good. It's structured quite unconventionally. There's a big hook line that comes in later on when you least expect it. It works really well, but it's not your average metal chorus. I think the three guitar players here are fantastic. It sounds live, as if they've kind of tracked it live. In other words, there's a lot of live energy to it, with an aggressive delivery from Bruce, and more obtuse chord progression towards the end. And then it slows down and gets atmospheric.

ROSENBERG: The ones where Steve has sole writing credit have dark and doomy themes. It's like, "Steve, are you feeling okay?" But no, that's nothing too out-of-character for him. This one addressed the concept of armed children, children of war. I've heard people call this song somewhat hopeful, but I didn't really get a hopeful vibe off it. But again, it's another one about the current state of geopolitics. If you go through all the lyrics, they are really quite weighty, and for the most part they're kept mysterious enough so that you don't know what time period they're addressing, which keeps them, I guess by definition, timeless.

POPOFF: Alright, any closing thoughts?

FRIEDMAN: Well, I want to reiterate this point I made about the band's consistency, and how *Senjutsu* delivers on this pact that they have with their fans. With people who love Iron Maiden and follow them, it's like AC/DC. I love it and I don't want them to change. Musically, I am hearing the exact same things that I heard back at the third album. But the fans recognize every slight deviation. If you're a fan, you think it sounds different. I'm a big Ramones fan, and even though all the songs have the exact same chords, I will notice a little pick scratch that's different on a live version from the studio version, right? Because I'm nuts. So an Iron Maiden fan will listen to this album and say, but no, there's these little nuances that are new. And that's the best thing that you can wish for as a band. That's why they're a super band. They don't stray off their formula and I have the ultimate respect for that. But like I say, after listening to it again, it dawned on me that Bruce is really the centerpiece of the whole thing.

DAVENPORT: Well, I'll just add that one important part of Iron Maiden's legacy is that their commercial impact—as well as [their] impact on the reputation of heavy metal—has been huge, as they've evolved, and especially since Bruce came back. It can't be understated. When they did the *Ed Hunter* tour and the reunion tour, that did a huge favor for every old-school metal band. And I know, because on a very small scale, I was playing in an old-school metal band throughout the late '90s into about 2001.

And we were trying to not jump on any bandwagon, but maybe add a bit more of a Metallica feel to the guitar sound and not sound like a throwback. But we just could not get arrested. And we had some label interest, actually from Sanctuary, but we were too old-fashioned, basically. We actually got a review that said, "This is what used to be called heavy metal," in 2001 [*laughs*].

And then when Maiden came back, that style of metal got a huge boost. You gradually saw traditional metal bands doing a lot better. And some of the ones who'd stayed together through the '90s and gone grunge, they eventually edged back more towards the old school, like Queensrÿche, for example. I remember going to the Download Festival in 2003 and Maiden headlined it and the rest of it was nu-metal. And within a couple of years, you know, you had Priest and Kiss and now it's a very diverse festival. But there were a lot of old-school bands who've come back in Maiden's wake and done very well.

Another part of their legacy is that Maiden promoted the idea that you can be progressive without being a prog band. Plus, they had a lot to do with the development of traditional metal throughout the '80s. And then, since they've come back, I think it shows what a good manager Rod Smallwood is, because he's managed it very skillfully. What we were saying earlier about celebrating the legacy and moving on with new music, I mean, they've not done a *St. Anger*, for example. They've not chased any bandwagons. Since Bruce came back, certainly, they've not made any albums that have damaged the legacy.

So I think in terms of defining what we all think of as old-school metal, and in terms of the songwriting, the musicianship and the vocal style as well, they've set the blueprint in a lot of ways. And again, in the reunion era, they've certainly cemented the commercial and merchandising legacy too, and added to it very well. And then on the records, they've taken the progressive element even further, and usually with great success. A lot of people who haven't kept up with the band perhaps don't realize how progressive they got in the new era and how different they are from the sort of traditional metal sound they're associated with from the '80s. So yes, overall, even from the approachability of the guys in the band through to the business and always making records and celebrating traditional metal—all of it—I'd say they've been the definitive band in terms of how to do all that relatively gracefully and successfully and with integrity. If only we could all be doing so much and working so hard in our advanced years as Steve and Bruce and those guys have been managing. Really, we should take it as a source of inspiration.

About the Author

At approximately 7,900 (with over 7,000 appearing in his books), **MARTIN POPOFF** has unofficially written more record reviews than anybody in the history of music writing across all genres. Additionally, Martin has penned approximately 115 books on hard rock, heavy metal, classic rock, prog, punk, and record collecting. He was editor-in-chief of the now-retired *Brave Words & Bloody Knuckles*, Canada's foremost heavy metal publication for fourteen years, and has also contributed to *Revolver*, *Guitar World*, *Goldmine*, *Record Collector*, bravewords.com, lollipop.com, and hardradio.com, with many record label band biographies and liner notes to his credit as well.

Additionally, Martin has been a regular contractor to Banger Films, having worked for two years as a researcher on the award-winning documentary *Rush: Beyond the Lighted Stage*, on the writing and research team for the eleven-episode *Metal Evolution*, and on the ten-episode *Rock Icons*, both for VH1 Classic. Additionally, Martin is the writer of the original metal genre chart used in *Metal: A Headbanger's Journey* and throughout the *Metal Evolution* episodes.

Then there's his audio podcast, *History in Five Songs with Martin Popoff*, and the YouTube channel he runs with Marco D'Auria, *The Contrarians*. The community of guest analysts seen on *The Contrarians* has provided the pool of speakers used across the pages of this very book. Martin resides in Toronto and can be reached through martinp@inforamp.net or martinpopoff.com.

About the Contributors

BLAZE BAYLEY is a singer/songwriter, proudly birthed in Birmingham, England. Having started his professional music career in Wolfsbane in 1984, his career elevated to global heights when he joined Iron Maiden with whom he released two albums and toured worldwide between 1995 and 1998. After leaving Iron Maiden, Blaze embarked on a solo career, during which he has released nine albums and has enjoyed an enviable reputation as one of the hardest-working artists touring worldwide. In 2015 Blaze celebrated the fifteenth anniversary of his first solo release, *Silicon Messiah*, and in 2016 saw a significant worldwide resurgence of interest in his career, not least with the release of the first two instalments of his *Infinite Entanglement* trilogy. A third emerged in 2018, capping off a project that serves as Blaze's crowning achievement.

RICH DAVENPORT is a UK-based music writer (*Record Collector, Rock Candy, Powerplay, Fireworks, Metal Shock Finland*), musician (Atomkraft, Radio Stars, Martin Gordon, Black Sheets of Rain, See Red) and radio DJ (*Total Rock*). A fan of Iron Maiden since buying the "Run to the Hills" seven-inch single at the age of nine in February 1982, he still maintains that the B-side, "Total Eclipse," would have been a better fit on *Number of the Beast* than "Invaders." Rich has seen the band live with three different lineups and even managed to catch a rare show by Adrian Smith's short-lived, unrecorded solo band in 1992. His favorite incarnation of Eddie is from the *Piece of Mind* album cover.

For forty-three years, **BOBBY "BLITZ" ELLSWORTH** has united and educated the heavy metal community with his love for the music and for the fans as the lead singer of New York thrash legends Overkill, who in 2023, issued their twentieth studio album, *Scorched*.

MARTY FRIEDMAN began his career as a Shrapnel solo recording artist and later joined forces with Jason Becker to form the unrivalled dual guitar unit, Cacophony. Amassing worldwide acclaim as a guitar superstar, he came to the attention of Megadeth, joining the band in 1990. Racking up sales of over ten million records with Megadeth—in the process, shredding his way through *Rust in Peace*, one of the top thrash albums of all time—Friedman continued to record solo records, often embarking on adventurous musical forays far removed from his work with Megadeth, including an album with Golden Globe winner Kitaro. In a bold move, he left the legendary Megadeth to pursue new musical goals and has succeeded tremendously. Friedman's many accomplishments make him currently the only musician to be a fixture in the top class of the Japanese domestic as well as international music scene. His music performance on national TV with the Tokyo Philharmonic Orchestra and charting high with his own music and with Japan's top artists, has spurred Friedman into new celebrity territory. Long residing in Tokyo, Friedman has become a television celebrity appearing as a regular on five major networks, and on mainstream TV programs on nearly a daily basis across Japanese airwaves. In North America, however, Friedman is simply known as one of heavy metal's greatest guitarists, which he proves on regular tours. Friedman's fourteenth solo album, *Tokyo Jukebox 3*, was issued in 2021.

Born in Japan, **MATT HEAFY** is lead vocalist and guitarist for well-regarded Florida-based thrash metal outfit Trivium. Trivium currently have issued ten records, all but the debut for Roadrunner Records. Trivium's third album, *The Crusade*, was promoted through tour dates supporting Iron Maiden, a fond memory for Heafy, a lifelong Maiden fan.

"Metal" **TIM HENDERSON** is Canada's top heavy metal mover and shaker. From McMaster University (where he gathered up two BA degrees), Henderson began promoting heavy metal on college radio, moving on to the Toronto flagship HMV superstore, where he ran what was ranked as one of the world's biggest heavy metal departments. Internships at MuchMusic's Power Hour followed as well as various radio stints and a long run at M.E.A.T. magazine, Drew Masters' respected metal magazine of the late '80s and early '90s. Henderson's main claim to fame, however, would be the founding of *Brave Words & Bloody Knuckles*, in print from 1994 to 2008. The magazine went digital virtually at the start of the Internet as well, continuing to this day at which point BraveWords.com has become one of the world's top handful of heavy metal sites. A lifelong Maiden devotee, Henderson has interviewed and met the band over twenty times.

CHRIS JERICHO grew up in Winnipeg, Canada, dreaming of becoming a rock star and professional wrestler. He would first conquer the world of professional wrestling, honing his craft all over the world, specifically in Mexico, Germany, and Japan, before landing permanently in America as part of ECW in 1996. He would then transition to WCW, and then to World Wrestling Entertainment where he is still an imperative member of the WWE roster to this day. While dominating the world of professional wrestling, Jericho found the time to pursue his other dream of becoming a rock star. Founding member of rap metal band Stuck Mojo, Rich Ward met up with Chris in San Antonio, Texas, in 1999 and invited him to jam with his band. This invite birthed a band devoted to producing eight albums of what can best be described as arena rock soaked in blood. Since its inception, Fozzy has gone on to tour with acts such as Shinedown, Metallica, and Avenged Sevenfold. Chris has also become a *New York Times* bestselling author while writing three autobiographies. He has been a frequent contributor to VH1 specials, G4's Attack of the Show!, and was a contestant on *Dancing with the Stars*. In 2013, Chris started his own podcast, *Talk is Jericho*, a fortress of solitude for his never-ending creative juices.

JIMMY KAY is the producer, editor and host of the online YouTube show *The Metal Voice.com*, on which he has done over 1,000 shows, reviewed hundreds of albums and interviewed most major hard rock and metal bands including Judas Priest, Scorpions, Saxon, Accept, Iron Maiden, Anthrax, Slayer, Exodus, Blind Guardian, King Diamond, Overkill, Queensrÿche, Nightwish, and many more. Kay has also produced documentaries on Blaze Bayley, Graham Bonnet, and Riot, and has covered major metal festivals and events all around the world including Heavy MTL, Sweden Rock, The NAMM Show, Cathouse Live festival, The Hall of Heavy Metal History Awards, and Motofiesta Festival.

SEAN KELLY is a Toronto-based guitarist, songwriter, author, educator, music director, and producer. Sean has toured the world as lead guitarist for Nelly Furtado and has recorded and/or toured with a number of award-winning artists, including Lee Aaron, Alan Frew, Helix, Gilby Clarke, Carole Pope and Rough Trade, Honeymoon Suite, Emm Gryner, Howie D, Coney Hatch, The Canadian Brass, The Kenyan Boys Choir, Wild Strawberries, and many others. He was cast in Dee Snider's *Rock & Roll Christmas Tale* as well as *Rock of Ages* and has authored the books *Metal on Ice: Tales from Canada's Hard Rock and Heavy Metal Heroes* and *Don't Call It Hair Metal*. Sean has twenty years experience as a vocal music teacher with the Toronto Catholic District School Board and is a graduate of the University of Toronto's Music Program, where he studied Classical Guitar under Eli Kassner.

Storied percussion legend **MIKE PORTNOY** is probably the first name that comes to mind when people thing of an heir to Neil Peart's "drummer's drummer" throne of distinction. Through his work with Adrenaline Mob, The Winery Dogs, myriad progressive acts over the years, and most notably Dream Theater, Mike has vaulted to the ranks of the handful of the most celebrated drummers in the media and drum community in history, or certainly at least in the last twenty-five years. Mike is proud to have performed the entire *The Number of the Beast* album with Dream Theater, as well as having played on stage with both Paul Di'Anno and Bruce Dickinson.

FRANC POTVIN is a long-term Iron Maiden fan and expert, and past guest guitarist for Blaze Bayley. He first became aware of the band back in 1980 but did not become a devoted disciple until Iron Maiden played his hometown of Chicoutimi, Quebec, back in 1983. He's been a diehard since and has seen and met the band on numerous occasions, witnessing them live dozens of times. He now lives in Kitchener, Ontario where he juggles a corporate job by day and all things music and metal by night.

KIRSTEN ROSENBERG is a noted animal rights activist, having worked with both the Genesis Awards and The Animal Rights Agenda. She is also the former co-owner of Sticky Fingers, an all-vegan bakery in Washington, D.C. Rosenberg performs as Bruce Chickinson, lead singer in America's all-female and most famous and ass-kicking Iron Maiden tribute band, The Iron Maidens.

BRIAN SLAGEL is the legendary stocker of heavy metal albums at Oz Records. He also is the founder of one of the first metal-mad fanzines, *The New Heavy Metal Revue*. While giving Metallica their first break by putting them on his first record project, landmark compilation *Metal Massacre*, Slagel went on to found Metal Blade Records, the world's longest-running heavy metal record label, o'er which he still lords over enthusiastically as its CEO.

NITA STRAUSS was recently ranked #1 in Guitar World's "10 Female Guitarists You Should Know." Formerly performing as Mega Murray with The Iron Maidens, in 2014, Strauss replaced Orianthi in Alice Cooper's band. She is now a successful solo artist.

AHMET ZAPPA is a musician with three albums to his credit, as well as a TV and film actor, and author of a novel for young readers. As the son of music legend Frank Zappa, he is the executor of the Zappa Family Trust.

Author Bibliography

Kiss at 50 (2023)

The Who and Quadrophenia (2023)

Dominance and Submission: The Blue Öyster Cult Canon (2023)

Wild Mood Swings: Disintegrating The Cure Album by Album (2023)

AC/DC at 50 (2023)

Pink Floyd and The Dark Side of the Moon: 50 Years (2022)

Killing the Dragon: Dio in the '90s and 2000s (2022)

Feed My Frankenstein: Alice Cooper, the Solo Years (2022)

Easy Action: The Original Alice Cooper Band (2022)

Lively Arts: The Damned Deconstructed (2022)

Yes: A Visual Biography II: 1982–2022 (2022)

Bowie at 75 (2022)

Dream Evil: Dio in the '80 (2022)

Judas Priest: A Visual Biography (2022)

UFO: A Visual Biography (2022)

Hawkwind: A Visual Biography (2021)

Loud 'n' Proud: Fifty Years of Nazareth (2021)

Yes: A Visual Biography (2021)

Uriah Heep: A Visual Biography (2021)

Driven: Rush in the '90s and "In the End" (2021)

Flaming Telepaths: Imaginos Expanded and Specified (2021)

Rebel Rouser: A Sweet User Manual (2021)

The Fortune: On the Rocks with Angel (2020)

Van Halen: A Visual Biography (2020)

Limelight: Rush in the '80s (2020)

Thin Lizzy: A Visual Biography (2020)

Empire of the Clouds: Iron Maiden in the 2000s (2020)

Blue Öyster Cult: A Visual Biography (2020)

Anthem: Rush in the '70s (2020)

Denim and Leather: Saxon's First Ten Years (2020)

Black Funeral: Into the Coven with Mercyful Fate (2020)

Satisfaction: 10 Albums That Changed My Life (2019)

Holy Smoke: Iron Maiden in the '90s (2019)

Sensitive to Light: The Rainbow Story (2019)

Where Eagles Dare: Iron Maiden in the '80s (2019)

Aces High: The Top 250 Heavy Metal Songs of the '80s (2019)

Judas Priest: Turbo 'til Now (2019)

Born Again! Black Sabbath in the Eighties and Nineties (2019)

Riff Raff: The Top 250 Heavy Metal Songs of the '70s (2018)

Lettin' Go: UFO in the '80s and '90s (2018)

Queen: Album by Album (2018)

Unchained: A Van Halen User Manual (2018)

Iron Maiden: Album by Album (2018)

Sabotage! Black Sabbath in the Seventies (2018)

Welcome to My Nightmare: 50 Years of Alice Cooper (2018)

Judas Priest: Decade of Domination (2018)

Popoff Archive–6: American Power Metal (2018)

Popoff Archive–5: European Power Metal (2018)

The Clash: All the Albums, All the Songs (2018)

Pink Floyd: Album by Album (2018)

Lights Out: Surviving the '70s with UFO (2018)

AC/DC: Album by Album (2017)

Led Zeppelin: Song by Song (2017)

Tornado of Souls: Thrash's Titanic Clash (2017)

Caught in a Mosh: The Golden Era of Thrash (2017)

Metal Collector: Gathered Tales from Headbangers (2017)

Rush: Album by Album (2017)

Beer Drinkers and Hell Raisers: The Rise of Motörhead (2017)

Hit the Lights: The Birth of Thrash (2017)

Popoff Archive–4: Classic Rock (2017)

Popoff Archive–3: Hair Metal (2017)

Popoff Archive–2: Progressive Rock (2016)

Popoff Archive–1: Doom Metal (2016)

Rock the Nation: Montrose, Gamma and Ronnie Redefined (2016)

Punk Tees: The Punk Revolution in 125 T-Shirts (2016)

Metal Heart: Aiming High with Accept (2016)

Ramones at 40 (2016)

Time and a Word: The Yes Story (2016)

Kickstart My Heart: A Mötley Crüe Day-by-Day (2015)

This Means War: The Sunset Years of the NWOBHM (2015)

Wheels of Steel: The Explosive Early Years of the NWOBHM (2015)

Swords and Tequila: Riot's Classic First Decade (2015)

Who Invented Heavy Metal? (2015)

Sail Away: Whitesnake's Fantastic Voyage (2015)

Live Magnetic Air: The Unlikely Saga of the Superlative Max Webster (2014)

Steal Away the Night: An Ozzy Osbourne Day-by-Day (2014)

The Big Book of Hair Metal (2014)

Sweating Bullets: The Deth and Rebirth of Megadeth (2014)

Smokin' Valves: A Headbanger's Guide to 900 NWOBHM Records (2014)

The Art of Metal (co-edit with Malcolm Dome; 2013)

2 Minutes to Midnight: An Iron Maiden Day-By-Day (2013)

Metallica: The Complete Illustrated History (2013); update and reissue (2016)

Rush: The Illustrated History (2013); update and reissue (2016)

Ye Olde Metal: 1979 (2013)

Scorpions: Top of the Bill (2013); updated and reissued as *Wind of Change: The Scorpions Story* (2016)

Epic Ted Nugent (2012)

Fade to Black: Hard Rock Cover Art of the Vinyl Age (2012)

It's Getting Dangerous: Thin Lizzy 81-12 (2012)

We Will Be Strong: Thin Lizzy 76-81 (2012)

Fighting My Way Back: Thin Lizzy 69-76 (2011)

The Deep Purple Royal Family: Chain of Events '80–'11 (2011)

The Deep Purple Royal Family: Chain of Events Through '79 (2011); reissued as The *Deep Purple Family Year by Year (to 1979)* (2016)

Black Sabbath FAQ (2011)

The Collector's Guide to Heavy Metal: Volume 4: The '00s (2011; co-authored with David Perri)

Goldmine Standard Catalog of American Records 1948–1991, 7th Edition (2010)

Goldmine Record Album Price Guide, 6th Edition (2009)

Goldmine 45 RPM Price Guide, 7th Edition (2009)

A Castle Full of Rascals: Deep Purple '83–'09 (2009)

Worlds Away: Voivod and the Art of Michel Langevin (2009)

Ye Olde Metal: 1978 (2009)

Gettin' Tighter: Deep Purple '68–'76 (2008)

All Access: The Art of the Backstage Pass (2008)

Ye Olde Metal: 1977 (2008)

Ye Olde Metal: 1976 (2008)

Judas Priest: Heavy Metal Painkillers (2007)

Ye Olde Metal: 1973 to 1975 (2007)

The Collector's Guide to Heavy Metal: Volume 3: The Nineties (2007)

Ye Olde Metal: 1968 to 1972 (2007)

Run For Cover: The Art of Derek Riggs (2006)

Black Sabbath: Doom Let Loose (2006)

Dio: Light Beyond the Black (2006)

The Collector's Guide to Heavy Metal: Volume 2: The Eighties (2005)

Rainbow: English Castle Magic (2005)

UFO: Shoot Out the Lights (2005)

The New Wave of British Heavy Metal Singles (2005)

Blue Öyster Cult: Secrets Revealed! (2004); update and reissue (2009); updated and reissued as *Agents of Fortune: The Blue Oyster Cult Story* (2016)

Contents Under Pressure: 30 Years of Rush at Home & Away (2004)

The Top 500 Heavy Metal Albums of All Time (2004)

The Collector's Guide to Heavy Metal: Volume 1: The Seventies (2003)

The Top 500 Heavy Metal Songs of All Time (2003)

Southern Rock Review (2001)

Heavy Metal: 20th Century Rock and Roll (2000)

The Goldmine Price Guide to Heavy Metal Records (2000)

The Collector's Guide to Heavy Metal (1997)

Riff Kills Man! 25 Years of Recorded Hard Rock & Heavy Metal (1993)

See martinpopoff.com for complete details and ordering information.

Index

A

AC/DC, 112, 121, 126, 259
"Aces High," 70, 72–74, 78, 91, 93, 120, 246, 256
Aerosmith, 121
"Afraid to Shoot Strangers," 78, 131–132, 140, 186
"Alexander the Great," 93–95, 97, 126
"The Angel and the Gambler," 156, 156–157, 165
Angel Witch, 22
"Another Life," 25
"The Assassin," 116, 126–127

B

"Back in the Village," 70, 75
Bayley, Blaze
    departure from band, 168–169
    entry into band, 142, 145, 147
    as singer, 148–152, 159–160, 169
    as songwriter, 143
    Steve Harris and, 168–169
    treatment of, 159–160, 162
    vocal issues of, 156, 169
"Be Quick or Be Dead," 131, 133, 134–135
Birch, Martin,
    co-producing role, 128
    Di'Anno and, 37
    The Number of the Beast and, 40
    as producer, 10, 22, 24–26, 28, 96, 111, 132
    as producer of other bands, 30
    sound of Iron Maiden and, 29–30
Black Sabbath, 10, 26, 28, 30, 44, 83
"Blood Brothers," 165, 166, 168, 174–175, 179
"Blood on the World's Hands," 149, 152
Blue Öyster Cult, 25, 30
"The Book of Souls," 241–243
The Book of Souls, 230, 232–235, 237–238, 240–245, 249
Bradstreet, Tim, 209
"Brave New World," 174
Brave New World, 104, 124, 164, 170, 172–179, 181–183, 186
"Brighter Than a Thousand Suns," 202, 210
"Bring Your Daughter . . . to the Slaughter," 55, 116, 121–123
Burr, Clive, 47, 49, 60

C

"Can I Play with Madness," 100, 104, 123
Card, Orson Scott, 103, 108
"Caught Somewhere in Time," 85, 93
"Chains of Misery," 128, 132
"Charlotte the Harlot," 10, 20
Charlotte the Harlot character, 29, 55, 88
"Childhood's End," 131
"Children of the Damned," 41, 53–54, 256
Churchill, Winston, 73–74, 256
"The Clairvoyant," 105, 108
"The Clansman," 80, 149, 160, 162–163, 256
"Coming Home," 214–215, 218, 221
"Como Estais Amigos," 157, 168
cover artwork, 11, 59, 73, 88, 91, 128, 145, 156, 184–185, 209–210, 214, 218, 234
Crack the Sky, 38
Crowley, Aleister, 105

D

"Dance of Death," 184, 197–198
Dance of Death, 160, 184–188, 190–191, 193–199
"Darkest Hour", 248, 256
"Days of Future Past," 248, 255
"Death of the Celts," 256
"Death or Glory," 234
Deep Purple, 28, 44, 83
"Deja-Vu," 85, 88, 94
Diamond Head, 22
Di'Anno, Paul
    departure from band and, 39, 40, 43
    as frontman, 8, 16–17
    Killers and, 28
    as singer, 16–18, 28, 31, 37, 67, 254
Dickinson, Bruce
    Accident of Birth, 170
    The Chemical Wedding, 170, 173
    departure from band, 141
    fencing and, 75–76
    as front man, 49
    literary inspirations of, 77
    as live presence, 199, 245
    move to join band and, 46
    on No Prayer for the Dying, 116
    personality of, 183
    reception of as lead singer, 43–45
    return to band, 124, 156, 170, 172, 260
    in Samson, 40, 43–44
    as singer, 33, 45, 50, 67, 97, 101, 120, 140, 151–152, 199, 246, 248–250, 252–253, 255–260
    solo career, 114, 141, 170, 172–173
    Somewhere in Time and, 85, 97
    as songwriter, 44, 46, 80, 101, 220–221, 232, 245
    Tattooed Millionaire, 114, 141
"Die with Your Boots On," 56, 67
"Different World," 202, 210
Dio, Ronnie James, 183
"Don't Look to the Eyes of a Stranger," 157, 166
"Dream of Mirrors," 164, 168, 172
"Drifter," 25
"The Duellists," 73, 75, 80

E

Ed Hunter (video game), 156, 164, 165
Eddie (mascot), 11, 22, 251
    Ed Hunter (video game) and, 156, 164, 165
    Ed Hunter (tour), 159
    Fear of the Dark cover, 128, 133
    and Killers, 29
    killing of Dickerson and, 145
    lobotomy of, 56–57, 64
    A Matter of Life and Death and, 209–210
    and other metal band mascots, 22–23
    "The Reincarnation of Benjamin Breeg" and, 206
    World Slavery Tour and, 73
Eddie Rips Up the World Tour, 200
"The Edge of Darkness," 154
"The Educated Fool," 159, 166
"El Dorado," 214–215, 218, 220–221
"Empire of the Clouds," 72, 233, 240–241
"The Evil That Men Do," 100, 108

F

"Face in the Sand," 185
"Fates Warning," 116, 125, 127
"Fear Is the Key," 131
"Fear of the Dark," 131, 139–140, 166, 190
Fear of the Dark, 112, 124, 128, 131–137, 139–141
"Final Frontier," 218, 219
The Final Frontier, 194, 210, 214–215, 218–221, 223, 226–229, 237

"Flash of the Blade," 70, 73, 75–76
Flight 666, 221
"Flight of Icarus," 56, 65
From Fear to Eternity, 215
"Futureal," 156–157, 160, 163–165

G
"Gangland," 40–41, 53
"Gates of Tomorrow," 190
"Genghis Khan," 31
Gers, Janick
    entry into band, 114
    as guitarist, 34, 123–124, 133–134,
        139, 223, 258
    on live presence of, 154–155, 177
    as songwriter, 114, 116, 128, 155, 211
    vocals of, 177
"Ghost of the Navigator," 178
Grant, Melvyn, 128, 133, 214, 218
"The Great Unknown," 237
Green, Nigel, 147
grunge, 114
guitar arrangements, 22, 34, 37–38, 50,
        81–82, 110–111, 134, 173, 190–191,
        196–197, 203, 226
guitar synthesizer, 86–87, 90, 112

H
hair metal, 92, 100, 114
"Hallowed Be Thy Name," 41, 46–47, 50, 53
Harris, Steve
    as bass player, 20–21, 33–34, 49, 68,
        96, 111, 195–196, 205, 244,
        246, 248–251, 253–254,
        256–257, 259, 260
    Blaze Bayley and, 168–169
    folk music inspiration, 210
    "Hallowed Be Thy Name" and, 50
    literary inspirations of, 72, 77
    No Prayer for the Dying and, 116, 118
    as original band member, 8
    on Paul Di'Anno, 39
    as producer, 128, 132–133, 160, 162,
        193–194, 229, 237
    progressive rock and, 20, 172
    progressive rock influence and, 31
    religious themes and, 197
    on *Seventh Son of a Seventh Son*,
        112–113
    Slagel on, 43
    as songwriter, 21, 24, 29, 31, 42, 55,
        80, 88, 95, 214, 232
    success of band and, 22

TV inspiration and, 54
writing on *The X Factor* and,
        142–143, 145, 147, 149
"Heaven Can Wait," 84, 87, 94–95
heavy metal, 86
    backlash against, 112
    black metal bands, 101
    hair metal, 92, 100, 114
    melodic death metal, 101
    New Wave of British Heavy Metal
        (NWOBHM), 8, 11, 14, 22,
        30–31, 83, 98, 112–113
    nu-metal, 181
    prog metal, 113
    thrash metal, 114
"Hell on Earth," 258
"Holy Smoke," 116, 119, 120
"Hooks in You," 116, 118, 121, 123

I
"I Live My Way," 143
"The Ides of March," 31
"If Eternity Should Fail," 230, 234–235, 237
"Infinite Dreams," 104–105
"Innocent Exile," 24–25, 32
"Invaders," 40, 53, 148
"Iron Maiden," 19
Iron Maiden (album), 8, 10–11, 13–14, 16,
        18–23, 37
"Isle of Avalon," 226–227

J
"Journeyman," 186
"Juanita," 94
"Judas Be My Guide," 139
Judas Priest, 10–11, 33–34, 86–87, 92,
        98, 260
"Judgement Day," 143
"Judgement of Heaven," 152–153
"Justice of the Peace," 143

K
Kenney, Michael, 156
keyboards, 100, 112, 119, 156
"Killers," 25, 32–33, 166
Killers, 13, 24–34, 37–39, 248

L
Lackey, John, 11
Led Zeppelin, 83
Legacy of the Beast World Tour, 250, 252
"The Legacy," 208
"Lightning Strikes Twice," 167
Live After Death, 214

"The Loneliness of the Long Distance
        Runner," 93–94
"The Longest Day," 203
"Lord of Light," 208
"Lord of the Flies," 143, 149–150
"Losfer Words," 82
"Lost in a Lost World," 248, 255

M
Maiden Japan (EP), 32, 246
Malone, Will, 8, 10
    Iron Maiden album and, 21
"Man on the Edge," 143, 151
"The Man Who Would be King," 218, 227
A Matter of Life and Death, 184, 194–195,
        200, 202–203, 205–206, 208–213
McBrain, Nicko, 47, 49
    as drummer, 57, 60, 62, 86, 111, 248,
        253–254, 256
    entry into band, 56
    on *A Matter of Life and Death*, 202
    personality of, 60, 97
    as songwriter, 185
    use of double bass, 185
Megadeth, 24, 37
Metal for Muthas, 8, 24
Metal for Muthas Tour, 11
Metallica, 22, 39, 83, 96, 126, 132,
        165–166, 249, 260
"Montségur," 184, 194, 196
"Moonchild," 93, 103–105, 110
"Mother of Mercy," 218, 228
"Mother Russia," 116, 119, 126–127
"Murders in the Rue Morgue," 24, 31, 33,
        54
Murray, Dave, 26–27, 34, 50, 81, 123–124,
        139, 223
music videos, 65, 135

N
"New Frontier," 190
New Wave of British Heavy Metal
        (NWOBHM), 8, 11, 14, 22, 30–31,
        83, 98, 112–113, 248
"No More Lies," 184, 190–191
"No Prayer for the Dying," 119
No Prayer for the Dying, 112, 114, 116,
        118–127, 132
"Nomad," 172
nu-metal, 181
"The Number of the Beast," 41, 53, 149, 190
The Number of the Beast, 29, 40–47,
        49–50, 53–55

O

occult, 105, 108
"Only the Good Die Young," 108
"Out of the Shadows," 206, 208
"Out of the Silent Planet," 178
Overkill, 13, 18, 22, 24
Ozzfest 2005, 179, 198, 203

P

"The Parchment", 246, 257–258
"Paschendale," 184, 194
Patchett, David, 184–185
"Phantom of the Opera," 10, 18, 27
Piece of Mind, 29, 56–60, 62–65, 67–69,
  72–73, 186
"The Pilgrim," 202, 210–211
political themes, 119, 125–126, 140, 157,
  168
"Powerslave," 72, 76, 249
Powerslave, 58, 70, 72–78, 80–83,
  255, 257
"The Prisoner," 41, 54
The Prisoner (TV show), 75, 77
"Prodigal Son," 24, 33
progressive rock, 77, 98, 190, 260
"The Prophecy," 105, 108
"Prowler," 10, 19, 27
"Public Enema Number One," 124–125
"Purgatory," 25

Q

Queensrÿche, 98, 132, 260
"Quest for Fire," 56

R

radio play, 93, 141, 206
"Rainmaker," 186–188, 190
"Reach Out," 75, 94
"The Red and the Black," 234, 242
"The Reincarnation of Benjamin Breeg,"
  200, 206
religious reaction, 55, 105
religious themes, 55, 65, 110, 116,
  196–197
"Remember Tomorrow," 10, 19–20, 53,
  125
"Revelations," 56, 58, 62, 67–68
reverb, 118
Riggs, Derek, 64–65, 98, 100, 128
"Rime of the Ancient Mariner," 70, 72,
  76–78, 80–81, 249
Rock in Rio, 181
Roy Z, 170, 172

"Run Silent Run Deep," 116, 127
"Run to the Hills," 41–42, 44–46, 53, 166,
  181
"Running Free," 10, 14, 16, 18

S

Samson, 40, 43–44, 46
Samson, Doug, 47
"Sanctuary," 8, 11, 17, 26, 37
"Satellite 15 . . . The Final Frontier," 214,
  218–219
"Sea of Madness," 85, 94–95
Senjutsu, 246–261
"Senjutsu", 252
"Seventh Son of a Seventh Son," 104
Seventh Son of a Seventh Son, 72, 84, 90,
  92, 94, 98, 100–101, 103–105, 108,
  110–113, 116, 118
"Shadows of the Valley," 244
Shakespeare, 108
Shirley, Kevin, 172, 173–174, 184, 191,
  193–194, 197, 200, 214, 228–229,
  246, 248, 253, 257
"Sign of the Cross," 80, 143, 148–149,
  151, 163
Slayer, 44
Smallwood, Rod, 8
  on cover art, 133
  hiring of Dickinson and, 40
  Piece of Mind and, 68
  success of band and, 22, 260
  Virtual XI and, 156
Smith, Adrian, 24
  departure from band, 114, 116
  as guitarist, 26–27, 34, 50, 81, 141,
   223
  return to band, 124, 156, 170
  as singer, 75
  songwriting and, 24, 42, 54, 55, 74,
   85–86, 88
  on writing for Iron Maiden, 119
Somewhere in Time, 84–88, 90–97, 100
The Soundhouse Tapes, 8, 13
"Speed of Light," 230, 234
"Starblind," 215
"Still Life," 56, 62, 67, 68
"Strange World," 10, 19–20, 125
"Stranger in a Strange Land," 54, 84–86,
  93–95
"Stratego", 248, 253
Stratton, Dennis, 24
"Sun and Steel," 56, 68
Syme, Hugh, 143

T

"Tailgunner," 116, 120–121, 256
"The Talisman," 215, 226
"Tears of a Clown," 232, 238, 244
"That Girl," 94
"The Alchemist," 218
"These Colours Don't Run," 202, 210
"The Thin Line Between Love and Hate,"
  178
Thin Lizzy, 50, 139, 202, 256
"The Time Machine", 248, 256
"To Tame a Land," 56, 58, 62, 68, 258
"Total Eclipse," 41, 53
"Transylvania," 10, 19
"The Trooper," 56, 62–64, 159, 179, 181
"22 Acacia Avenue," 41, 54–55
"Twilight Zone," 37
"2 Minutes to Midnight," 70, 72–75

U

"The Unbeliever," 148, 149, 206

V

video games, 156, 164, 165
Virtual XI, 151, 156–157, 159–160,
  162–169
vocals, 05, 100–101, 104–105, 126, 140,
  148–149, 178

W

"Wasted Years," 54, 74, 84–86, 91–93, 95
"Wasting Love," 128, 131, 135
"Weekend Warrior," 128, 131, 137
"When the Wild Wind Blows," 215, 228
"When Two Worlds Collide," 167
"Where Eagles Dare," 57, 58, 62, 67
Whitesnake, 30
"The Wicker Man," 175–176, 194
"Wildest Dreams," 186–187, 190
Williams, Robin, 232, 238
Wishbone Ash, 195, 256, 259
Wolfsbane, 142
World Slavery Tour, 72, 84
"Wrathchild," 8, 24, 31–33, 190
"The Writing on the Wall", 246, 248,
  253–254

X

The X Factor, 59, 142–145, 147–149,
  151–155

Photo Credits

A=all; B=bottom; L=left; M=middle; R=right; T=top

ROBERT ALFORD: p71; p79; p80. **ALAMY STOCK PHOTOS:** p23, Trinity Mirror/Mirrorpix; p85, RT Marino/MediaPunch; p212, WENN Ltd.; pp216–217A, © Southcreek Global/ZUMApress.com; p219, ITAR-TASS Photo Agency; p220, ITAR-TASS Photo Agency; p221, WENN Ltd.; ZUMA, p247; Sipa USA, p248; Jan-Erik Eriksen, p250; Jan-Erik Eriksen, p251; Jan-Erik Eriksen, p252; Anne-Marie Forker, p258. **AP IMAGES:** p78; p168T, Michel Euler; p180T, Dario Lopez-Mills; p183, Dario Lopez-Mills; p188, Mark Allan; p195, Robert E. Klein; p240, Sipa via AP Images. **GETTY IMAGES:** p1, Mick Hutson/Redferns; p4, Annamaria DiSanto/WireImage; p9, Martyn Goddard/Corbis via Getty Images; p15, Virginia Turbett/Redferns; p16, Virginia Turbett/Redferns; p17, Virginia Turbett/Redferns; p18, Virginia Turbett/Redferns; p25, Robert Ellis/Hulton Archive; p27, Fin Costello/Redferns; p28, Paul Natkin; p29, Paul Natkin; p30, Paul Natkin; p32, Ebet Roberts/Redferns; p41, Paul Natkin; p42, Peter Still/Redferns; p48, Michael Putland; p50, Ebet Roberts/Redferns; p57, Chris Walter/WireImage; p58, Michael Putland; p59, Paul Natkin; p61, Peter Still/Redferns; p63, Paul Natkin; p64T, Michael Montfort/Michael Ochs Archives; p69, Richard E. Aaron/Redferns; p75, Popperfoto; p76, Richard E. Aaron/Redferns; p82, Paul Natkin; p88, Graham Tucker/Redferns; p90, Ebet Roberts/Redferns; p92, Ebet Roberts/Redferns; p94, Ebet Roberts/Redferns; p99, John Mahler/*Toronto Star*; p102, Ebet Roberts/Redferns; p106, Brian Rasic/Hulton Archive; p109, Brian Rasic/Hulton Archive; p110, Michael Putland; p113, Larry Hulst/Michael Ochs Archives; p115, Michael Linssen; p117, Jim Steele/Popperfoto; p118, Jorgen Angel/Redferns; p121, Mick Hutson/Redferns; p124, Ebet Roberts/Redferns; p125, Ebet Roberts/Redferns; p130, Kevin Cummins; p131, Kevin Cummins; p134, Brian Rasic; p136, Stuart Mostyn/Redferns; p137, Odile Noel/Redferns; p143, Brigitte Engl/Redferns; p144, Mick Hutson/Redferns; p146, Mick Hutson/Redferns; p147, Mick Hutson/Redferns; p148T, Mick Hutson/Redferns; p157, Mitchell Gerber/Corbis/VCG via Getty Images; p158, Mitchell Gerber/Corbis/VCG via Getty Images; p167T, XAMAX\ullstein bild via Getty Images; p168, Paul Bergen/Redferns; p171, KMazur/WireImage; p175, Tim Mosenfelder; p176, Paul Natkin; p182, Dave Hogan; p185T, Mick Hutson/Redferns; p187T, Matt Carmichael; p188, Mick Hutson/Redferns; p196, Frazer Harrison; p199, Annamaria DiSanto/WireImage; p201, Annamaria DiSanto/WireImage; p203, Annamaria DiSanto/WireImage; p204, Annamaria DiSanto/WireImage; p207, Dibyangshu Sarkar/AFP; p223, Martin Philbey/Redferns; pp224–225, Martin Philbey/Redferns; p229, Francesco DeGasperi/AFP; p233, David M. Benett; p235B, Feature China/Barcroft Media via Getty Images; p236, Archivio Francesco Castaldo\Mondadori Portfolio via Getty Images; p239, Archivio Francesco Castaldo\Mondadori Portfolio via Getty Images; Torben Christensen/AFP, p261. **REX FEATURES:** p10, Eugene Adebari; p21, Andre Csillag; p97, Ilpo Musto; p129, Ilpo Musto. **QUARTO COLLECTION:** p8; p10A; p11; p13A; p14A; p19A; p20; p22A; p24; p31; p33; p34A; p37A; pp38–39A; p41; p43; p44; p45A; p46; p49; p55; p56; p62A; p64B; p65A; p66B; p70; p72A; p74; p81B; p83B; p84; p86A; p87T and M; p91B; p93A; p98; pp100–101A; p103; pp104–105A; p108; p114; p116; p119A; p120; pp122–123A; p128; pp132–133A; p135; p138; pp140–141A; p142; p145, p148M; p149; p152; p153; p154A; p156; pp162–163A; pp164–165A; p166A; p167B; p168B; p170; pp172–173A; p174; p177; pp178–179A; p181; p184; p185M; p186A; pp190–191A; p194; p197; p198; p200; p202; p205; p206; pp210–211A; p213; pp214–215A; p218A; pp226–227A; p230; p234; p235T; p238A; p241; pp242–243; p244. **FRANK WHITE PHOTO AGENCY:** p35, Kevin Hodapp; p36, Kevin Hodapp; p47, Frank White; p51, Frank White; p52, Frank White; p66, Frank White; p83T, Frank White; p87B, Frank White; p89, Frank White; pp105–106, Frank White; p127, Frank White; p150, Frank White; p151, Frank White; p161, Frank White; p180B, Frank White; p192, Frank White; p193, Frank White; p208, Frank White; p209, Frank White; p231, Frank White. **WYCOVINTAGE.COM:** p54; p68T; p73; p81T; p95A.

Quarto.com

© 2018, 2024 Quarto Publishing Group USA Inc.
Text © 2018, 2024 Martin Popoff

First Published in 2018. Second edition published in 2024 by Motorbooks,
an imprint of The Quarto Group, 100 Cummings Center, Suite 265-D,
Beverly, MA 01915, USA. T (978) 282-9590 F (978) 283-2742

Motorbooks titles are also available at discount for retail,
wholesale, promotional, and bulk purchase. For details, contact the
Special Sales Manager by email at specialsales@quarto.com or by mail at
The Quarto Group, Attn: Special Sales Manager, 100 Cummings Center,
Suite 265-D, Beverly, MA 01915, USA.

28 27 26 25 24   2 3 4 5 6

ISBN: 978-0-7603-8927-0

Digital edition published in 2024
eISBN: 978-0-7603-8928-7

Library of Congress Cataloging-in-Publication Data available

COVER DESIGN: Cindy Samargia Laun
PAGE DESIGN AND LAYOUT: Brad Norr Design
PHOTO RESEARCH AND CAPTIONING: Tom Seabrook
ON THE COVER: Andrey_Kuzmin/Shutterstock
ON THE ENDPAPERS: Mikesilent/Shutterstock

This book has not been prepared, approved, or licensed by Iron Maiden, its
individual members, or its representatives. This is an unofficial publication.

Printed in China